Freeway

Englisch für berufliche Schulen

Ausgabe Sozialpädagogik (Neubearbeitung)

von
Rosemary King
Wolfgang Rosenkranz
Graham Tucker

Ernst Klett Verlag
Stuttgart Düsseldorf Leipzig

Freeway – Ausgabe Sozialpädagogik (Neubearbeitung)

Englisch für berufliche Schulen

von
Rosemary King M.A., Wesel
OStR Wolfgang Rosenkranz, Bad Oeynhausen
Graham Tucker B.A., Castrop-Rauxel

Beratung durch Hellmut Imsel, Stuttgart

1. Auflage 1 5 4 | 2008

Alle Drucke dieser Auflage können im Unterricht nebeneinander benutzt werden, sie sind untereinander unverändert. Die letzte Zahl bezeichnet das Jahr dieses Druckes.

Internetadresse: http://www.klett.de

Redaktion: Volker Wendland, Astrid Keller (Assistenz)
Gestaltung: Thomas Gremmelspacher, Ulrike Wollenberg
Umschlaggestaltung: Nikolaus Keller
Reproduktion: Meyle + Müller Medien-Management, Pforzheim
Druck: Schnitzer Druck GmbH, 71404 Korb
Printed in Germany.
ISBN 3-12-809932-4

Freeway

Freeway, das einbändige Lehrwerk für den Englischunterricht an berufsbildenden Schulen führt aufbauend auf der Fachoberschulreife zur Fachhochschulreife. Es entspricht den Richtlinien und Lehrplänen für berufliche Schulen der verschiedenen Bundesländer.

Freeway – Ausgabe Sozialpädagogik (Neubearbeitung) – ist insbesondere an sozialpädagogisch ausgerichteten Fachoberschulen und Höheren Berufsfachschulen sowie in entsprechenden Kursen an Fachschulen und Berufsschulen einsetzbar.

Freeway – Ausgabe Sozialpädagogik (Neubearbeitung) – ist wie folgt aufgebaut:

Units 1 – 5	**Basic structures**
Units 6 – 10	**Advanced structures**
Units 11 – 15	**Exam preparation**
Units 16 – 20	**Exam preparation (Further reading)**

Dem unterschiedlichen Kenntnisstand und den verschiedenen Voraussetzungen bei Schülerinnen und Schülern der angesprochenen Schultypen wurde durch eine flache Strukturprogression in den ersten fünf Units Rechnung getragen. Damit wird auch schwächeren Lernenden der Zugang zu den Themen erleichtert.

In den Units 6 – 10	werden Aufbaustrukturen in einem berufsbezogenen Kontext vermittelt. Es findet hier bereits eine intensive Vorbereitung auf die Anforderungen der schriftlichen Abschlussprüfungen statt.
In den Units 11 – 15	werden schwerpunktmäßig sozialpädagogische Inhalte behandelt. Die Grammatikschwerpunkte der vorherigen Units werden hier noch einmal wiederholt und gefestigt.
Die Units 16 – 20	bieten ein erweitertes Textangebot zum Themenbereich Sozialpädagogik und bereiten ebenfalls auf die Prüfungen vor.

Im Anhang befindet sich eine ausführliche Grammatikübersicht, der vorausgesetzte Grundwortschatz, das kapitelbegleitende Vokabular mit Phonetik, die alphabetische Wortschatzliste sowie eine Liste der unregelmäßigen Verben.

Die Hörverständnistexte der einzelnen Units sind ebenfalls am Ende des Lehrwerks abgedruckt.

Freeway – Ausgabe Sozialpädagogik – zeichnet sich durch folgende Merkmale aus:

■ Übersichtlichkeit und schnelle Orientierung durch das Doppelseitenprinzip.
Die Units 1 bis 10 bestehen aus:

Starter	Einführung in das Thema	Auf der mit Fotos und Zeichnungen illustrierten Motivationsseite findet eine erste Annäherung an das Thema der Unit statt. Bereits vorhandene Kenntnisse werden durch einfache Übungen aktiviert.
Teil A (Doppelseite)	Textarbeit	Anhand von Texten, Statistiken und Übersichten wird in das Thema der Unit eingeführt. Die Grammatikschwerpunkte werden kontextualisiert vorgestellt und imitativ bzw. reproduktiv geübt.
Teil B (Doppelseite)	Grammatik	Im B-Teil wird der Grammatikschwerpunkt der Unit trainiert. Die Übungen sind inhaltlich an die Unit angelehnt, das Niveau des Wortschatzes wird hier aber bewusst niedrig angesetzt, um die Grammatik flexibel einsetzen zu können. Der B-Teil wird immer durch eine anspruchsvolle Aufgabe abgeschlossen, die mit Advanced gekennzeichnet ist.
Teil C (Doppelseite)	Textarbeit	Der C-Teil dient der Vertiefung des Unitthemas, wobei in der Regel ein längerer Text zu bearbeiten ist.
Teil D	Hörverständnis	Der D-Teil schließt jede Unit mit Übungen zum Hörverständnis ab. Dazu werden hier neben handlungsorientierten Aufgaben Sprechanlässe zur Verbesserung der Kommunikationsfähigkeit geschaffen.

■ Flexible Handhabung
Um den Vorkenntnissen und Interessen der Lernenden gerecht zu werden und um die Ziele der jeweiligen Schulform optimal zu erreichen, soll der Unterrichtende die Möglichkeit haben, flexibel mit Freeway zu planen.

Dabei sind z. B. folgende Varianten denkbar:
- Bei leistungsstarken Klassen könnte es sich z. B. bei den ersten fünf Units anbieten, nur die C-Teile zu bearbeiten (Vertiefung des Themas).
- Ebenfalls wäre es möglich, jeweils nur den A- und B-Teil (Einführung des Themas und Grammatikschwerpunkt) zu behandeln.
- Soll verstärkt die Grammatik geübt werden, dann ist auch ein Schnelldurchgang möglich, indem lediglich der B-Teil durchgenommen wird.
- Die Hörverständnisübungen und weiteren Aufgaben im D-Teil können natürlich mit allen Varianten kombiniert werden.

◼ Klare grammatikalische Strukturierung

Der Schwerpunkt der Grammatik liegt in den ersten Units auf der Wiederholung der wichtigsten **Tenses**, in den folgenden Units in den Bereichen **Conditional, Passive voice, Reported speech, Participle, Gerund und Infinitive**.

Um die Übersichtlichkeit im Lehrbuch zu erhöhen, wurden Übungen zu Nebenstrukturen in das Workbook ausgelagert. Eine benutzerfreundliche Grammatikübersicht mit Erklärungen befindet sich im Anhang.

◼ Intensive Prüfungsvorbereitung

Auf der Grundlage eines längeren Textes dient der C-Teil in den Units 6–10 der systematischen Vorbereitung auf die schriftliche Prüfung mit gezielter Hinführung zur Textproduktion (z.B.: Skills: Writing a summary) Eine Info-Box zum schnellen Nachschlagen gibt eine Übersicht über die wichtigsten Schritte zur Bearbeitung von **Comprehension questions, Summary, Vocabulary, Translation und Comment**.

In den Units 11–20 (Exam preparation) liegt der Schwerpunkt der Prüfungsvorbereitung auf sozialpädagogischen Inhalten.

◼ Weitere Merkmale

- Die Themen und der Wortschatz haben einen festen Bezug zur Arbeitswelt.
- Ein inhaltlicher und kommunikativer Schwerpunkt wurde auf die Bedeutung und Verwendung der englischen Sprache in einem zusammenwachsenden Europa gelegt.
- Unter Berücksichtigung des handlungsorientierten Ansatzes wurde versucht, die Lernenden anhand unterschiedlicher Situationen an adäquate Kommunikationsformen heranzuführen.
- Fester Bestandteil der ersten 10 Units ist die Schulung des Hörverständnisses unter Verwendung einer Vielzahl von Sprechern mit verschiedenen Akzenten (auch non-native speakers). Ausgewählte Texte des Schülerbuches wurden ebenfalls von verschiedenen Sprechern gelesen und befinden sich ebenfalls auf der CD.

Freeway setzt circa 1350 Wörter als Grundwortschatz voraus. Diese werden systematisch wiederholt und durch maßvolle Neueinführungen auf einen Gesamtwortschatz von circa 2700 Wörtern erweitert.

Das Lehrwerk Freeway – Ausgabe Sozialpädagogik (Neubearbeitung) umfasst das vorliegende **Lehrbuch**, ein **Arbeitsbuch** mit einem sozialpädagogischen Teil zu den Units 1–15 und weiteren schriftlichen Übungen zu Wortschatz und Grammatik, einen **Lehrerband** mit didaktisch-methodischen Hinweisen und Hintergrundinformationen sowie dem Schlüssel zu allen Aufgaben des Schülerbuches und des Arbeitsbuches. Eine **CD** mit allen Hörverständnisaufgaben und ausgewählten Lesetexten des Lehrbuches begleitet das Lehrwerk.

Wir wünschen Ihnen viel Spaß und Erfolg bei der Arbeit mit Freeway – Ausgabe Sozialpädagogik (Neubearbeitung).

Autorin/Autoren und Redaktion

General topics

Social topics

Audio-CD

Listening comprehension

Reading texts

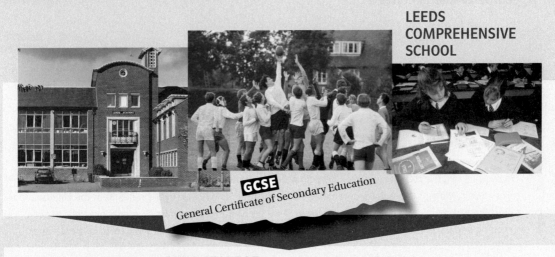

LEEDS
COMPREHENSIVE
SCHOOL

GCSE
General Certificate of Secondary Education

LEEDS COLLEGE

Engineering studies

Social studies

Business studies

BTEC
National Diploma

Public Service

Company

University

a Look at the photos and answer these questions.
1. What do the photos show?
2. What can the students from Leeds Comprehensive School do at Leeds College?
3. What possibilities do they have after college?

b Why are you at college?

1 Come to Leeds College

INFORMATION PROGRAMME OF STUDY LINKS

COURSES NEWS OPEN DAYS

LEEDS COLLEGE

EMAIL: INFO@LEEDS-COLLEGE.AC.UK
WWW.LEEDS-COLLEGE.AC.UK

Our college is one of the largest in the country. We employ over 400 teachers, both full-time and part-time. Our students are of all ages. About half of them are under 20, but we even have one who is 86 years old. The college runs over 200 courses at all levels. Most of the study programmes take place between nine and five, but we also offer evening and part-time courses.

BTEC National Diploma courses
These full-time courses lead to higher job qualifications. Successful students can also go on to university. Changes are taking place in Europe. On these courses students can learn a lot about Europe and study a European language. This is a great start for a career in a modern Europe!

Costs:
The courses are free for students under 18. Students who live over 3 miles from the college receive a free bus pass. Students over 18 can get a grant to cover part of their costs for books and equipment.
For further details see our homepage, send us an e-mail or write to:

Leeds College
Shaftesbury Road
Leeds LS2 45   Tel. 0532/449536

2-YEAR-PROGRAMME OF STUDY

Engineering Studies (Electrical, Mechanical or Civil)
- Mathematics
- General science
- Electrical/mechanical principles
- Computer studies
- English
- European language (French or German)
- Engineering applications of computer systems (CAD & CAM)
- Industrial control and instrumentation

Business Studies
- Mathematics
- General office skills
- Accountancy
- Computer studies
- English
- European language (French or German)
- Statistics
- European business and finance

Social Studies
- Sociology
- Psychology
- Principles of education
- Health care
- Statistics
- Computer studies
- European language
- English

a Answer the questions below. Start your answers with expressions like:

"In the text/brochure it says …"
"In the second paragraph you can find out …"
"In line … of the first/second … paragraph you can read …"

1. How do you know that Leeds College is very big?
2. How old are the students there?
3. When do most of the students have their lessons?
4. Why do the students learn a European language?
5. What can you get if you live far from the college?
6. How can people get in contact with Leeds College?

b Talk about your college. Think about:
size of college / teachers / students / courses / your course / costs

c Make a small brochure or a homepage for your college.

2 Two students meet on the campus

Terry: Hello, Sally. Long time no see. What are you doing here?

Sally: I'm doing a BTEC course.

Terry: And how are you finding it here?

5 **Sally:** Right now my big problem is mathematics. There are so many new formulas to learn. And then of course, there's the money.

Terry: I know what you mean. I've got a part-time job with my old firm. I work four hours in

10 the evenings in the packing department. It's hard work, but it helps me pay for my flat.

Sally: Oh, it's easier for me. I still live with my parents. But I've got a weekend job in a restaurant. That gives me a little more pocket

15 money. You know what I mean.

Terry: Which department are you in, by the way?

Sally: I'm in the Electrical Engineering department. First year. And you?

Terry: I'm in the Business Studies department.

20 In my second year. We're studying accountancy, statistics and subjects like that at the moment.

Sally: What foreign language are you learning on your course?

Terry: This year I'm doing German for beginners

25 – and that's my problem. There are so many new words to learn. Guten Tag. Ich … heiße Terry. … möchtest du …

Sally: Wow, look at the time. It's eleven o'clock. I've got a science lesson at five past. I have to

30 rush. See you.

Terry: Bye. … eine Tasse Kaffee?

a Copy the information sheet about the two students and complete it.

	Student 1 (female)	Student 2 (male)
Name?		Terry
Course?		
Department?		
Home?		
Problems?		

b Now write about the two students using the information above.

c Use the expressions in the dialogue and make a new dialogue between these two students.

Mike
- 1st year BTEC course in mechanical engineering
- bedsitter (one-room apartment)
- weekend job as a tennis coach
- problems with French/money

Linda
- 2nd year BTEC course in social studies
- house with three other students
- evening job as a waitress at a local club
- problems with statistics/money

d Now write about your college, home and any work you do.

1 Jill is a student

This is what she says about herself:

"I'm eighteen and I go to Leeds College. I don't have any brothers or sisters. I live in Leeds with my parents. My parents give me £100 a month. I spend most of the money on books and things for college. In the evening I work at Pete's Pizza Palace. I need the money, because I buy quite a lot of clothes. In my free time I don't go out very often.

I usually go to college by bus. Sometimes a friend takes me there in his car. At college we have a lot of subjects. I'm in the second year. I like English and mathematics best, but I don't like French. We don't have German. Very often I do my homework with a friend. Normally we both work hard for our course. It leads to higher qualifications and I hope to find a good job afterwards."

a Now talk about Jill.

Example:

"Jill is eighteen and she goes to Leeds College. She doesn't have any brothers or sisters. She ..."

b Do you remember? Ask your partner(s) questions about Jill. Do not look at the text on the left.

Example:

Where – Jill – live?
Where does Jill live?
Jill lives in Leeds.
Who – live – with her parents?
Who lives with her parents?
Jill lives with her parents.

1. Where – Jill – go to college?
2. Who – give – her – £100 a month?
3. What – Jill – do – in the evening?
4. Why – she – work?
5. How – she – get – to college?
6. Which subjects – Jill – like best?
7. Who – do – homework – together with her?
8. How – they – work – for their course?
9. Which subject – they – not – have?
10. What – Jill – hope to find?

2 In the cafeteria

a Guess what the students in the picture are doing.

Example:
Helen's writing.

b What do you think? Ask your friends questions about the students in the cafeteria. What are they doing exactly?

Use: What • How many • Where
What ... about • Who ... to

Example:
What is Helen writing?
I think she's writing a letter.

3 People at Leeds College

- usually	- do homework
- normally	- organize meetings
- on weekdays	- help visitors
- from Monday to Friday	- listen to teachers
- every day	- take a lot of calls
- often	- do tests

John is a student and Lucy is a secretary.

■ Talk about John and Lucy.
1. What do they normally do?
2. What are they doing at the moment?

today …
right now …
at the
moment …

4 On the phone

■ Fill in the right tense.
Sally: Hi, Tom. Are you busy at the moment?
Tom: Yes, sure. Why?
Sally: What **1. (do)** you?
Tom: I **2. (do)** my homework, of course.
Sally: What again? You never **3. (do)** anything else, Tom. Why you **4. (stay)** home all the time?
Tom: You know that I **5. (prepare)** for my exams and right now I **6. (try)** to do my mathematics. Our teacher **7. (give)** us more than 20 exercises every day.

Sally: And what about me? I **8. (wait)** for your call every evening.
Tom: I'm really sorry about that. Why you **9. (not go out)** with Susan sometimes?
Sally: I **10. (not see)** her very often, because she **11. (study)** for a different exam this year. And Anna **12. (live)** in France at the moment, because she **13. (work)** on her French project. I'm so unhappy …

5 Money problems   **Advanced**

■ Fill in the right tense. Use the bubbles for help.
"As you **1. (know)** life **2. (get)** so expensive these days, especially for poor students like us. I always **3. (tell)** Jack – why **4. (go)** you shopping at the corner shop? Things **5. (cost)** much less at the supermarket near the college. It **6. (annoy)** me because I **7. (get)** the feeling that he **8. (not listen)** to what I **9. (say)**. It's terrible. We always **10. (have)** arguments about things like that. Sometimes I **11. (think)** he just **12. (be)** lazy. On the other hand there are other things where Jack **13. (think)** we can save. We **14. (own)** a little car for example. Jack **15. (say)** we **16. (not need)** it. He **17. (be)** quite right. And so we **18. (think)** of selling it. We **19. (have)** to do something. Money **20. (not grow)** on trees."

"Is your daughter having a good time at college?"

"You know, students are always complaining about money but every third student owns a car."

"Nowadays a lot of students are thinking seriously about their future and things are getting more expensive. And as you know, money makes the world go round."

1 Leeds and Dortmund: An exchange programme

a Look at the picture which goes with the newspaper article below. Who do you think the people are?

b Read the article and check if you are right.

c Use information from the text and make a list of four
1. things on the programme in Leeds this week.
2. people the students expect to meet during the week.
3. things the students may worry about before they leave Germany.

City plays host to German guests

by Marigold Prince

"For these young people it's quite an adventure" says head of department Willi Schmitz from the Berufsbildende Schulen in Dortmund, Germany. His group of 16 students are just getting to know
5 their English host partners at a reception at Leeds College.

"For many of them it's their first visit to Britain and their first chance to put their
10 English to the test." Indeed, the group of 18–20 year-old students don't know very much about each other before their first meeting.
15 Usually students in both groups receive a passport photo of their partners and a short introduction form before the exchange. This
20 form gives them information about their partner's leisure interests, plans for the future and their favourite food and music.

"I hope mine's not a smoker who's only into heavy metal!" remarks one young Leeds student to his
25 friend as he passes me with some coffee and biscuits for the visitors.

As well as the new situation with their partners and the language, for one week the group has to cope with the different way of life in an English family.
30 "But," adds Willi Schmitz, who is on his fourth visit to Leeds, "after they get to know each other on the first evening, they usually all get on like a house on fire."

This week their programme includes visits to a number of local firms, trips out to the Yorkshire
35 Moors and the Lake District (including a stop at Borwick Hall on the way) as well as a joint project in the College workshops. "This year both groups are working together on a business studies and technology project on local environment prob-
40 lems," says Peter Stewart, Leeds College's exchange organizer.

"We find that working
45 together on a project is certainly one of the best ways of making really good friends. Many of the students from past exchanges still visit their
50 partners or go on holiday with them and every year there are always one or two students who are especially unhappy when it is
55 time to leave," Peter tells me.

As I leave the staffroom at the College, the German students are collecting their luggage and leaving for the first night with their partners and their families. Already it seems to me that some of
60 their earlier ideas about Britain and the British are changing. I hear a couple of comments from some of the German students. One of them says, if I understand his German correctly, "They seem really friendly." "Yes, and it's not raining, either,"
65 replies his friend and smiles. Maybe travel really can broaden the mind! **435 words**

d Which of these statements are true and which are false? Use information from the text.

1. The first exchange visit to another country is always an exciting experience.
2. Exchange students are well-informed about each other before the visit.
3. One of the Leeds students wants a smoker as a partner.
4. After one meeting, the exchange students generally like each other very much.
5. There are visits to local sights on the week's programme.
6. Students who work together get to know each other well.
7. There are two projects this year, one for the business students and one for the technology students.
8. Students who take part in these exchanges do not often see each other again.

e Which three of the true statements in exercise "d" represent the main ideas in the text?

f In these sentences from the text, who or what do the words in bold type refer to?

1. ... **it's** quite an adventure ... (line 1)
2. For many of **them** it's their first visit ... (line 7)
3. ... **he** passes me with some coffee ... (line 25)
4. ... who is on **his** fourth visit to Leeds ... (line 30)
5. As **I** leave the staffroom ... (line 56)
6. ... **they** seem really friendly ... (lines 63/64)

g Find in the text the opposites of these words

guest; work; same; last; arrive; alone

h Here are some words from the text and their dictionary definitions.
Find the matching pairs.

1. host	a) something people do together
2. to get to know	b) when things or people change places
3. leisure	c) to make something wider or bigger
4. to cope with	d) person who has guests
5. exchange	e) to meet someone for the first time
6. joint (project)	f) something difficult or dangerous
7. to broaden	g) to manage a situation well
8. adventure	h) free time

i Now answer these questions.

1. Why is an exchange visit such an adventure?
2. Why is Willi Schmitz sure that his students can have a good time in Leeds?
3. Why is it important for the students to work together on a joint project?
4. Why do students from the past exchanges still visit each other?
5. Why does one student say "Yes, and it's not raining, either"?

j Translate lines 56 to 66.

2   An informal letter

You are taking part in an exchange scheme that your college is organizing.
You already have some information about your partner and now you want to write to him or her to introduce yourself.

■ Write an informal letter in English.
Begin with 'Dear ...' and end with 'Yours ...' or 'with love from ...'

Include these points:
- yourself and your family
- your interests
- what you like/dislike
- your personality and what you look like
- your town
- the weather in your area

Use these expressions:
I am ... /in my family we usually ...
I am interested in ...
I like/love/can't stand ...
Some people say I am .../I look ...
There's .../we've got ... in our town
it's sometimes .../often ... here

1 An exchange visit

 a Listen and then answer these questions.

1. Who are the speakers?
2. Who is talking about what? Look at the pictures for help.

 b Listen again and correct these statements.

1. The exchange students are working on the environment project at the end of the week.
2. John thinks that visits to local firms and factories are boring.
3. Klaus thinks you learn more about the British as a tourist.
4. John's mother is not very enthusiastic about the exchange.
5. John believes that the Germans are all serious and hard-working.
6. Klaus finds living in an English family strange.

c Complete the sentences with the phrases in the box below.

1. … it's really great that we have the chance to see places like that.
2. …, that's why these exchanges are such a good idea.
3. Oh yes, … with you.
4. … that tourists learn half as much.
5. They don't have enough contact with the locals, …
6. They still think, …, that all the Germans are serious.
7. …, isn't it a bit strange for you, Klaus, living in a foreign family?
8. …, you're all so friendly to me.

> I suppose • I think • I believe • I'm sure • in my view • I agree • in my opinion •
> I'm quite certain • I don't think • for example • for instance • I mean

2 Giving your opinion

a Now try to find more arguments for exchanges.
Use the expressions in the box above for your arguments.

b Comment on the following statement using the expressions in the box above.
"Learning a foreign language at college is a waste of time."

Are people always asking you what you want to be when you leave school?
Try our special chart to help you discover which is the job for you!

■ Work out the best job for your partner. He/she should answer 'yes' or 'no' to
the questions. It's more interesting if your partner closes his/her book.
When you reach one of the symbols, look at the list below for a suitable job.

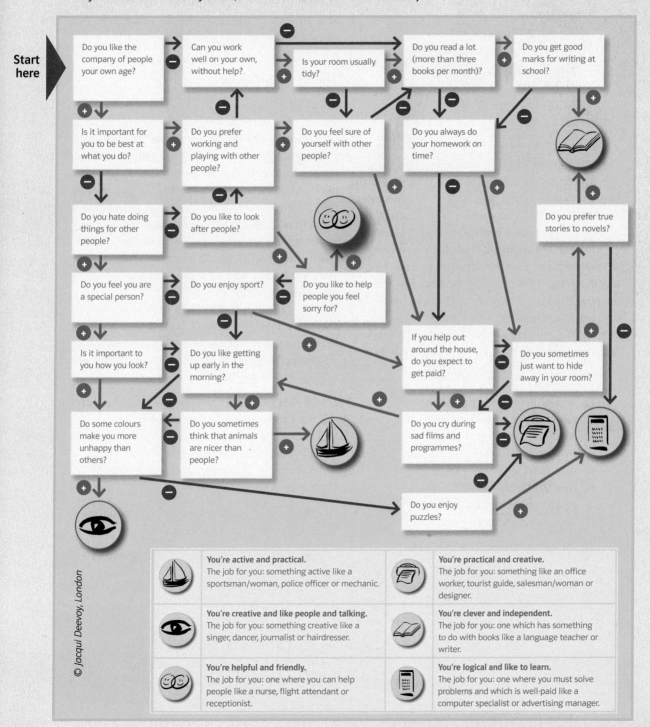

Start
here

© Jacqui Deevoy, London

1 "Computers Unlimited"

a Look at the photo and describe what you can see.

me   my boss

The American dream is alive and living in North London. John Sanson started his own business, Sanson Computers, 6 years ago in a small flat above his parents' butcher's shop. However, in the last few years his sales have increased so enormously that his company now has a turnover of £13.5m. At 28 Mr Sanson has already become a very rich man. Only 2 weeks before he opened his computer shop, he graduated from Nottingham University with a degree in Electrical and Computer Engineering. "A lot of people in my family were self-employed and I wanted to do the same. I have always been interested in computers and while I was at university I saw the possibilities of a growing market in personal computers. So, when I left university, I decided to take the risk," John explains. However, there were not a lot of risks for him; he lived with his parents and was used to life on a student's grant. Moreover, he only had a staff of one, so he didn't have a high wage bill. Sanson's firm is now called 'Computers Unlimited'. He employs more than 80 people who sell and service PC software and hardware. "Nowadays you can go out and buy a computer like a TV or video recorder," says Sanson. As a result his business has expanded enormously. In his first year he made a profit of only £11,000. In the meantime his profits have reached £2.3m a year. Naturally enough, he has moved from his small shop in North London and has now rented a large store in a business park just outside London. He sums up his success story like this: "Of course it has been hard work. But the secret is that I still enjoy the work and my boss likes me, too."   302 words

© Roger Trapp, The Independent, London (adapted)

b Answer the following questions.
1. Where did John Sanson open his first shop?
2. What did John study at university?
3. Why did he decide to start his own business?
4. Why didn't John have a lot of risks at first?
5. How has his business developed?
6. Where has he moved to?
7. Why, do you think, has he moved?

c The following words are in the text. Match them with their definitions.

d Find words or expressions in the text which have the same meaning as the following.
1. company 2. little 3. grown
4. left university with a degree 5. workers
6. computer equipment 7. up to this time
8. employer

e Say whether the words you have found are nouns, adjectives, adverbs or verbs.

f Use the words to talk about John Sanson.

1. to employ (line 22)	A. the technology of electricity (n.)
2. electrical engineering (line 10/11)	B. to give work to. They … 150 workers in that factory (vt)
3. self-employed (line 12)	C. to a great extent (adv.)
4. enormously (line 26)	D. (good fortune) to have great … in life (n.)
5. to increase (line 5)	E. to make or become bigger in size or number (vt)
6. success (line 31)	F. having your own firm or company (adj.)

🎧 2 A radio interview

"Young people in Southampton" is a popular programme on Radio Solent, the local radio station. Des Jacky is talking to Roberta Crumb.

DJ: Welcome to "Young people in Southampton". Today we have Roberta Crumb with us in the studio. Roberta, you are 24 and you ran a small video production service here in Southampton.
5 Now could you tell our listeners a little about what has happened to you and your business?
RC: Well, it all started when I saw an advert in the local paper. At that time I was employed at a large electronics firm near here.
10 **DJ:** And what was the advert for?
RC: "Starting your own business." The local bank offered to give advice to young people who wanted to start up their own business. At first I didn't take it all that seriously. But the more I
15 thought about it, the more interested I became. I talked to my parents and my boyfriend about it. They said I should do what I really wanted to do, which was to start up a small video production service. So, after some time I went to the bank
20 and had a talk with the bank manager. He explained all the advantages and also the risks of being self-employed.

DJ: What happened then?
RC: Well, after a lot of thought I made up my mind to start up the business. We recorded customers' weddings, birthday parties – anything like that, but I didn't earn as much as in my old job.
DJ: And what happened then? 30
RC: Well, I still had to pay back a lot of money to the bank for the video equipment, and advertising cost me a lot, too. I couldn't live on the income from my work. So I decided to close down the business. I think my main mistake 35 was that I didn't watch the market development carefully enough. People nowadays have their own video cameras and don't need a professional service.
DJ: And where are you working now, Roberta? 40
RC: I've got a job in a photographer's shop. The pay's not bad, but the problem is I have to pay back the money to the bank. I haven't had a holiday for 2 years now. I just can't afford one.

a True or false?
1. Roberta worked in a photographer's shop.
2. The local bank put an advert in the newspaper.
3. Roberta earned enough money from her business.
4. The bank manager gave her some advice on starting her own business.

b Complete these sentences. Choose from the nouns and verbs in the boxes.
Use the same tenses as in the dialogue.
1. Roberta … a video production …
2. She … an … in the local newspaper.
3. She … a talk with the …
4. Roberta … up the business.
5. She (not) … the market … closely enough.
6. Roberta (not) … enough customers.
7. She … down her …
8. She … in a … shop.

| have (2) • see • run • start • watch • work • close |

| advert • development • service • business • bank manager • photographer's |

c Join the sentences with the linking words in the box.
Example:
1. In the interview we hear that Roberta ran a video production service.
2. First she …

| In the interview we hear that … |
| Then … After that … |
| However … As a result … |
| So … Now … First … |

1 Softright Systems

Jane Topper moved to Glasgow seven years ago. There she met Harry Coe who didn't like his old job in an import company. As they were both interested in computers they **1. (decide)** to start a small software company. First they only **2. (write)** computer programs for Harry's old import company, but soon they **3. (see)** that a lot of other companies also **4. (need)** special software. So they **5. (hire)** some young programmers who **6. (work)** in small teams and **7. (develop)** a lot of new ideas.

The company **8. (be)** profitable from the start. Although other companies **9. (have)** their problems Softright **10. (not lose)** money. In their third year in business they **11. (make)** a profit of £150,000. Then they **12. (try)** some advertising and it **13. (work)**. That is why they **14. (spend)** more on marketing in the following years. At the beginning Jane and Harry only **15. (have)** two small rooms for their work. After some time they **16. (rent)** offices in several different buildings. But last year they **17. (buy)** a warehouse in central Glasgow. The move **18. (not be)** easy and it **19. (take)** more than two months. "We **20. (lose)** quite a lot of money when we **21. (move)**," Jane said. "But we **22. (not want)** to work in different places any more. That **23. (be)** a good decision!"

a Complete the sentences in the past tense.

b Find the missing parts in the following statements about Jane and Harry's company. Ask a classmate about it. He/she should give you an answer with the help of the information in the box below.

Example:
1. When did Harry's parents move to Glasgow? They moved to Glasgow in 1976.
2. Where …

1. Harry's parents moved to Glasgow in …
2. After college in Glasgow Harry worked at …
3. The company imported …
4. He enjoyed his … very much.
5. But one day Harry left because …
6. He met … on a computer course.
7. She told him …
8. Of course, they needed … for their new company.

- some money
- that she wanted to start her own business, too
- he wanted to be his own boss
- his partner
- 1976
- his father's company
- electronic parts
- work

2 Times have changed

Describe what has happened to the following two companies in the last few years.
Example:
Evans & Sons have been in Sheffield since 2000. Linda Graves has …

	be in Sheffield	sell	make a loss	expand	buy a company abroad
Evans & Sons	since 2000	120 million DVDs so far	never	three times	already
Linda Graves	for five years	about 1,000 cars up to now	once	just	not yet

3 A job interview

Mary Wilson has applied for a job in the export department of Kwik-Fit. In an interview she talks about her life and career.

a Take her role. Use the verbs and the information below.

Example:

"I was born in Leeds in 1979. I went to school from …"

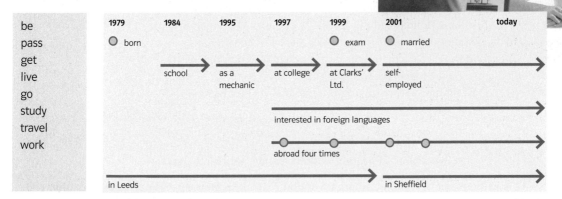

be	1979	1984	1995	1997	1999	2001	today
pass	○ born				○ exam	○ married	
get							
live		school	as a mechanic	at college	at Clarks' Ltd.	self-employed	
go							
study				interested in foreign languages			
travel							
work				abroad four times			
		in Leeds				in Sheffield	

b Ask your classmates about:

date of birth / school / college / important exams / address / trips abroad / experience in English / experience at work / hobbies

c Complete the following report about Kwik-Fit. Put the verbs into the simple past or present perfect tense.

Example:

35 years ago Tom Farmer opened two garages in Edinburgh. In 1974 he …

Kwik-Fit

35 years ago Tom Farmer **(open)** two garages in Edinburgh. In 1974 he **(sell)** to G.A. Robinson. Shortly afterwards Robinson **(get)** into difficulties. Then Farmer **(buy)** the company again. Since then the company's name **(be)** Kwik-Fit. In the beginning most of the business **(be)** with private cars, but in 1987 Kwik-Fit **(begin)** a service for companies. In the last few years customers **(include)** ICI, Avis and British Petroleum. Up to now Kwik-Fit **(keep growing)**.

4 How long …? **Advanced**

a Answer the following questions.
1. How long have you been working with this book? **for … weeks/since …**
2. How long have you known about this college? **for … years**
3. How long have you been learning English? **for … months/since …**
4. How often have you visited England? **once, twice, … times, never**

b Translate the following sentences. Watch out for the correct tenses.
1. Peter arbeitet seit Januar bei Seafood Limited.
2. Er kennt den Manager seit einigen Jahren.
3. Sie planen seit drei Monaten ein neues Projekt.
4. Peters Frau hat sich 3-mal um eine Stelle beworben.
5. Sie wartet schon seit langem auf eine Antwort.
6. Sie sind schon lange nicht mehr zusammen im Urlaub gewesen.

1 Workers – past and present

a In one sentence say what subject these texts have in common.

For the people who lived in the East End of London in the middle of the nineteenth century, life was hard. Often a whole family lived in one room and even 12-year-old children went out to work. Working days were long, often from five in the morning until nine at night. There were no holidays until 1871 when the government introduced the first Bank Holidays. At this time 77% of the population of Britain belonged to the working class and so had to live in such conditions. Even to buy the most basic food could cost a man three days' pay. When a man lost his job, which could happen at the end of the week, the day or even the hour, or when he became sick, he had nothing except his family and friends to help him.

5

Europe's workers – underpaid but happy!

This is the result of a survey which a London firm has completed for the managers of a number of multinational companies who have employees all over Europe. The survey shows companies what they can expect from the workers in each country. More than 500,000 workers answered the questions about attitudes to pay, workmates and benefits.

5

The survey shows that in general Europe's workers enjoy what they do, get on well with their workmates and identify with the company they work for.

10

However, attitudes to pay are less positive. Although 57% of workers in the Netherlands are satisfied with their wages, in Switzerland only 44% of the workers are happy with their pay. In Britain the number is much lower, 35%. Moreover, the Dutch also feel happiest about their working conditions and benefits.

15

Workers there receive paid sick leave after two days at 70% of their pay for one year.

20

The European Union has introduced laws about the maximum number of working hours. However, working hours within Europe still vary quite a lot. In Britain and Luxembourg the maximum is 48 hours, but in Denmark it is much lower, 37 hours.

25

There are also laws in the EU about the minimum amount of paid holiday a worker can have. The average in Britain is usually 23 days. However, German workers can expect a lot more than this.

30

Finally, on the question of job satisfaction, the survey's results are positive. Most of Europe's workers are happy with their workmates as well as with the job they do.

35

The European, London (adapted)   **262 words**

Are you happy with your pay?

Netherlands 57%	
Switzerland 44%	
Belgium 42%	
United Kingdom 35%	

Are you satisfied with your job?

Switzerland 77%	
Netherlands 76%	
Belgium 75%	
United Kingdom 64%	

b Which of these pictures show conditions of work which are mentioned in the texts? Name them.

1  2  3  4  5  6

c The following numbers appear in the texts. What information do they give?
500,000; twelve; 2; thirty-five; 5; twenty-three

d Answer these questions.
1. When did 77% of the British population belong to the working class?
2. How many hours per day did people often work in the past?
3. What help did workers in the past receive when they became ill?
4. Why did the London firm carry out its survey?
5. The survey shows that most workers in Europe agree about some conditions of their work. Which ones?
6. Which two conditions of their work are the Dutch the happiest about?
7. Which conditions of their work do you think the British are unhappy about?
8. Job satisfaction depends on pay. Do you agree? Use the charts to help you with your answer.

e How has the situation of workers in Europe changed in the last one hundred years?

f Translate lines 1 – 8 (Europe's workers – underpaid but happy!).

2   What about you?

a Talk about your experiences.
1. Have you ever worked full-time or in your free time?
2. Have you ever had a job you enjoyed?
3. Is it important for you to enjoy your job?

b Choose five things in this list which you think are important.

	workmates	pay	travel	holidays	working hours	to help other people	to be independent	to have a secure job
important								
not important								

In my job	I want to ... it's important to me to ... I would like to ... I hope that ...	because in order to ... so that ...

Job advertisements

A leading European engineering company requires responsible people to work in several departments:

TECHNICAL ASSISTANT
EXPORT ASSISTANT
CHILDCARE ASSISTANT

The successful candidates must be aged 21–30, have a BTEC National Diploma or similar qualifications and some work experience.
A good knowledge of English and German is essential in our international business.
Technical and export assistants should be willing to travel overseas. The childcare assistant should have experience in caring for children under 5.
The company offers interesting jobs with attractive salaries and excellent working conditions.

Applications with full CV to the personnel manager
Mr Len Linscott.

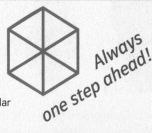

Always one step ahead!

IEP Industries
105–110 Oldham Road
Manchester M13 9PL
Tel: 0161-8342707
www.iepinfo.co.uk

a Answer the following questions.
1. What is the firm looking for?
2. What qualifications must the applicants have?
3. What advantages can you find in the jobs?

b Apply for one of the jobs above. Complete the missing information in the letter below. Use your own personal details, where possible.

```
name and address                                          your address
of employer above                                                 date

Dear Sir/Madam/Mr …/Ms …,

With reference to your advert in today's newspaper, I would like to apply for
the vacancy of (job). I am (age) and of (...) nationality. I have attended (college in ...)
since (date). In (date) I hope to pass my examination in (department).
While I was at college/Before college I was employed at (name of firm/institution) from
(date) to (date) as a (job). In my job there I (tasks). I am applying for the job as
(name of job) in your company because (reasons for applying). Enclosed please find my CV and
copies of certificates.
I look forward to hearing from you soon.

Yours faithfully/Yours sincerely, (name)
```

c After you have written the letter of application, the next step is to write a curriculum vitae (CV). Write your own CV including the following information:

personal data, education, qualifications, job experience, interests, references

d Mr Linscott is interviewing two candidates for the job of Technical Assistant. Listen and find out:
1. names of the candidates
2. their favourite subjects at school/college
3. their present jobs
4. why they have applied

e Decide who you would choose for the job. Give reasons.

A survey in Europe: Do you feel European?

A survey released by the European Commission in 2003 shows how Europeans feel about this question. This is what they said:

Source: Standard Eurobarometer 2003

"I'm not interested in Europe." 41%

"I feel first European and then citizen of my own country." 7%

"I feel European only." 3%

"I feel first citizen of my own country and then EU citizen." 49%

a Put the letters of these words in the right order to find the names of some European countries.
canfre; dianler; laity; yemnarg; desnew; umigleb; cegeer; lopdna

b Answer the following questions.
1. Which letters on the map show which countries?
2. What is the capital city of each country?

3. What are the most important languages in Europe?
4. Which of the countries on the map are now in the European Union?

c Do you feel European? Look at the statistics above and make a similar survey for your class. Compare the results.

d Find reasons for the differences.

1 Studying in Europe

Nowadays it's becoming more and more important to spend some time abroad, so if you want to study or train for a job, why not do so in another European country?

"When I arrived in Warsaw they had already organized everything for me," says 20-year-old Sven Berglund from Stockholm in Sweden. "A friend was waiting for me at the station and he took me 5 to the student hostel where I stayed for the first three months. Now I share a beautiful flat with two other students. It's much more comfortable and costs much less than I would have to pay at home. Living in Poland is quite cheap, you know.
At the university in Warsaw, where I'm studying social studies, 10 my sociology lectures are in English and German so I don't have to speak Polish. What I found a little strange in the beginning was that if you want to talk to your professor or practise discussions in seminars you have to wear a suit. I hadn't brought a suit with me so I had to buy one. But normally I wear jeans, of course." 15

"Don't take everything too seriously," says Brian Auger from Bristol. "That's what I first learned when I started my engineering studies in France. Most of the lectures are in French but I soon got used to that and, of course, it helped a lot that I had learned the language at school for many years. 20
I spent the first three weeks at a youth hostel here in Lyon because it wasn't easy to find a place to live. Then I got a couple of addresses from a students' organisation and was able to rent a small room. Also I didn't expect such a lot of bureaucracy in France – you have to fill in a lot of forms if you want to live here, and you need several kinds 25 of insurance – and that's not cheap. But if you insure with a students' insurance company you get discounts in fast food restaurants and supermarkets. Isn't that great?"

"Studying in Great Britain can be expensive so money is the most important thing if you want to study here," says Esther Rosenkranz from Frankfurt. "First 30 I applied for a place at Oxford University, but I didn't pass the entrance exam. Now I'm at the London School of Economics and I have to pay quite a lot of money a year, but on the other hand you study in small groups right from the start. That means that your professor knows you by name, which wasn't possible in Germany because there are often hundreds of students in the 35 seminars there.
When I applied for a place in business studies I had to take a language test in English first, but I didn't find that too difficult. I've always enjoyed English. I'm really happy here and feel quite at home in the student hostel where I'm living. Luckily it's not too expensive and also it's very international, because 40 quite a lot of the places are reserved for students from abroad, which I find exciting."

a Find at least 3 examples of each of the following in the text:
1. countries
2. cities
3. subjects
4. languages
5. places to live

b Answer the following questions.
1. Why did Sven Berglund move out of the student hostel in Warsaw?
2. What did Sven Berglund find strange at first and how did he solve the problem?
3. Why isn't it a problem for Brian Auger that his engineering lectures are in French?
4. What disadvantages are there if you study in France?
5. What benefits do you get in France if you insure with a students' insurance company?
6. Why isn't Esther Rosenkranz studying at Oxford University?
7. What differences are there between studying in Germany and Britain?
8. What does Esther Rosenkranz like about the hostel where she is living?

c Find verbs or adjectives in the text which go with the nouns in the box below. Say where you have found them and whether they are verbs or adjectives?

Example:
I have found the word 'train' on line 2. It is a verb.

> training • organisation • practice • insurance • application • payment • knowledge
>
> importance • beauty • stranger • possibility • difficulty • excitement

d Use the nouns above to complete these sentences.
1. Sven, Brian and Esther recognised the … of spending time abroad.
2. Sven had no problems with the … of his trip, everything had been done for him.
3. Esther had no … with her English language test.
4. Esther's … for a place at Oxford wasn't successful.
5. In Germany there is very little … that a professor knows his students by name.

e Would you like to live and work or study in another European country? Why? Why not?

2   The European Union

European unity has been a slow and sometimes difficult process. After the 2nd World War most people in Europe dreamed of a United States of Europe: democratic, peaceful and wealthy. However, many governments put their own political and national interests first. These factors have often slowed down the building of European unity. On the right you can read about some of the important steps on the road to a united Europe.

a Complete the sentences in the left column with the information in the right column.

b Now give a report on the history of the EU in the past tense. Use the linking words on page 19 to join the sentences.

c What has happened in the EU since 2005?

1957 Belgium, France, Germany, Italy, Luxembourg and the Netherlands …	… join the EU.
1958 The European Community …	… sign the Treaty of Rome.
1973 Denmark, Ireland and Great Britain …	… become members of the European Union.*
1979 First direct elections for the European Parliament …	… welcomes 10 new members.
1981 Greece …	… comes into operation.
1986 Portugal and Spain …	… joins the EU.
1993 The twelve member states …	… becomes the single currency of many EU states.
1995 Sweden, Finland and Austria …	… take place.
2002 The Euro …	… introduce the Single European Market (The European Union).
2004 The EU …	… enter the EU.

* "EC" before November 1993.

1 Travelling in Europe

Last summer Robert Page, a computer salesman, travelled around France by train. Here are his travel notes.

JULY

12 Monday
18.00 Paris Gare du Nord
evening - hotel (Montmartre)

13 Tuesday
morning - Eiffel Tower, Notre Dame
13.15 John Walters / business lunch
(Café des Artistes)

14 Wednesday
morning - shopping
13.10 train to Marseilles (Dan and Mike /
workmates)

15 Thursday
morning - old port (very hot)
14.00 meeting / Martin Turner

16 Friday
11.00 breakfast / Hôtel du Roi, rest of day on beach
18.30 flight to Manchester

17 Saturday

a Answer these questions.
1. What time did he arrive in Paris?
2. When did he go to the hotel?
3. What sights did he see in Paris?
4. Where did he meet John Walters for lunch?
5. What did he do on Wednesday morning?
6. Who did he meet on the train to Marseilles?
7. When did he visit the old port?
8. What did he do on Friday morning?

b Make complete sentences with the following words:

Example:
after/arrive/Paris/go to/hotel
After he had arrived in Paris he went to the hotel.

1. after/be to/Eiffel Tower/meet/John Walters
2. after/meet John Walters/have/lunch
3. catch/train to Marseilles/after/do/some shopping
4. after/get on/train to Marseilles/meet two workmates
5. after/arrive/in Marseilles/visit/the old port
6. have/a meeting with Martin Turner/after/see/the old port
7. after/have/breakfast/spend/day on beach
8. catch/plane to Manchester/after/spend/day on beach

2 Some business trips do not go as well as others

Andy Williams met Robert Page and told him about what had gone wrong on his trip.

■ Use past perfect in one clause and simple past in the other. Use the words in brackets to join your sentences.

1. get to platform	train - leave already	(when)
2. the next train - be late	the engine - break down	(because)
3. at the hotel - find	leave my case on bus	(that)
4. get to bus station	it - shut already	(by the time)
5. ask a friend to meet me at hotel	he - not arrive	(although)
6. later - remember	give my friend the wrong address	(that)
7. leave the hotel to go for a meal	lose credit card	(after)
8. return to hotel	someone else - take my room	(by the time)

Example:
arrive at station - ticket office close already (when)
When I arrived at the station the ticket office had already closed.

3 At the airport

Mr Jones, a businessman from Cardiff, went to the airport last week to get his plane to Brussels.

a Make sentences about these situations.

Example:
drive to airport / start to rain
As/While he was driving to the airport it started to rain.

1. show ticket at airport / passport fall out of pocket
2. look around bookshop / meet a friend
3. plastic bag break / he and friend go upstairs
4. friend get coffee / he sit down at table
5. they call his flight to Brussels / he and friend drink coffee

b Jason Norman is a journalist for the "Evening News" in Seattle. Two weeks ago he travelled to Frankfurt. At the airport he went to the bank to change some money.
Put the verbs in these sentences into simple past or past continuous. Be careful, some sentences have both verbs in the simple past. Join your sentences with one of these words: *while, as, when* or *and*.

Example:
A lot of passengers (wait) at the counter – Jason Norman (walk) into the bank
A lot of passengers were waiting at the counter when Jason Norman walked into the bank.

1. he (look) at the exchange rates – man behind him (ask) to borrow a pen
2. he (stand) in line – he (count) his money
3. he (get) to the counter – Jason (hand) the money to the assistant
4. he (talk) to the assistant – there (be) an announcement
5. Jason (listen) to the announcement – the assistant (leave) the counter
6. she (return) – she (give) him a form
7. she (count) his money – Jason (sign) the form
8. she (give) him the money – he (put) it into his pocket

4 On the boat   **Advanced**

Put the verbs in brackets into the correct form of the past tense (past simple, past perfect, or past continuous).

While Tim Smith **1. (stand)** and **2. (look)** over the side of the boat which **3. (take)** him to Ostend, he **4. (try)** to imagine the people who **5. (travel)** below him in the Channel Tunnel. Although the tunnel **6. (open)** many years ago and he **7. (have)** enough time to get used to the idea, he still **8. (find)** it difficult to imagine the journey to the Continent by rail and not by boat. Before they **9. (complete)** the tunnel, Britain **10. (always be)** an island and many people still **11. (want)** it that way.

1 Europe's cities lead the way

A long time ago, before people had even thought of ideas like the EU, Europe consisted of a number of independent nations. Nowadays, with more and more countries in the EU, the question
5 is, what developments will tomorrow bring?

For some people, the most exciting aspect is its cities. And why? Well, look at any number of European cities even today and you can see that they are enjoying the greatest growth, energy and
10 activity.
London for example, is exciting and the most cosmopolitan city in the world – the bridge between Europe and America. Berlin, on the other hand is the link between Western and
15 Eastern Europe, its glass-walled Reichstag a symbol of the new European democracy. And it's not only in Europe's western capitals that you can feel this energy. The former eastern capitals – Prague, Warsaw and Budapest now

not only look better after the neglect of the 20
communist era, they also show a desire for the ideals of a modern Europe: tolerance and new ideas. Each city has its own strengths. Talinn in Estonia is rediscovering its strength as one of the great Baltic trading centres, while places like 25
Marseilles, Barcelona and Liverpool are changing their run-down port areas into new centres which will link people to the sea. The diversity of each city is also one of its strengths. Each city is developing its own ideas. In Paris, a mayor 30
once turned one of the main roads into a huge beach with sand and sunchairs instead of cars. The London Eye, also known as the Millennium Wheel, which was put up as a joke for the 2000 millennium, has now become a permanent 35
attraction in London.
Even more exciting are the links between cities. High-speed trains and low-cost airlines are connecting more of these cities with each other. Such links mean that millions of Europeans can 40
afford both the time and the money to visit places they could not have visited before. These links are also bringing Europe's cities closer to each other than to their own countrysides. Londoners will go shopping in Barcelona, while Parisians take the 45
Eurostar to visit the free museums or the clubs in London. City leaders will talk to each other without waiting for the OK from governments. In future Europe will have to look to its cities for new ideas, new jobs and new leadership. The 50
growing links between cities will help to speed up the disappearance of national boundaries and each city and its people will gradually realize that their interests lie with each other.   **431 words**

a Describe what you can see in the photo. It shows something you can find in one of the cities mentioned in the text. Which city do you think it is?

b Which of the following arguments can you find in the text?
1. Europe's strength is its independent nations.
2. The growing number of member states in the EU will increase the importance of Europe's cities.
3. Europe's future lies in its cities because they are places of growth and energy.
4. London is exciting because people from many different countries live there.
5. Berlin is important as a bridge between Europe and America.

6. The neglect of cities during the communist era means that they are not as important as the capitals of western Europe.
7. The strength of each city lies in their common ideas.
8. As a result of better rail and air links, more and more people are able to visit foreign cities.
9. The differences between cities will slowly disappear as a result of links between their people.

c Which of the arguments you found in the text do you agree with and why?

d Answer the following questions on the text in complete sentences.
1. How has the view of Europe changed over the years?
2. What do London and Berlin have in common?
3. Why are Europe's eastern capitals also exciting?
4. What examples can you find of some new ideas?
5. What strengths do cities have individually and in general?
6. What advantages will new transport links between cities bring?

e Translate lines 37 to 54.

f Project: Write about a European city you know, saying what you like and dislike about it.

2 How Europeans go on holiday

a Say which of the two photos below shows what kind of holiday you take and say why.

Country	Holidaymaking rate (at least a trip of four nights)	Domestic trips	Outbound	Holidaymakers within the EU	Holidaymakers outside the EU
Belgium	40.2%	17.9%	82.1%	73.9%	26.1%
Germany	76.9%	34.0%	66.0%	66.2%	33.8%
Spain	37.3%	89.7%	10.3%	59.4%	40.6%
Italy	46.3%	77.2%	22.8%	55.3%	44.7%
Netherlands	67.9%	37.0%	63.0%	74.7%	25.3%
Finland	51.9%	71.5%	28.6%	61.0%	39.0%
United Kingdom	60.9%	55.0%	45.0%	65.8%	34.2%

eurostat 2002

b Find out about the following:
1. Which holidaymakers travel most/least?
2. Which holidaymakers stay in their home countries most/least?
3. Which nationalities travel within the EU/outside the EU most/least?

c Answer these questions. What do you think?
1. Why do some people travel more than others?
2. Why do some people stay in their home countries, why do others prefer to travel abroad?
3. Why do many people stay within the EU, why do others take their holidays outside the EU?
4. Is holidaymaking different in central and southern Europe? Why/why not?

d Write a text about holidaymaking in Great Britain, Germany and Italy. Use the results from above.

1 Voting systems

a First listen to these two European politicians who are talking about their own political careers and find out about the following points:
1. Name   2. Country   3. Political party   4. Special interests
5. Constituency   6. Former job   7. Member of Parliament since

b Now describe the two politicians in complete sentences.

c The politician went on to talk about the following statistics. What do you think he said?

The election 2001

Labour	40.8%
Conservative	31.8%
Liberal Democrats	18.3%
Others	9.1%

Distribution of seats

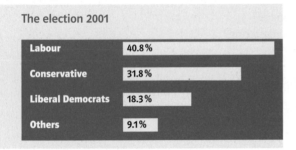

Others
Conservative
28
166
Labour
413
52
LibDem

2 The British parliamentary system

■ Describe the diagram of the British parliamentary system.

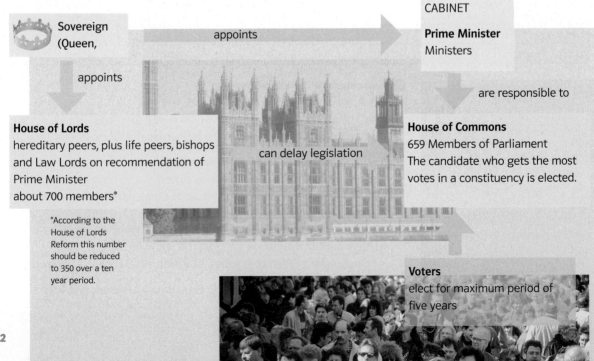

Sovereign
(Queen,

appoints

CABINET
Prime Minister
Ministers

appoints

are responsible to

House of Lords
hereditary peers, plus life peers, bishops and Law Lords on recommendation of Prime Minister
about 700 members*

can delay legislation

House of Commons
659 Members of Parliament
The candidate who gets the most votes in a constituency is elected.

*According to the House of Lords Reform this number should be reduced to 350 over a ten year period.

Voters
elect for maximum period of five years

Telecommunications/Advertising

■ Answer the following questions.

1. What can you see in the pictures?
2. Do you own or use any of the devices shown?
3. Are they useful?
4. What advantages do they have?
5. What developments do you think we will have in the future?
   Think of office technology and communications.

1 A virtual future?

Since the invention of the computer technologists have promised us a world in which we will have more control over our lives – in short a technological paradise in the real world. Unfortunately this technology is sometimes still much too complicated and often not user-friendly enough. We can't even control the technology in our own homes; for example our PC systems still crash whenever we need them most.

But now a new trend in user-friendly technology is
15 coming as engineers combine computers, consumer electronics and the media. Super appliances and services will change all our lives. Firstly, powerful computers are becoming smaller and smaller. Secondly, information transmission has gone digital. A new world of easy-to-
20 use communication with higher speed data networks will open up for us all. People all over the world, not only the western world, will be able to send and receive multimedia documents that combine texts, sound and pictures. This computer revolution will be even bigger
25 than the PC revolution of the 1980s. Why? The computer revolution of the 1980s reached only about 15 % of

homes, mainly because people didn't really need expensive and complex machines to store addresses and telephone numbers, for example. The next revolution will introduce computer 30 technology into most products that people need. The big difference will be that people will actually be able to use the devices because they will be more user-friendly. In future it will also become even easier to communicate with other 35 users through wireless connection systems. Using digital devices people will be able to call up special computer programs. For example "VirtualTown" will then appear on the screen of your digital TV set. Here people will meet 40 in virtual schools, make virtual trips to exotic countries, watch a football match and even talk to other users while they are watching. Of course, some virtual activities like shopping or banking via the Internet have already become reality and 45 in future more people will make use of this new technology.

So we will all get the technology – and the future which we always wanted. It still won't solve the big problems, such as war and poverty. But at least we 50 will have powerful devices that we will be able to use and not ones we do not really understand.

377 words

a Match the words in the box, according to the text.

> networks • multimedia • wireless • systems • transmission • digital • documents • data • information • connection • PC • devices

b Answer the following questions.
1. Do we live in a "technological paradise"? Why (not)?
2. Which two developments have led to the new computer revolution?
3. What do we mean by "multimedia documents"?
4. Why will this new development be more important than the PC revolution of the 1980s?
5. How will "VirtualTown" work?
6. What big problems won't this technology solve?

c Find the words or expressions in the text from these definitions and then make four new sentences in which they appear.
1. electrical devices you use at home, e.g. a DVD player
2. apparatus for receiving and showing television transmissions
3. a complex system which connects and transmits information
4. a device used in the home or office which stores and processes information

d From the information in the text explain the technological revolution in your own words.

e In your opinion, what else could people use computers in their homes for?

f "We will all get the technology which we always wanted." Do you agree?

2 Who is in touch?

The bar graph shows the percentage of electronic communication devices in five European countries.

(2001) households with

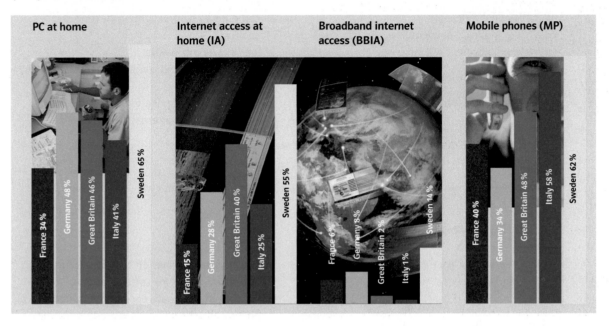

a Compare countries in the following way. Use the phrases in the box on the right.

Example:
IA – S / GB
The graph shows that the percentage of homes with internet access in Sweden is higher than it is in Britain.

1. PC – F / G
2. BBIA – I / S
3. MP – GB / G
4. IA – F / I
5. PC – S / F

The graph shows	that	the number of	(device) owners	is higher	in (country A) than it is in (country B).
The figures show		the percentage of	households who have	is lower	
We can see from the statistics					

b What could be the reasons for these differences? Use the following phrases.

I'm pretty sure that …
That may be because …
A possible reason is that …
I'm sorry, but I've no idea why …

1 Life in the future – what will it be like?

a Ask your classmates what they think about the following ideas about the future.
The words in the box below can help you.

Example:
unemployment / increase
What do you think, will unemployment increase?
I think unemployment will increase.

> I'm of the opinion; I think/don't think;
> I expect; I suppose

1. people / read / books any more
2. computers / control lighting, heating and cooking
3. we / have / more wars
4. television, DVD, and computer games / replace / sport
5. there / be / more pollution
6. all houses / use / alternative energy

b Now answer the questions in short form and give reasons.

Example:
What do you think, will unemployment increase? Yes, it will because computers will do all the work.

2 In the office of the "Daily News"

■ Make sentences like this:

Example:
The phone is ringing. A secretary is walking towards it. She is **going to** answer the phone.

1. Jim Price has sat down at his computer. His notes for a story are in front of him.
2. Sally Jones is looking at her address book. She picks up the phone.
3. Two secretaries have left their desks and are putting money in the coffee machine.
4. Sam Smith, the head reporter, has invited a local politician to the office. He is preparing some questions.
5. It is eleven o'clock in the morning. Jim is taking some biscuits out of his bag.
6. The receptionist and her friend are in the restaurant. They have chosen their food and are standing at the till.

3 Office Electronics Ltd

Sam Smith wants to write an article about developments in the modern media for the "Daily News". He has invited James Bradshaw, manager of "Office Electronics Ltd", for an interview. Here is part of their conversation.

■ Put the verbs into the correct form of the future.

Sam Smith: Come in, Mr Bradshaw, sit down. **I'll take** your coat and I expect **Janet will** bring us some coffee in a minute.
James Bradshaw: Thank you, Mr Smith.
Sam Smith: Now, as I said on the phone **I'm going** to do an article on media developments and I'd like to ask you a few questions. Don't worry about that noise, by the way, it's one of the old fax machines. **It's going** to break down any minute.

James Bradshaw: Oh dear, I hope it's not one of ours.
Sam Smith: Oh no, of course not. Now, Mr Bradshaw, how is business? Do you think this year **1. (be)** as successful for you as last year?
James Bradshaw: Well, I certainly hope so. I have our most recent sales report here and the figures show that the firm **2. (do)** very well again this year.
Sam Smith: Of course, the market is growing all the time, isn't it? In the next few years I expect we **3. (see)** an even bigger increase in the use of communications technology. But do you think this **4. (be)** a good thing?
James Bradshaw: Well, for me and my company certainly!
Sam Smith: But what about the customers? It's an expensive business, isn't it? I've certainly decided that I **5. (not spend)** any more money on the latest developments.
James Bradshaw: Well, just a minute. I **6. (show)** you our brochure …

4 The trainee journalists

Two new trainee journalists have started work at the "Daily News" newspaper in London. They are on a one month test period. Ken Brown, the head of the foreign news department, has to write a report on them. He has used the following system:

++ excellent / + good / – bad / –– terrible

	General work	Computer skills	Shorthand	French	Communication skills
Duncan	+ +	+	–	++	––
Tina	+	–	+	–	++

a First make sentences about Duncan. Use the verbs in the box.

> speak – use – communicate – write – work

Example:
Duncan's general work is excellent. He works excellently.

b Form adverbs from the following adjectives.

> careful, slow, fast, accurate, polite, quick, correct, hard, wonderful

c Now choose from these adverbs to compare the trainee journalists in the following way:

Example:
general work
Duncan works more carefully than Tina does.
Tina doesn't work as carefully as Duncan does.

5 A report   **Advanced**

■ Look at the adjectives and adverbs. Then complete Ken's report on two other trainees.

On the whole I can say Phillip's work in the office has been **fairly good**. **Unfortunately**, he speaks French **terribly**. On the other hand, his computer skills appear to be **very good**. In comparison, Charlotte has worked **extremely well** over the last four weeks. Although she speaks French **(real) (bad)**, her computer skills are **(extreme) (good)**. Nevertheless, she seems to be the **(good)** of all our trainees. **(General)**, she keeps **(calm)** in a crisis and doesn't get **(nervous)**. All in all, I think she will **(probable)** make an **(excellent)** journalist. But she must learn to speak more **(polite)** on the phone. I **(certain)** cannot say the same about …

Entwicklung der Werbung
Development of advertising

US Advertising Expenditures (dollars per head) 1900 – 2000

Share of all advertising dollars in the US

	Magazines	Newspapers	Outdoor	TV	Radio	Internet
1995	19 %	24 %	2 %	53 %	3 %	n/v
2000	18 %	23 %	2 %	50 %	4 %	3 %

a Answer the following questions.

1. How did the amount of money which was spent on advertising per head change in the 20th century?
2. Whose share of the advertising market fell between 1995 and 2000?
3. Which of the media had a bigger share of the advertising market in 2000 than in 1995?
4. What could be the reason for this development?

b Read the text on the next page and answer the following questions.

1. Which of the media in the chart above are mentioned?
2. What could the headline of the following text be?

If you see a big yellow M on TV, will you recognize it and – more importantly – will you know what product it stands for? Most people will recognize it, according to an international survey. They be-
5 lieved that the M was one of the best known logos in TV advertising.

For the companies that had spent millions on the production of commercials and on airtime the results of the survey were quite important. The companies
10 whose products came first were pleased. But the problem is that compared to every commercial that becomes popular 100 others fail.

Indeed, according to the survey, one of the main disadvantages of TV advertising is that only a third
15 of commercials receive our full attention. One in five plays to empty rooms, while people are making tea or going to the toilet. Two in five act as background while people are eating, reading or even sleeping. With the help of "hidden" video cameras in a number
20 of homes, the survey showed what surprising things people actually do during the break – one man even practised his tennis serve.

According to the survey even people who stay in the room during commercials do not always watch them.
25 A new generation of viewers has arrived – people who watch with remote control in hand and switch to another channel when the commercials come on. Reports from America, where this habit is much older, say that in this way companies waste a quarter
30 of the money which they spend on TV advertising.

Of course, it was not the TV companies which paid for this international survey, it was the newspapers. They used it for an £8 million advertising campaign. The message was simple: Advertisers overestimate the value of TV commercials. The reason why 35 newspapers started their campaign is also easy to see; their share in the advertising market has been decreasing worldwide, and is down to about 15% in Britain.

Newspapers and TV stations have different view- 40 points on advertising. On the one hand, Bert Hardy, who is the manager of the newspapers' campaign, argues: "The most expensive time in TV advertising costs around £60,000 a minute, whereas a full page in a national newspaper only costs £20,000 45 and lasts all day. The companies could use some of the money that they waste on TV advertising to increase their profits and cut prices." On the other hand ITV manager Malcolm Wall points out the fact that newspapers themselves spend millions on TV 50 advertising.

Today many advertising managers are sure that a mix of the advertising media will be the best way to reach consumers. Some companies have already changed their advertising campaigns. Many more 55 are planning the same and are going to advertise not only on TV in the future but also on the radio, in newspapers and on the internet.   465 words
(The Telegraph plc, London)

c Find the expressions with the same meaning in the text.
1. 20 per cent   2. 25 per cent
3. 33 per cent   4. 40 per cent

d Try to make some more expressions in the same way.
1. 66 per cent   2. 75 per cent
3. 10 per cent   4. 80 per cent

e Read the text again and answer the following questions in complete sentences.
1. Are all companies happy with the results of their TV advertising? Why (not)?
2. What percentage of the commercials on TV do viewers really watch?
3. What do people do during the commercial break?
4. Who paid for the international survey on TV commercials? And why?
5. What financial advantage do firms have when they advertise in newspapers?
6. What media will many companies use to advertise in the future?

f Give your opinion.
If advertising on TV is so expensive, why are firms willing to spend so much money on it?

g Translate lines 40 to 51.

1 Radio advertising

 a Listen and find out:
1. the product
2. the name of the product
3. the price
4. the name of the shop that sells it

 b Listen again and find adjectives from the ones below which describe the products. Say which of the products they describe.

careful • cheap • superfast • superb • modern • safe • excellent •
popular • polite • wonderful • light • accurate • good • quick •
easy to use • comfortable

2 Analyzing advertisements

Who says you can't afford paradise?

Prices from London
Jamaica £ 299
Barbados £ 333
Antigua £ 399
All other destinations
on request

BT

Budget Tours 44 Euston Road / London NW1 2BT / www.budgettours.co.uk

a Try to analyze the advertisement on the left.
1. Say what this advert is for.
2. Identify
   – the slogan/key words.
   – the logo/brand name/name of the company.
3. Say what other information is given in this advert.
4. Describe what the picture shows.
5. Say what ideas and lifestyle you associate with this picture.
6. What target group could the advert be aimed at?

b With reference to what you have found out above do you think this advert could be successful?

3 Writing an advertisement

a Look at the photo on the left and think of a product/service you could sell with it. Choose a suitable target group.

b Now write a short advertisement for your product/service. Refer to the points in D2.

c Present your advertisement to the class. Say why you have designed it in this way.

a Describe the situation in the photo.

b How do the people in the cars feel?

c Decide which of the following comments in your opinion best describe the situation in the photo and say why.
1. People in cities don't need their cars.
2. Private transport will be the death of us.
3. If you want to reduce your stress level, leave your car at home.
4. It's quicker on foot.

d What is your view of the traffic situation in our towns and cities?

1 Traffic

Every day we can hear reports of cities which are congested by traffic and this situation is getting worse day by day. The congestion of roads and motorways causes major problems for drivers and the environment. These problems have grown with the development of private transport. We have got used to a lifestyle we find hard to change. More and more people who own cars are not able to imagine a life without them. The question is how to find a solution people would accept. Some people believe public transport should be the answer. Others are looking into technological innovations such as electronic navigation systems.

109 words

a Match the following words with their definitions.

1. congestion	A. the world around us
2. environment	B. a way to travel for people in large groups, e.g. bus, tram, train
3. navigation system	C. the state of being too full or overcrowded, especially on roads
4. public transport	D. a device which helps you find your way

Here are some statements we heard at a transport planning meeting.

b Complete these statements with the words used above (1. – 4.).

1
"During the rush-hour the ... on the M25 leads to long traffic jams every day."

2
"The fumes from cars pollute the ..."

3
"A ... can help drivers to avoid congested traffic without having to look at a map."

4
"I believe we should use ... and leave cars at home."

2 Car navigation systems

Car navigation systems are no longer a high-tech dream. You can find them in many cars as a standard device. If you miss a traffic report, there is no need to worry. Your navigation
5 system saves it for you in text and audio form and will give it to you at the touch of a button. It can even recalculate your chosen route using the latest traffic information. Life couldn't be easier!

Drivers can relax as they are guided to their 10 chosen destination, be it a city centre or a small suburban street, without having to look at a single map. A quick look at the display and you can see how much longer your journey will take and how many miles you have to drive. All this 15 is made possible by satellites that can pinpoint your car's location, if it is equipped with a Global Positioning System (GPS).

The Trafficmaster system is an additional aid in
20 avoiding traffic congestion. Instead of relying
on radio reports, Trafficmaster obtains its
information from sensors installed on motorways
and road networks which monitor traffic speed.
Trafficmaster transmits this information to its
25 users at regular intervals. The system is available
as part of the navigation system from some car
manufacturers, but is not normally a standard
feature and you have to buy it as an extra.
So, is there anything navigation systems cannot
30 do? Well, they cannot regulate traffic flow to avoid
traffic jams and slow moving traffic in the first
place. They can only help find a way out of the
congestion and suggest a diversion. The other
disadvantage with most navigation systems

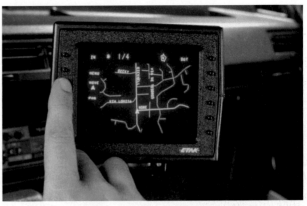

35 at present is the slow and rather complicated
method of entering your destination, especially
when you are driving. However, this is all going to
change. A leading technology company and a car
manufacturer have produced a navigation system
40 that uses voice recognition. For example drivers
who suddenly realize that they are running out of
petrol can press the 'talk' button on their steering
wheel and give commands like "find the nearest
petrol station". The system is programmed to
understand around 150 commands and a number 45
of different accents. This makes programming
your system a lot easier and safer, for example,
when you are driving along the motorway or
looking for the nearest fast food restaurant.
However, all this only helps the individual driver 50
and does not really solve the general problem of
traffic congestion and pollution. **406 words**

a Look at the text.
1. Describe how you can find where the nearest petrol station is through a car navigation system.
2. Explain how this is possible.
3. Show how the Trafficmaster system works.
4. Point out two disadvantages of car navigation systems.
5. Explain why the newer navigation systems are safer.

b Here are some radio travel news announcements. Find nouns in the text to complete them.
1. Traffic … on the M1 near Nottingham is causing problems for drivers.
   Try to avoid the M1 near Nottingham if possible.
2. Due to motorway repairs on the M4 there is a 5-mile … in both directions near Bristol.
3. Road works on the A58 south of Rochdale. The police advise drivers to follow the … signs.
4. Due to an accident on the A30 near Exeter there is 3 miles of …
   So take care when driving on the A30 near Exeter.
5. Fog on the M62 ! Drivers should reduce their …

c Rewrite lines 10 – 18 and replace some of the expressions with those in the cloud. Start like this:

Example:
Drivers can take it easy as …

monitor · **take it easy** · route ·
glance · just one · find exactly ·
how far · fitted · position ·
shown the way

1 Getting around

a Look at these pictures and the information below. Then make sentences like this:

Example:

1. The train which is standing at the station is going to the Docklands.
2. The students who are waiting for the ferry …

- go to the Docklands
- go on a bike tour
- phone his wife
- be a London tourist bus

b Now describe the other pictures in the same way.
Example: The train which is going through the Eurotunnel …

- go to Paris
- travel to Italy
- read newspaper
- go to Paddington

2 Travelling home

Complete the following story. Fill in "who" or "which" where necessary.

At 5.30 Henry arrived at the station **(–)** he knew so well. He showed his ticket to the man **who** was standing at the gate. Then he got on the train **which** was waiting at platform 7. He politely greeted the woman **(1)** was sitting next to the door. She put down the book **(2)** she was reading. They both smiled and then he walked to the seat **(3)** he always chose. He sat down and filled the pipe **(4)** he had taken out of his jacket. This was the time of day **(5)** he liked best. After some minutes he started to read the paper **(6)** he had bought at the station. The couple **(7)** were sitting next to him were talking about the plans **(8)** they had for the weekend. He listened for a while and then he looked out of the window at the countryside **(9)** was passing by. What a nice day it was! Henry started to think about the work **(10)** he had done at the bank. He smiled. He remembered all the years **(11)** had passed and all the people **(12)** had worked with him. When the train arrived at the station he at once saw the woman **(13)** was waiting for him. He walked up to her and kissed her. It was the first time his wife had met him at the station. She had bought him the flowers **(14)** he liked so much and he knew it would never be the same again. This had been his last day at work after 48 years.

3 A guessing game

a Guess who or what it is.

1. It's a person who goes on a journey for pleasure.
2. It's an electronic appliance which helps you to find your destination.
3. It's a place where trains arrive and leave.
4. It's a piece of paper you buy when you want to travel by train or bus.

b Now describe other persons, places, vehicles etc. in the same way. Don't mention their names. Your classmates should find out who/what they are.

4   Changes in travelling

■ Compare travelling today, in the past, and in the future. Make sentences like this:

Example:

Lots of people must/have to wait in traffic jams today. 100 years ago most people had to walk.
In 100 years' time I think people will …

Today …	100 years ago …	In 100 years' time (I think) …
lots of people/wait/ in traffic jams (must/have to)	most people/walk	people/use/public transport in cities
passengers/travel/to America in a few hours (can/be able to)	passengers/get/to America in a week	passengers/travel/around the world in minutes
drivers/stop/at most European borders (needn't/not have to)	drivers/have/a driving licence	drivers/stop/at any borders
travellers/enter/some countries without showing their passports (can/be allowed to)	travellers/take/their cats and dogs into Britain	travellers/enter/all countries freely
man/fly/to Venus (can't/be not able to)	man/fly/to the moon	man/fly/to the stars
people/drive/ faster than 70 mph on British motorways (mustn't/be not allowed to)	people/drive/without a person carrying a red flag in front of their vehicles	people/drive/cars in city centres

5   A day in the life of Harry S.   **Advanced**

Harry **(1)** works in London. But he lives in Bacon End **(2)**. Every day he has to travel one and a half hours to the computer firm **(3)**. At 7.30 when he leaves his house, he gets into the car and drives to the station **(4)**. Harry arrives there at about 8 o'clock and he gets on the train **(5)**. On the train he reads the newspaper **(6)**. Sometimes he talks to the passengers **(7)**. When he arrives in London he takes the underground line **(8)**. Sometimes he meets his colleague **(9)** and together they walk to work. On his journey home **(10)** he often uses his mobile phone to text his friends or listens to his CD player.

■ Complete the text about Harry S. with the information below. Use relative clauses.
Decide if the relative clause is necessary or not and find out if you can replace "who" or "which" by "that".

Example:

Harry, who is 24, works in London. But he lives in Bacon End, which is 35 miles away.
Every day he has to travel one and a half hours to the computer firm he writes programs for. At 7.30 …

Some more information on Harry S.:

a) The journey home takes about one and a half hours.
b) The line goes to Cannon Street Station.
c) Harry is 24.
d) He writes programs for the computer firm.

e) He usually buys a newspaper at the station.
f) Bacon End is 35 miles from London.
g) The passengers are sitting next to him.
h) His colleague also works at the computer firm.
i) The station is in Harlow.
j) The train leaves at 8.05.

1 From jam to tram

1 Peter Wood used to travel to his office in Manchester by car. Every morning the journey took longer and longer because the roads were too congested. One day he decided to try the tram and the journey
5 was half an hour shorter. Thanks to the town's tram system, his journey only takes 16 minutes. "It really is a very good service," says Wood. Other commuters are happy too. One of them, Mike Pulman, adds "I stopped using my car years ago simply because
10 the tram is so convenient."

2 Their views of the tram are quite different to the ones people in Britain had after the war. At that time people thought that the trams were noisy and slow and so they got rid of them. In the 1920s, Britain
15 had over 14,000 trams in more than 100 towns, but by the 1960s the tram remained in only one town. At that time the attractive alternatives were the bus and the car. The bus because it provided a more flexible alternative to the fixed-route tram and the
20 car because of the freedom it gave to the individual driver. Of course, in those car-crazy days, "nobody thought about the congestion and pollution which all those petrol engines would produce," says Don Roach, who is head of London's traffic department.

Today however, environmentalists 25
and city planners are welcoming back the electrically-driven, new-style tram or 'light-rail system' as they now call it. They see it as an efficient and ecological solution to 30 inner city traffic chaos.

3 Today's trams are most profitable in cities which have populations of half a million or less and no more than 20,000 passengers an hour at 35 peak times. Although one alternative – an underground system – may be a good solution to the traffic problems of large cities, Mary Browning, a British environmentalist says "it doesn't make sense for 40 medium-sized cities and is much more expensive to build than a tram system." In fact, a team of traffic experts has estimated that building one kilometer of underground costs 11 times more than building the same length of tramway. "The main reason trams are 45 coming back is not just because they are good for the environment," says Browning, "it's because they are cheaper and more efficient."

4 However, the fact that there are two good arguments for trams doesn't mean that they are easy 50 to introduce. Public transport of any sort is unpopular with car drivers and the car industry so that governments do not always support it. As a result, it is difficult for town planners to put tramway projects into practice. This helped to slow down the opening of 55 Manchester's system by nine years and may also slow down progress on similar projects. However, since statistics show that there will be twice as much road traffic by the year 2025, sooner or later governments will have to look at light rail systems as one possible 60 solution to the transport problems which European cities are facing in the 21st century. **498 words**

a Find the forms of transport mentioned in the text.

b Match four of these headings with the paragraphs in the text.

Trams – an old idea made new • Trams – a danger to private transport? •
Trams reduce journey time • Trams – too noisy and dirty •
Trams save money for medium-sized towns

c Now do these tasks.

1. Describe the difference which Manchester's tram system has made to commuters.
2. Say why trams were unpopular in Britain after the war.
3. Explain the advantages which today's modern 'light-rail systems' have.
4. Compare the costs of a tram system with an underground system.
5. Give reasons why it is often still difficult to introduce tram systems.

d Complete these sentences with information from the text. Use your own words.

1. As a result of road congestion in Manchester commuters …
2. Traffic planners are in favour of the tram because …
3. Although Britain had 14,000 trams in the 1920s …
4. Buses became more popular than trams because …
5. Although there are two good arguments for trams …
6. As a result of the increase in road traffic in the future …

e Translate lines 11 to 31.

2 Solutions to traffic problems

Two traffic experts are talking about possible solutions to traffic problems:

A: But **don't you think the best thing would be to** improve the public transport system?
B: Certainly, but that's not enough. People will never give up private transport completely. They would lose their freedom and industry would suffer. **I think the answer to the problems of** congestion for example, is technology.

Why not make car computers cheaper, then everyone could have one?
A: Yes, but that doesn't solve the problem of pollution, does it? **One solution to that problem could be** a tram system. It's the quickest and most convenient means of transport and **I would definitely suggest it** for a medium-sized town.

■ Discuss the solutions you can see in the pictures below in the same way and any others you can think of. Use the expressions in bold type in the dialogue or similar ones.

1 Travel announcements

a Listen to the announcements. Where could you hear these announcements?

b Listen to the announcements again and answer the following questions.

1. Where is the train to Liverpool?
2. Where does it stop?
3. What must passengers do who want to travel to Leeds?
4. Where is the plane with flight number BA98 flying to?
5. Which gate should the passengers go to?
6. What was the reason for the delay?
7. Why is there trouble on the M4?
8. How long is the traffic jam?
9. According to the police, what should the motorists do?

2 Welcome to Wakefield

It's so simple to get here!

Since the great coaching days of the 18th century Wakefield has always been at the "crossroads of the north". This fact is now even more important in a world where fast and easy communications are a must. In any part of the Wakefield district you are only minutes away from a motorway, the M62 to the two main ports of Hull and Liverpool, and the M1 to London which is only a three hour drive away.

Moreover, you can reach Wakefield by rail from all parts of the country. Regular train services operate from most cities in England, Scotland and Wales. Again London is only two hours away.

On top of all this, Wakefield has two major airports nearby: Manchester (only an hour's drive on the M62) and Leeds (only minutes away via the M1). These fast growing airports provide links with four major intercontinental airports – London, Amsterdam, Paris and Dublin.

An ideal base. Discover Wakefield yourself. It could work for you.

For further information write to:

Wakefield
Tourist Information Centre
Town Hall
Wood Street
Wakefield WF1 2HQ

Or visit our website:
www.city-visitor.com/wakefield

162 words

a With the help of the text and the map answer these questions about Wakefield.

1. Why do you think Wakefield is called the "crossroads of the north"?
2. How can you get to continental Europe from Wakefield?
3. Why are the Manchester and Leeds airports so important for Wakefield?
4. Why do you think Wakefield has produced this promotion brochure?

b Design a promotion brochure in English for your town.
Concentrate on road/rail/air/sea connections.

Umwelt

Waste management

In one year the average family of four throws away 112 pounds of metal, 90 pounds of plastics and an amount of paper equal to six trees. We produce more than 25 million tons of waste each year. Where does all this waste go?

Waste Management in Europe (per cent)

Country	Landfill	Energy recovery	Composting	Recycling
Denmark	11	58	2	29
France	49	39	6	6
Germany	54	18	5	23
Italy	80	7	10	3
The Netherlands	12	42	7	39
Spain	74	6	17	3
UK	85	8	1	7

a Describe what you can see in the picture.

b Answer the following questions.
1. What kind of waste do you think it is?
2. Where, in your opinion, does this waste come from?
3. What will happen to the waste?
4. What else could they do with it?

c Talk about the information in the chart on the left.

d What are the current developments in waste management in Europe?
Compare the latest figures (e.g. from the internet) with the figures in the chart.

1 Everyone can help to save the world

1 We are all environmentalists now. We all know about acid rain and the ozone hole. But what are we doing about these problems? As consumers we have the power to make decisions which will
5 contribute to a better world. For example, when we walk into a supermarket we can choose to buy environmentally-friendly products and refuse products which damage our planet. In this way we also have the power to influence retailers to
10 sell us these so-called 'green' products.
2 The supermarkets have understood the message and are now trying to improve their environmental image. They are turning to less wasteful and recyclable packaging. The range
15 of 'green' products will continue to expand to meet the growing demand. This message has also reached the manufacturers. Companies are now developing environmentally-friendly products which mean no decrease in quality or increase
20 in price. They have realized that protecting the environment may start as an advertising campaign but in the hands of intelligent people it can become a very profitable business.

3 We also know there are other areas where all of us can make a positive contribution to a 25 cleaner, healthier and safer environment. We can all reduce energy consumption at home and so cut the emissions from power stations. There are a number of ways we can do this. For example, we now know how important it is to insulate our 30 houses well. In the use of electrical appliances and lighting we should choose the best energy-efficient technology, such as modern light bulbs which can reduce electricity consumption by 80% over the older ones. Rubbish is another 35 area where we can act. We all produce tonnes of rubbish and so waste disposal is becoming a big problem. As an environmentally-conscious consumer we should buy products which do not have so much packaging. We should avoid non- 40 returnable goods at all costs. In Scandinavia and Germany, for example, plastic bottles and cans are now returnable goods.
4 In conclusion it is important to emphasize once again the rise of consumer power. We 45 must realize that we are all part of the problem. Nevertheless we must also realize that we have the responsibility to be part of the solution.

363 words

a The text above has four paragraphs. Find headings for each paragraph in the following bubbles.

> The influence of consumers on supermarket products

> The use of public transport

> The introduction of 'green' products and price increases

> The problems of acid rain and the ozone hole

> The reaction of retailers and manufacturers to environmental problems

> Everybody's duty to contribute to a cleaner world

> Other ways to protect the environment

b Answer the questions on the text.
1. Which decisions can a consumer make in a supermarket?
2. How have supermarkets reacted to these decisions?
3. Why have manufacturers become more interested in environmentally-friendly products?
4. How can we reduce our consumption of energy?
5. How can we help to avoid waste?

c Give your opinion.
1. What is the message of the text?
2. In what other ways can you protect the environment?
3. What other examples of 'green' products can you think of?

d Look at the following nouns and find the verbs in the text. Say which line in the text.

1. choice
2. reduction
3. insulation
4. production
5. emphasis
6. sales

e Now find the nouns from the following verbs in the same way.

1. to consume
2. to demand
3. to decide
4. to contribute
5. to waste
6. to solve

f Find synonyms in the text for the following words.

1. shop owners
2. 'green' products
3. waste
4. to manufacture
5. to cut
6. to make better

2 Pollution

a Read the statements and match them with the photos.

A Emma Shaw, chemist: "I've just read a book about acid rain. Did you know it was a Scottish chemist, Robert Angus Smith, who invented the expression 'acid rain' in an 1852 article on the air and rain in Manchester? Moreover, according to him air pollution damages buildings and forests more quickly in countries where people use more fuel than elsewhere."

B Paul Jenkins, environmentalist: "It's true that this government is doing a lot to reduce the level of air pollution here in Britain. However, in my opinion, we consumers have the power to make the biggest improvement. We should buy cars which don't pollute the environment so badly or we should use public transport."

C Jill Kemp, journalist: "As I see it, we, the people of Britain, have been using our rivers as waste disposal channels for hundreds of years. I'm convinced that our government must act. Furthermore, we need better pollution control over companies, farmers and even local government."

D Richard Palmer, politician: "I think the ozone hole is the greatest danger to our planet. It isn't true that we can afford to wait. The ozone hole will cause serious dangers to our health. In addition all over the world people must stop making household products with CFCs* in them."

*CFC = chlorofluorocarbon

b Why did you make those decisions? Answer in the following way:

Example:
I chose the photo of … for text A because Emma Shaw says/tells us …

c Report what each person says and introduce each reported sentence with a different verb. Use the table below.

	Direct speech	Reporting verbs
Opinion	"In my opinion …"	be of the opinion
	"As I see it …"	take the view
	"I think/believe …"	think/believe
Emphasis	"I am (I'm) convinced …"	maintain
	"We should/ought to/must …"	emphasize
Agreement/ Disagreement	"It is (It's) true …"	agree
	"It is not (It isn't) true …"	not agree
Additional Information	"Moreover …"	point out
	"Furthermore …"	go on to mention
	"In addition …"	add

1 Protect your environment

For a project on the protection of the environment, the consumer magazine 'What?' interviewed some people in Birmingham. Here are some of the answers they got.

1. "We are fighting for more cycle paths here." **Joe Straw, member of Green party.**

2. "I'm joining the WWF tomorrow. People don't give enough money to help with their work." **Roger Williams, bank clerk.**

3. "I don't buy cans." **Mrs Black, housewife.**

4. "I ride my bike to school every day." **John Smith, teacher.**

5. "We are closing some streets to traffic in the city centre next year." **Ray Peters, town planner.**

6. "My husband doesn't wash his car here in the street any longer." **Mrs Rivers, housewife.**

7. "We always buy bottles we can return to the shop." **Fred and Jim, college students.**

8. "Well, I'm just taking my old newspapers to the container like I usually do on Saturdays." **Peter Bone, old man.**

9. "We don't buy goods which aren't environmentally-friendly." **Anna and Rob Nelson, young married couple.**

10. "We must all save a lot more energy in the home. We're buying an energy-efficient heating system tomorrow." **Mr Field, farmer.**

■ Report the answers like this:

Example:
1. Joe Straw, a member of the Green party, said that they were fighting for more cycle paths there.
2. Roger Williams, a bank clerk, said that he was joining the WWF the next day. People didn't give …

2 Retailers and the environment

The manager of a large supermarket group gave the following statement to 'What?' magazine about retailers and the environment:

"We opened our first supermarket just ten years ago and we have had a lot of success since then. We have always kept our prices low and our quality high. We will of course continue to do this in the future. However, and I know you are interested in this, we have always had a special interest in environmental matters. Right from the start we sold goods with as little packaging as possible and placed bottle banks and containers in all our car parks.

As from next month we won't hand out free plastic bags any more and we will stop selling all drinks in plastic containers. Over the last few years we have introduced more and more 'green' products and we certainly haven't felt sorry about this. Two years ago, when we started to plan our second store here in this area, there wasn't a bus service. But after we wrote to the council they agreed to introduce one. All in all I think I can say that we are really doing our best for the environment."

Chris Hawkings, who reported this statement for the magazine, began his article like this:

Example: The manager of Dippy Supermarkets spoke to me yesterday … He told me that they had opened their first supermarket ten years before and that they had had a lot of success since then. He went on to say … that they had always … and that they would of course …

■ Complete his article.

3 Interview with "Whiz Bang Electronics"

Chris Hawkings' next job was to interview the head of "Whiz Bang Electronics" about their new washing machine, which they want to sell as an environmentally-friendly model. Here is his list of questions:

1. Do you plan to replace all your old models with environmentally-friendly ones?
2. How many models will you produce per year?
3. Why do you call it environmentally-friendly?
4. Do you think the new model will sell well?
5. When did you begin to develop this model?
6. How many litres of water does it use?
7. What is the energy consumption like?
8. What plans have you made to recycle these washing machines?

Later at lunch, the head of "Whiz Bang" told one of his colleagues about the interview and that the reporter had wanted to know a lot about their new model.

Example:

1. He wanted to find out if we planned to replace all our old models with environmentally-friendly ones.
2. He also wanted to know how many …

■ Now you go on.

4 The inner city traffic situation   **Advanced**

Last night there was a meeting in the town hall to discuss the inner city traffic situation. Here is part of this discussion:

Town planner: … and so in my opinion, the only solution is to close the centre to traffic completely.

Shop owner: What will happen to our trade? No one will want to come into town at all then. And we already have enough competition from these big out-of-town superstores.

Town planner: But we have already introduced a number of highly successful park and ride schemes and I'm sure people will prefer shopping without all the noise and exhaust fumes from cars.

Shopper: That may be true, but we don't like carrying heavy bags of shopping for miles and miles before we can get them into the car.

Shop owner: You see, we must discuss the problem in more detail. Do you realize the problems we will have with deliveries?

Town planner: We do, Mr Black, and as long as lorries can deliver before 10 in the morning, there won't be a problem.

Shopper: I suppose shopping is more pleasant with no traffic. I will certainly feel better about bringing my children into town then. In some cities they even have special play areas for children. Can't we have something like that here, too?

■ Now report this discussion. Use as many different reporting verbs as possible.

Vehicles go round again

The three R's of waste management

Randy Newbury, manager at an international car company, has a dream. "In thirty years our company will be 100% environmentally friendly. On the one hand we will not pollute air or water any more during
5 the production process, on the other hand we will only produce cars from recycled material. And I hope we will then be able to recycle these cars completely." This sounds unlikely? Not to Newbury, who is responsible for such environmental problems. What
10 is more, lots of other international companies are actively trying to find solutions to make this dream come true. While they are already re-using waste heat and raw materials, they are reducing the amount of waste in the production process. Moreover, they are
15 trying to increase the number of parts they can re-use. And of course, the products themselves must be recyclable. To be more precise, these companies are employing the new 3 R's to protect the environment: reduce, re-use, recycle.
20 The 3 R's were not always part of the companies' vocabulary. In fact, until the late 1980s, companies wishing to go 'green', installed filters in the factories and then tried to get rid of the waste they had

collected there. "People were just shifting their pollution from one place to another," states Ron 25 Humber for Friends of the Earth in London. "What we need is a completely new approach to waste management."

"I'm dreaming of a factory," says Randy Newbury, "in which scrap vehicles enter through the back door for 30 100 per cent recycling and leave as new cars through the front door."

"At the moment this is only a dream," he quickly adds, "but we must do something now. Every year millions of cars in Europe go to the scrap dealers." 35

"In the past, industry was only able to recycle the metal parts. But after they had taken them out they still had up to 250 kg of mixed waste – plastics, glass, rubber and engine oil. The scrap dealers had to pay £50 a tonne to dump this waste – and the costs were 40 rising. Now special firms collect and dismantle old vehicles and return as many parts as possible to the car manufacturers.

We code the plastic parts of each car so it is easier to separate material for recycling. In this way we reduce 45 the amount of mixed waste, but there is still some left. So our engineers and suppliers are working on this problem to find substitute materials for the rest. Ideally car parts should be made from one family of material. All this adds to the cost of a new car but, 50 of course, we are able to save money by re-using or recycling the parts.

This means that one day we will produce a car which is 100% recyclable, which allows us to use the same materials over and over again. As we see it every 55 new vehicle we design in this way helps us to solve tomorrow's problems today."

493 words

a Before answering the following questions on the text, look at the "steps" on the opposite page.
1. What is the manager for environmental problems dreaming of?
2. How are other firms attacking the waste problem?
3. In what way did companies try to solve the problems of pollution in the 1980s?
4. How can special firms improve the work of the scrap dealers?
5. How can car companies help to solve problems of pollution when they are designing new cars?

Follow these steps

Example (Question 1):

1. Read the text carefully.

2. Find the lines in the text which contain the information necessary to answer the questions.

lines 29 – 32

3. Look up all the words (in a dictionary or below) you must understand to answer a question.

scrap = metal from …

---

dealer (n) **1.** A **dealer** is a person who buys and sells things. **2.** A **dealer** in a game of cards is the person who gives out the cards to the other players.

dismantle (v) If you **dismantle** a machine, you carefully take it to pieces.

dump (n) A **dump** is a place where rubbish is left.

dump (v) **1.** If you **dump** something, you throw it away carelessly. **2.** If a company **dumps** goods, it sells large quantities at very low prices, usually in another country.

recycle (v) If you **recycle** things that have already been used, such as bottles or paper, you process them so that people can use them again.

reduce (v) To **reduce** something means to make it smaller in number, size, price etc.

re-use (v) When you **re-use** something, you do not throw it away. You use it again.

scrap (n) **1.** A **scrap** of paper is a very small piece of it. Usually you do not want it any more. **2. Scrap** or **scrap** metal is metal from old or damaged machines, cars, etc. which is melted so that it can be used again.

shift (n) A **shift** is a change from one position to another.

shift (v) If you **shift** something, you move it or change its position.

substitute (n) A **substitute** is a person or thing that takes the place of another.

substitute (v) If you **substitute** a thing, you put the new thing in the place where the old thing was.

---

4. Use part of the question as an introduction to your answer, if possible.

The manager for environmental problems …

5. Use synonyms and paraphrases.

The manager for environmental problems has a vision of …

6. Write your answer in complete sentences. Be careful with the tenses and use the phrases below.

It says in the text that the manager for environmental problems has a vision of a factory in which old cars become fully recycled new cars.

In the first (second, …) paragraph the author mentions that … / In line one (two, …) we read that … / It says in the text that …

b Translate lines 44 – 52.

Info-Box: How to answer questions on a text

Remember:
1. Read the text carefully.
2. Find the information necessary to answer the questions.
3. Look up all unknown words which are important for your answers.

4. Now answer the questions.
   - If possible, use the question as an introduction to your answer.
   - Use the main facts that you have found in the text.
   - Write your answers in complete sentences.
   - Use your own words.

1 Ecology or economics?

 a Listen to the news report on Radio 4 and find the correct answers.

1. The news report is about
   a. a North Sea oil project
   b. a zinc ore mining project
   c. a coal mining project
2. The reporter mentions the effect of the project
   a. on the tourist industry
   b. on the air
   c. on the countryside
3. The people against the project are
   a. technologists
   b. hotel owners
   c. environmentalists

b Now listen to the recording again and find out more about the following points:

1. where the company has found the zinc ore deposits
2. why this area is especially interesting for the company
3. how many jobs the project will create
4. what this development will probably mean for nature in this area
5. the fears of the hotel owners

c Use your answers to write a short summary of the radio report.

2 Zinc UK project: A public enquiry

Zinc UK, a mining company, have found large deposits of zinc ore in the attractive coastal area of Cornwall. The ore is rich in zinc and is near the surface. This means mining will be relatively easy and
5 therefore profitable. The project will create new jobs for the area.
The problems are that this is a particularly beautiful area and it is the home to many wild plants and animals. It is also a tourist attraction for the visitors
10 to the small seaside resorts along the coast. The seaside resorts are small because of the poor road communications and there is no railway. The mining company has promised to build a new major road which will go directly to the motorway 25 miles away. Unemployment in the area is high. Most of the jobs 15 are on local farms and in the seaside resorts. However, in the last few years the seaside resorts have had fewer visitors. Local taxes for house owners are high and the local government wants to keep tax increases as low as possible in the future. Zinc UK would contribute 20 to the income of the area. The small town of St. Agnes has a new housing estate, but it only has a few shops, a coffee bar, a pub and a primary school. There is no public library, sports centre or cinema in the area.

228 words

a What advantages/disadvantages do you think the project could bring to the area?

b The local MP for North Cornwall has decided to hold a public enquiry to hear the views of the people concerned. The enquiry will help to decide whether Zinc UK should be allowed to start their mining project or not. The following people are at the meeting:

1. managers of the mining company
2. teenagers from the area
3. members of the local environmental group
4. hotel owners from the area
5. unemployed house owners from the area

Imagine you are one of these people.

1. List the advantages and disadvantages that the mining project might have for you personally.
2. Play your role at the meeting. Use expressions like "In my opinion" etc. to introduce your arguments.

c After you have discussed the issue write a report of the meeting. Use reported speech.

Energy

peat
mountains
forests

strong
winds

N
10 km

This is an island off the west coast of America. The island has strong winds from the west, high mountains with fast running rivers, thick forests along the west coast and peat bogs in the south east. There are no resources of coal, oil or natural gas on or near the island. At present only a few people live there.

■ You are in a project team which wants to develop the island.
Think about and discuss these ideas.
1. What material would you use to build homes on the island?
2. Which two materials could help you to produce heat to cook food?
3. What could you use to produce electricity to run machinery etc.?
4. Where would you build houses on the island? Give reasons.
5. What environmental problems will you cause when you use the natural resources on the island?
6. What conclusion do you draw from your study?

1 More wealth – less energy

Modern technology and relatively low prices have led to a situation in which most people feel relaxed about energy. Technology has made us believe that there will always be an answer to future problems
5 and the prices still create the impression that we have plenty of energy. But we have little reason to feel secure.

More than half of the world's population (mostly in the developing countries) lives without a commercial
10 supply of energy. The total energy consumption per head in countries such as India is only about 3 % of that in the United States. By 2100 the number of people in the world will rise to about 10 billion (compared with more than 6 billion today) and 85 %
15 of mankind will live in poor countries. Either billions of people will continue to live in poverty, or the demand for energy will grow enormously. Governments and companies will invest trillions of dollars in the next twenty or thirty years – more
20 than ever – in the developing countries. And if they do so, economic growth will mean much higher consumption of energy in the Third World.

Although the availability of fossil fuels is limited, experts predict that during this century the world
25 will still depend on them, especially coal which is plentiful in India and China – countries with the

highest populations. The problem is that developing countries care far more about the standard of living of their citizens today than they do about pollution and global warming. That is why they use the little 30 money they have to increase the production of goods. If they had enough money, they would be able to produce and use energy in an environmentally-friendly way.

On the other hand many wealthy industrialized 35 countries are introducing methods to save energy and they are further developing technologies which provide new sources of renewable energy such as solar power. Of course, it is not an easy job to transfer these expensive technologies to the poorer parts of 40 the world. But if we help the developing countries, they will be able to increase their energy efficiency. In this way these countries will manage to raise the standard of living significantly. At the same time they will consume only little more energy than today 45 and the production of this energy will not harm the environment so much.

The time to take action is now. The West is beginning to learn from the mistakes it has made. Surely it is important to help the developing countries so that 50 they can avoid the same mistakes. If we do not act now, what will life be like in 2100?   **435 words**

a Refer to the text and correct the following statements.
1. We must start to help the developing countries in the year 2100.
2. The number of people in the world is falling.
3. Today the United States consumes 5 times more energy per head than developing countries in South Asia.
4. In many developing countries people have developed methods to save energy.
5. The developing countries do not buy new energy technologies because they do not want to save energy.
6. The price of energy is very high today.

b Find the nouns in the text.
1. grow   2. consume   3. pollute   4. supply
5. demand   6. produce   7. poor   8. efficient

c Find antonyms in the text.
1. less   2. poor   3. high   4. a lot   5. past
6. industrialized (countries)   7. difficult
8. slighty   9. cheap   10. (the number will) fall

d Answer the following questions.
1. Which are the sources of energy mentioned in the text?
2. Which of them is a fossil fuel and which is a renewable source of energy?
3. Which of the following are fossil fuels, which are renewable sources: gas, water, wind, oil, peat?
4. Which advantages and disadvantages do fossil fuels and renewable sources of energy have? Think about these points: geographical position, availability, costs, pollution.

2 Talking about graphs

Graph 1: Development of world temperatures

Graph 2: Development of energy consumption (1970 – 2020), in Quadrillion Btu (British thermal units)

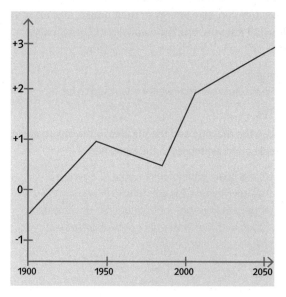

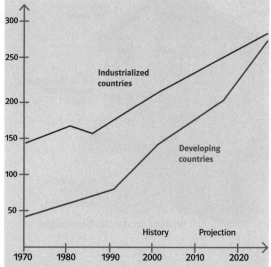

a Study the graph above and its description.
The graph shows the development of world temperatures.
Between 1900 and 1940 world temperatures rose significantly.
From 1940 to 1980 they fell slightly.
Since 1980 temperatures have increased constantly.
If this trend continues, temperatures will be about 3.5 degrees higher in 2050 than in 1900.

b Now describe graph 2.
Use the words in the boxes below.

Trends		
increase increase rise go up grow	**decrease** decrease fall go down drop	
remain stable steady constant at the same level		

Changes	
big changes significant(ly) substantial(ly)	**small changes** slight(ly) a little
fast changes sudden(ly) sharp(ly)	**slow changes** slow(ly) gradual(ly)

1 How to save energy in your house

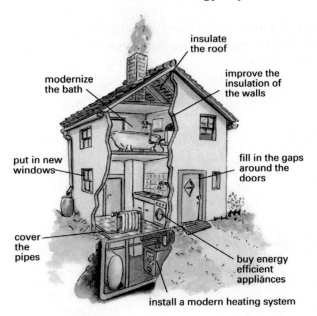

insulate the roof

modernize the bath

improve the insulation of the walls

put in new windows

fill in the gaps around the doors

cover the pipes

buy energy efficient appliances

install a modern heating system

Darren and Kate Palmer have just bought a house. The house is 25 years old and needs some repairs. The Energy Council has sent them a brochure on ways they can save energy in their house. Darren is showing Kate the brochure and says: "Look, it says here …"

Example:

"If we insulate our roof well, we will save a lot of energy."

■ Use the drawing and the phrases in the box to make at least eight sentences in the same way.

> lose less heat · save money · not use so much hot water · avoid a loss of heat · reduce our energy consumption · not pollute the environment so much · cut our water bill · not waste so much energy · save a lot of energy

2 The advantages of alternative energy

Cathy Johnson, a politician and expert on energy questions, is giving a talk at a local school. She is convinced that we depend too much on the use of fossil fuels (oil, gas and coal) as sources of energy.

She believes that we should save energy and also look into the possibilities of the use of alternative energies more carefully. Here are some of her notes for her talk.

■ Use the expressions in the box to express her opinions.

> 1. First of all – must say
> 2. Secondly – be of the opinion
> 3. Thirdly – think
> 4. At this point – must emphasize
>
> 5. Moreover – must add
> 6. In addition – believe
> 7. Furthermore – must say
> 8. Finally – be convinced

Example:
1. First of all I must say, if people used alternative forms of energy, they would contribute to …

1. people use alternative forms of energy – they contribute to a cleaner world
2. government spend more money on these alternatives – we all see the advantages in a few years
3. electricity companies replace old power stations in this area – they can produce electricity and not pollute the environment so much
4. firms produce more energy efficient appliances for the home – we not need so many power stations

5. house owners insulate their houses better – they can reduce their electricity bills
6. we use the sources of renewable energy in this part of the country – we save a lot of fossil fuels
7. people not travel by car so much – we not have such a big energy problem
8. we not waste energy as we do now – we have a cleaner and better world

3 Bob Flynn is thinking about his life

... didn't get good marks in the first year – because I didn't work hard.

... did well at college in the end – after I spent more time on my studies.

Bob Flynn is the manager of a small company which develops solar systems.

▪ Express his thoughts for him like this:

Example:

If I had worked hard, I would have got good marks in the first year. If I hadn't spent more time on my studies, I wouldn't have done well at college in the end.

1. I got a job as an electrician – after I wrote a lot of letters of application.
2. I went to university – after I attended evening classes three times a week.
3. I studied electrical engineering – after I looked at the good job possibilities.
4. I passed my examinations at university – because I worked hard.
5. I didn't go straight into my own business – because I wasn't sure what to do after university.
6. I started up my own business – after a friend gave me some tips.
7. I bought a workshop – after the bank lent me $50,000.
8. I became interested in alternative forms of energy – after I joined an environmentalist group.
9. I started to develop solar systems – because I learnt all about solar energy at university.
10. I didn't invest more money in the business – because I didn't have enough money at that time.

4 Save energy now   **Advanced**

Two students have started a "Save Energy Now" group. They are talking about the use of energy and how people have reacted to new developments.

▪ Put the verbs in brackets into the correct form.

Mary Jo: But we still aren't doing enough and if we **1. (continue)** to take so little care of our environment, soon we **2. (not have)** an environment at all.

John: I know. But if people **3. (know)** years ago about the damage that power stations can do to the environment, I'm sure they **4. (do)** something about it a long time ago.

Mary Jo: Yes, but now we all know about it and we can all help. If a lot of people **5. (not be)** as lazy as they are, they **6. (not waste)** so much energy in their homes. It's the little things that help.

John: Yes, you're right. I'm sure that if the school **7. (not help)** us with our project, then we **8. (never be able to start)** it, for example.

Mary Jo: That's true, and nowadays there are more people who are really interested in alternative forms of energy. If that **9. (not be)** so, we **10. (not find)** so many people at our meetings.

Renewable energy

In the mid-1970s fewer than 1,000 U.S. homes generated their own power. That number has grown to more than 100,000 and every year
5 thousands more will join those who are already off-the-grid. They are turning to renewable energies, such as wind, water and sunshine in order to generate power for their homes.

10 But why are more and more people doing this? Very often it is because these people live far away from the grid and cannot afford the cost of a power line to their home.

15 As a result of this strong interest, it has become big business to supply homes with renewable energy.

The yearly sales for the solar-energy industry alone have already reached $1 billion, and wind and hydro
20 systems for domestic users add millions more. Recently many off-the-grid homes in the USA opened their doors to show how they keep the beer cold, the shower warm and the reading lamp lit with no help from the local power station.

25 Wind power is generally used for industrial and commercial applications. However, the most popular off-the-grid technology for private homes is the use of solar energy. Although photovoltaic (PV) systems are nearly twice as expensive as wind power, the sun
30 provides energy for more than two thirds of America's off-the-grid homes. This is because solar energy is easy to install and doesn't need a lot of maintenance. In the past, makers of PV systems sold 60 % of

their equipment to the government. However, their main customers now are private homes and companies who have realized that PV systems are often cheaper in the end. For example, private companies can install a PV cell on phones or on highway signs which are far away from the grid and so it's not necessary to dig up roads and lay cables. Even the building industry has shown an interest, offering solar-equipped homes at no extra cost.

One of the most important developments recently is that some electricity companies are even using solar power to avoid the need to build more traditional 50 power plants. A Californian gas and electricity company has supplied 150 homes in California with electricity from a number of PV panels. In this way it saved the 55 $1 million it would have spent on a traditional system.

"All this is going in the right direction," says Tom Kelly, a solar research scientist, "but we must 60 still make a number of engineering improvements before we are ready for the mass market." In fact, research is going on all the time in order to find cheaper and better materials and to increase efficiency in solar energy installations. 65 Off-the-grid energy may even get some help from politicians, who may introduce an extra tax on fossil fuels in order to limit global warming. If they do this, fossil fuel prices will increase and solar energy will therefore become more attractive. However, the 70 energy of the future might come from a completely different source. Many experts believe that hydrogen-based fuel cell systems will provide the energy for the generations to come. Fuel cell powered cars are already on the roads and many companies are testing 75 fuel cell systems. They are relatively cheap, renewable and environmentally-friendly. So, let's see what the future holds for us! **536 words**

a Write a summary of this text.

Follow these steps	**Example for first section:**
1. **Read the text carefully and write the main idea in an introductory sentence.**	In his text "Renewable energy" the author discusses the increase in the use of alternative energy sources, such as wind, sun and water.
2. **Divide the text into six main sections and find headlines for each.**	Section I (lines 1–14) Off-the-grid energy increasing in U.S.
3. **For each section write key points (not complete sentences). These must contain the main ideas in each section. Be careful not to include any unnecessary information or details.**	since 1970s – more U.S. country homes – off-the-grid power. alternative sources of energy – cheaper for them
4. **Decide what function each section has, e.g. introduction to subject matter, presentation of arguments for and against, examples, further information, results, contrast and conclusion.**	Section I – introduction to subject matter.
5. **Choose expressions from the list below which help you to present the ideas in the six sections.**	Firstly, the author points out that …

Firstly / On the one hand / On the other hand / Furthermore / Consequently / As a result / For example / For instance / The reason for / Although / In conclusion / All in all	the author points out / claims / states / maintains / mentions / argues / adds / goes on to say / concludes that …

| **6.** **Now write a summary of the text using your key words and notes. It should be about half the length of the original text and you should use your own words.** | In his text "Renewable energy" the author discusses the increase in the use of alternative energy sources, such as wind and sun. Firstly, the author points out that it is mainly since the 1970s that U.S. country homes have turned to off-the-grid power. Alternative sources, says the author, are cheaper for them. |

b Translate lines 58 to 78.

Info-Box: How to write a summary

Remember:

1. Write the main idea of the text in an introductory sentence.
2. Divide the text into sections and find headlines for each one.
3. For each section write key points, giving the main ideas.
4. Decide what function each section has.
5. Choose expressions to present the ideas in each section.
6. Complete the summary in about half the length of the original text in your own words.

1 From poultry litter to electricity

John James, an engineer from Britain, is on a business trip to Minnesota in the USA.
He is talking to Chet Brown, production manager of an alternative power station
which runs on agricultural biomass, including poultry litter.
The pictures below show some things which are part of the production process.

 a Listen to their conversation and put the pictures
in the right order.

turbine

furnace

fuel on conveyor

litter lorries tipping

b Now describe the production process.

2 Writing a report

Here are the notes which John James made during his visit to the Minnesota
alternative power station.

1. generator produces 12.5 megawatts
2. fuel cheap and environmentally-friendly
3. government money still necessary to keep station competitive
4. lorries deliver 25 tons manure to storage hall daily
5. low manpower costs: 2 employees only
6. furnace burns manure at 800 °C
7. ash from furnace is quality fertilizer
8. turbine drives generator
9. greenhouse gas production 25% lower than from traditional power station
10. steam drives turbine
11. computer-controlled conveyor belts take poultry litter from storage hall to
   furnace
12. burning process produces steam

a From the notes make two lists to show:
1. the energy production process.
2. the arguments for and against the process

b Use John James' notes to write a report.
1. Explain the process in the correct order.
2. Write down points for and against the process
   in full sentences.

■ Answer the following questions.
1. What differences can you see between the two production methods?
2. When do you think the photos were taken?
3. Where would you prefer to work and why?
4. What changes in production methods will there be in the future? What do you think?

1 New production technologies

Modern life in the so-called civilized world needs all kinds of goods in increasing quantity and quality: computers, digital cameras, TV sets, toys, cars etc. There are many ways of producing goods, but for products that are sold in large quantities, the best way to make them is by mass production.

Manufacturers are constantly trying to improve their productivity. That is why automation has been introduced to work faster, more accurately and more economically. As a result factories and shop floors look very different from the way they did in the past.

a The following three paragraphs describe three important developments in new technologies which are used in modern factories.
Read the three paragraphs and find out from the box on the right which terms go with each paragraph.

robots, shop floors, Computer Aided Design (CAD), workers, research department, Computer Aided Manufacturing (CAM)

1
One of the latest developments in this area is that the "workers" are equipped with electronic sensors such as video cameras, microphones and touch sensors. Such a "worker" needs this equipment to do his work and also to send back information to the controlling computer. The computer is programmed to use this feedback to change its instructions to the "worker" if necessary.

2
With special programs designers can simulate on the computer what will happen if a particular design is chosen. In the past often unsuitable plans were drawn, just to find out later that they did not work. Now the computer helps to predict what will happen under different conditions – for example to a bridge in different winds. Moreover, these programs can also work out the most economical way of making something out of the materials available.

3
Machines that have to do the same job again and again can be operated automatically by this computer system. The computer programs in this system control the automated machines or tools. This software can be changed and so the machines can be programmed in different ways to make different products. The system is also used to monitor the production process and correct any faults.

b Answer the following questions.
1. What is the method of producing goods in large quantities called?
2. Why have most companies introduced automation in their factories?
3. How are technical drawings made nowadays?
4. What advantages does the CAD system have?
5. What does a CAM system control?
6. In what way is the CAM system flexible?
7. What electronic equipment do modern robots have?
8. Why are they equipped with these things?

c The most advanced systems link together CAD, CAM, robots and other automated machinery. One such system is called Computer Integrated Manufacturing (CIM). It is shown on the right.
Describe in your own words how it works.

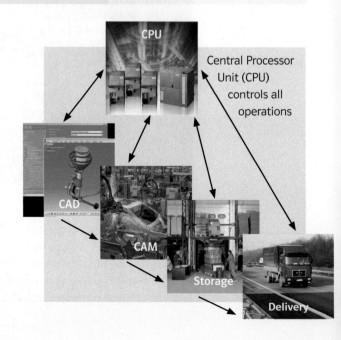

CPU

Central Processor Unit (CPU) controls all operations

CAD

CAM

Storage

Delivery

2 Describing a production system

a Match the words in the box with the parts of the car.

1. engine
2. doors
3. headlights
4. wheels
5. dashboard
6. windscreen
7. bumper
8. exhaust pipe
9. car body
10. steering wheel

b In the diagram below you can see how a car is made in a modern car factory.
Describe the production system. Use the vocabulary in the box.

Example:
First lorries deliver the different parts of the car to the factory.

lorries	
workers	assemble, add, test, dip, weld, dry,
machines	fit, deliver, drive away, put on
robots	

1

2

3

4

5

6

7

8

9

10

1 How is a car produced?

■ Describe the production process on page 67 in the passive voice.
Add "by" if necessary.

Example:
The parts are delivered by lorries. The body is …

2 How should production be improved?

In order to succeed on the international market a modern car has to be produced in only
a few hours today. How can this be done?
Here are some suggestions the workers have made.

■ Complete the sentences in the passive voice. *Must, should, can* or *could* should be used
at least once.

Example:
1. The workers should be trained more carefully.

1. workers / train more carefully
2. production process / organize better
3. cars / assemble / by groups of workers
4. important parts / make / by the workers

5. other parts / deliver "just-in-time"
6. better working conditions / introduce
7. a new kind of fast-drying paint / use
8. workers / give more responsibility
9. workers' suggestions / follow / by the management

3 Production in the past and today

Many years ago motor companies used only a few machines. So
the workers did most of the hard and dirty work. After Henry Ford
had invented the production line, motor companies started mass
production. In the last few decades companies have improved
the production process. Nowadays they are still developing new
production methods. If they did not do this, they would sell fewer
cars, because of growing international competition. So companies
have bought a lot of expensive machines. Today production lines
transport the car bodies and robots do most of the work. However,
machines cannot replace all workers and companies will still need
qualified staff in the future.

■ Describe the development of production in the passive voice.

Example:
Many years ago only a few machines were used by motor companies.
So most of …

4 A new job

Wesley Harding has applied for a job at a big motor company. This is what happened to him:

1. Before his interview/Wesley/a letter/send/the personnel manager
2. On the day of his interview/Mr Harding/questions/ask/about his qualifications/the personnel manager
3. While he was waiting/the applicant/a cup of tea/serve/the tea-lady
4. Then/he/the new machines/show/the head technician
5. Afterwards/Wesley/lunch ticket/give/a secretary
6. In the afternoon/he/result/tell/the personnel manager
7. Wesley/job/give/the personnel manager
8. Before he left/Mr Harding/£20 travel expenses/pay

■ Make sentences both in the active and passive voice.

Example:
1. Before his interview the personnel manager sent a letter to Wesley.
   … Wesley was sent a letter by the personnel manager.

5 Translation   Advanced

■ Translate the following text. Watch out for the tenses.

Die meisten Automobilfirmen wurden vor vielen Jahren gegründet. Zu jener Zeit wurden viele Arbeiter benötigt, um Autos zu produzieren. Es konnten pro Tag natürlich weniger Fahrzeuge als heute hergestellt werden. Aber nachdem neue Technologien eingeführt worden waren, wurden mehr und mehr Arbeiter entlassen (dismiss). Seit dem Beginn der Massenproduktion ist die Produktivität erhöht worden. Heute wird die Produktion von Robotern ausgeführt und von Computern kontrolliert. Der Prozess der Automatisierung kann nicht angehalten werden. In der Fabrik der Zukunft werden wahrscheinlich viele Produkte ohne Arbeitskräfte hergestellt werden. Allerdings werden auch dann qualifizierte (skilled) Arbeiter benötigt werden, weil nicht alle Tätigkeiten von Maschinen ausgeführt werden können. Zur Zeit werden Arbeitnehmer von verschiedenen Autoherstellern zu ihren Ideen befragt, wie die Produktion verbessert werden kann. Neue Technologien können auch zusammen mit den Gewerkschaften entwickelt und eingeführt werden. Aber natürlich weiß heute niemand genau, welche Autos in fünfzig Jahren produziert werden und wie der Produktionsprozess dann aussehen wird.

1 Team work works

Automation, computer-controlled robots, in recent years we have all seen pictures of modern production lines which are dominated by machines and where no humans can be seen.
5 However, in one German electronics firm in Cardiff, Wales, humans are making a comeback. Personnel manager Martin Wibberly told me "Nowadays we think of our workers not only as a cost factor, but as capital and so we invest
10 in them." And the company invests in them because their flexibility is needed in today's market. Martin added "Flexibility means a faster and more customer-orientated service. Of course, we still use robots but the production
15 lines of the past were too inflexible and complex and therefore too expensive to serve today's market. And so these methods have been replaced by much smaller and individual production units."
20 It's an arrangement which suits the workers equally well. Peter Brown, who was one of the 500 chosen from 25,000 applicants for jobs at the firm, explained the advantages of the new system for the workers. "As you know,
25 past production methods were all based on mass production where each worker on the production line performed one small monotonous task. Now however, the work is done in groups which are completely
30 responsible for one individual step in the production process. This arrangement is also more flexible for us because now we can arrange our own working schedules."

Today there are also opportunities for workers to train and get further qualifications so that
35 they can do different jobs when this becomes necessary. This too, means that the work is much less repetitive and boring than in the past. The groups also meet regularly to discuss problems in the production process, to suggest solutions
40 and to help to put them into practice. Peter Brown points out that when the workers have a say in the organization of their work, communication between workers and management is improved. He also enjoys the
45 feeling of responsibility not only for his own work, but also for the success of the whole process.

These changes have been supported by the unions. They too, recognize the opportunities
50 for personal development which workers will be given under this system. Lean management and productivity in the Japanese style can only be effective, they say, when all the employees have more say in the decision-making process.
55

387 words

a Name two methods of production mentioned in the text.

b Find three groups of people who support the new method.

c List the disadvantages of the old system.

d List the advantages of the new system.

e Give the meaning of the following expressions from the text.
1. customer-orientated service (line 13)
2. mass production (line 26)
3. working schedules (line 33)
4. further qualifications (line 35)
5. lean management (line 52)
6. decision-making process (line 55)

f Write a summary of the text.

g Translate lines 34 to 48.

2 Describing a process

a A large electronics firm in Germany has developed a new DVD recorder. They need the recording instructions in English. The production manager has given you these pictures.

Write the instructions in English for the export model.

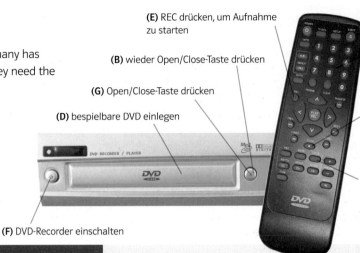

(E) REC drücken, um Aufnahme zu starten

(B) wieder Open/Close-Taste drücken

(C) gewünschten Kanal auswählen

(G) Open/Close-Taste drücken

(D) bespielbare DVD einlegen

(A) STOP drücken, um Aufnahme zu beenden

(H) Monitor-Taste drücken, um TV-Kanäle durch DVD-Recorder zu sehen

(F) DVD-Recorder einschalten

Follow these steps

1. **Put the instructions in the right order.**

2. **Translate the instructions using the words in the box below. If you need more help, use your dictionary.**

einschalten:	to switch on
drücken:	to press
einlegen:	to insert
auswählen:	to select
aufnehmen:	to record

3. **Use infinitives, modals or passive forms.**

4. **Ask your partner to test the instructions at home (if possible).**

Example:

(F) DVD-Recorder einschalten
(G) Open/Close-Taste drücken
(D) bespielbare DVD einlegen
...

Switch DVD on – Press OPEN/CLOSE button – Insert ...

First, the DVD recorder must be switched on. Then ...

b Here is a new cassette recorder which has been produced by the same firm.
Write the operating instructions for a recording.

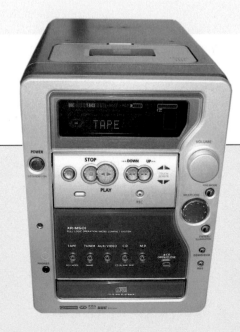

Info-Box: How to describe a process

Remember:
1. Put your information in the right order.
2. Use your dictionary to find exact meanings.
3. Write precise instructions. You can use infinitives, modals or passive forms.
4. Test out the instructions on the equipment.

1 Sales talk

 a Listen and find out the following things:
1. Who is talking ?
2. Where are they talking ?
3. What are they talking about ?

 b Listen again and find out about the following:
1. speed
2. paper
3. print quality (resolution)
4. installation
5. service
6. price

2 Installing equipment

You have just bought the new Pineapple ink jet printer.
Unfortunately the instructions in the handbook are only in English. You also discover that these instructions are completely mixed up.

a First find the correct headlines for the instructions. Choose from the headlines in the box below.

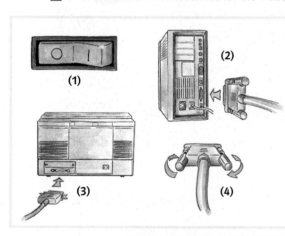
(1)
(2)
(3)
(4)

Instruction 1.
- Tighten the screws of the interface connector.
- Connect the other end of the interface cable to your printer.
- Make sure that both the computer and the printer are turned off.
- Connect one end of the interface cable to the computer.

Headlines:
- Printing
- Connecting the printer
- Functions
- Installing the ink cartridge
- Fault finding

Instruction 2.
- Put the printer cover back on.
- Press the cartridge down until it snaps into position.
- Take off the safety tape on the ink cartridge.
- Remove the printer cover.

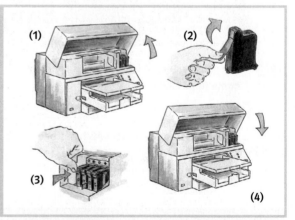
(1)
(2)
(3)
(4)

b Now put the instructions into the correct order. The drawings will help you.

c Translate the instructions into German.

d You still need help to install the ink jet printer. The supplier of the printer comes to your house and shows you how to do this.
Work out the conversation you might have with this computer expert. Play these roles.

Financial and legal services

LEEDS
We've got everything you need!

Publishing and printing

LEEDS BRADFORD INTERNATIONAL AIRPORT

UNIVERSITY OF LEEDS

LEEDS CITY MARKETS

Manufacturing

a What do the photos tell us about Leeds?

b Who do you think wrote the brochure and why?

c Compare your town / region with Leeds.

d Imagine you have to write a brochure in English for your town / region. Think of a slogan. What photos would you use? Give reasons for your choice.

1 Changes in the North of England

Coal industry

steel industry

textile industry

shipbuilding industry

Steel production reduced by 30 %!

Textile industry goes east!

NEWCASTLE SHIPYARD CLOSED!

4,000 jobs lost in coal industry!

■ Look at the industrial map of Great Britain in the 1960s and the newspaper headlines on the left. Now answer the following questions.
1. What kind of industries could you find in the Leeds/Newcastle area in the sixties?
2. What has happened to them?
3. What has happened to the workers?
4. Why do you think has there been such a development?

2 Newcastle takes off

Newcastle Business Park, the £100 million development of a former industrial area, was officially opened some years ago. The success of the Newcastle scheme was that 95 per cent of the
5 67,000 square metres of office buildings had been let immediately, mostly to computer companies and light industries. The management of the business park gave financial help to many of these new companies and provided them with the latest
10 communications technology.

The business park is ideally located, as the area has the advantage of excellent road, rail and air links. Today more than 4,000 people work on the 1.5km site.
15 Decades ago the site was occupied by a large factory which produced machinery and arms. When the factory closed down, nobody was interested in taking over the site. However, unemployment figures were so high in Newcastle
20 some years ago that the Newcastle Development Corporation decided to invest £100 million in this site. John Scally, the managing director, proudly said: "Newcastle Business Park is an outstanding example of what cities can achieve."
25 Newcastle City Council has also recently started an exciting £10 million partnership with Digitalbrain Plc to become Europe's first Digital City. This programme will provide businesses and citizens with a range of interactive electronic

services and information to improve the region's
30 economic growth. Newcastle upon Tyne is now one of the most wired cities in terms of broadband network coverage. This allows companies and private individuals access to large-scale data processing. Moreover, Newcastle City Council
35 is creating a Centre for Entrepreneurship and Innovation (CEI) in the middle of the Newcastle Business Park. These buildings will provide office space for new companies in the area of digital technology and will create over 400 jobs. As you
40 can see Newcastle is taking off!   **295 words**

a What has been done in the Newcastle area in the last few years?

b Answer the following questions.
Some answers cannot just be taken directly from the text.

1. What does a business park look like?
2. What was produced on the site of the new business park years ago?
3. Who (do you think) has given the money for the project to the Newcastle Development Corporation?
4. Why (do you think) has so much money been invested?

5. Why (do you think) are so many companies interested in the new office buildings?
6. Why (do you think) were they not interested in the old site?
7. In what way (do you think) is Newcastle becoming Europe's first Digital City?
8. Why (do you think) is Newcastle creating the CEI?

c Now think of the town/area where you live. Describe a similar project that you have seen or heard of.

1 A Canadian student at Newcastle college

Craig Russell, a Canadian student from Vancouver, is planning to go on a year's exchange visit to Newcastle College in the north of England. He has never been to Europe before. So yesterday he asked Calvin, another student who was on last year's exchange, for some help. Here are some of Craig's questions and the answers he received.

a Match the answers to the questions.

1. Who should I contact first at the college?
2. When should I write to my host family?
3. How should I travel from London Airport to Newcastle?
4. Where can I reserve a seat for that journey?
5. What should I give my host family as a present?
6. How much luggage should I take?
7. What should I wear at college?
8. Where can I find a good bank in Newcastle?

a) at a travel agent's
b) a month before you arrive
c) opposite the college
d) Ms Keegan, the head of department
e) not too much
f) by coach
g) casual clothes
h) something typically Canadian

b Now report Calvin's answers like this:
Example:
Calvin told him / advised him to contact Ms Keegan at the college.

c Craig has been at Newcastle College for one month now. This is part of Craig's letter home. As you can read the teachers **expect him to work** hard during his stay in Newcastle and sometimes they **make him do** some extra work. Complete the letter with the verbs in the box.

> let • expect • make • want • ask

Life at college is great. I am the second Canadian student to study here for a whole year. I get on well with the teachers here but they **(1)** me work quite hard. They **(2)** me to talk to the English students more about the Canadian college system. I didn't realize it was so complicated. In fact, the teachers **(3)** me to know a lot more than I actually do. Last week, for example, they **(4)** to show my photos of our college in Vancouver in order to give the English students a better idea of our work at Canadian colleges. But it is not all hard work. And if I want to do some sight-seeing at the weekend, the teachers **(5)** me go early on Fridays. By the way I have met …

2 Finding out useful information

a On the next page you can see parts of the students' Internet notice board at Newcastle College. Match the following sentences with the notices on the Internet notice board.

Example: Sentence 1 goes with notice D.

b Complete the sentences below. Use the -ing form of a suitable verb.

Example: I'm interested in knowing more about France so I'll go to the French Club.

1. I'm interested in … more about France.
2. I'm tired of … with my parents and I need somewhere to live.
3. Students who are afraid of … their final tests should ring 347168.
4. … is dangerous for your health.
5. Craig is going to the Sports Club because he is good at … basketball.
6. We'll leave the car at home … and … is stupid.
7. I'm looking forward to … you on Friday evening.
8. If Gary takes me in his car, I won't have any more problems in … to college on time.

3 Talking about friends

Craig has met a lot of new friends at Newcastle College. Here are some remarks they have made about themselves.

Sharon: "I play more hockey than volleyball at the Sports Club."
Kevin: "I go to the cinema every week."
Emma: "I don't smoke any more."
Bill and Ben: "We don't eat in the college canteen. The food's not very good there."
Sam: "That's one thing I hate – my alarm clock."

Mary Ann: "I'm very interested in foreign languages."
Gary and Sue: "We did the same test last year. "
Lisa: "I try not to be late for college. I take the early bus."
Mike: "I spend all my free time at the Sports Club."
Tina: "This book is very useful. I think you should read it."

■ Make statements about Craig's friends.
The verbs in the box will help you.

like • hate • prefer • remember • stop • enjoy • avoid • suggest • dislike • love

Example: Sharon prefers playing hockey to volleyball at the Sports Club.

4 Translation   Advanced

Imagine you were at Newcastle College on an exchange visit and that you had to write a report in English about your experiences there.

■ Translate these notes into English.
1. Meine Gastfamilie ist sehr nett. Ich wohne gern bei ihr.
2. Aber zuerst hatte ich Schwierigkeiten, ihr Englisch zu verstehen.
3. Am Anfang hatte ich Angst, Fehler zu machen.
4. Die englischen Schüler im College sind sehr interessiert, mehr über Deutschland zu hören.
5. Im College lassen die Lehrer mich ziemlich hart arbeiten.
6. Sie erwarten, dass ich viel über das deutsche Schulsystem weiß.

'Made in Britain' loses appeal

1 When he invented the bagless vacuum cleaner – among other things -, Britons looked upon James Dyson as just one more in their long tradition of inventors. When Dyson, who is now 54, turned his ideas into a private business with sales of $315 million in 2000 and an estimated value of $700 million, the inventor became an icon of innovative Britain. His name has become a brand name and is printed on all of the 8 million Dyson bagless vacuum cleaners his company has sold since 1993.

2 But things are changing. Although he had promised that he would never leave his home country, Dyson shifted production of all his vacuum cleaners to the cheaper labour markets of Asia last year. Moreover, he has just announced that he is planning to close an assembly line for washing machines in Britain and open a new plant in Malaysia. The move will eliminate hundreds of jobs at his relatively new plant in Great Britain, saving labour and other costs as Dyson prepares to introduce his products into the U.S. market this summer. "I have put £40 million of my money into this business to try and make manufacturing work here," Dyson said. "But I have to regard the law of economics. If we want to survive as a business, we have to go where manufacturing is economical. It is only in this way that we can keep more than 1,200 hi-tech jobs in research, design and engineering.

3 In the past three decades, manufacturers have seen their share of Britain's annual output go down by 50 percent while services such as banking or restaurants have prospered in a new kind of consumer economy that has given Britons jobs, low interest rates and huge spending power. "The country as a whole is in a two-speed economy where the consumer economy is roaring away and manufacturing is in a deep recession," said Eric Britton, an economist. "It is typical of developed economies that the manufacturing sector tends to go down. We must accept that manufacturing is a global industry."

4 But while much of Continental Europe is struggling with unemployment, the British unemployment rate is down to 3.2 percent. Britain, once called by Napoleon a nation of shopkeepers, has become a nation of shoppers: Consumer spending accounts for 60 percent of the economy.

5 Contrast that with the old-fashioned business of producing things to sell: Last year, 150,000 jobs were lost in the manufacturing sector as its share of national economic activity fell below 20 percent. By contrast, service industries such as call centres added almost 230,000 jobs. But does it matter? As long as consumers continue to spend the way they are doing – stores recorded an average increase of 7 percent for the Christmas holidays – growth will continue. **468 words**

a Each of the following sentences represents a paragraph of the text.
Put the sentences in the order of the paragraphs.
1. Dyson has to close down factories in Britain in order to save costs.
2. Compared to other European countries the economic situation in Britain is quite good.
3. Many jobs in manufacturing are replaced by jobs in the service industries.
4. Inventor James Dyson has become a well-known and successful businessman.
5. While the manufacturing sector is decreasing in Britain consumption is rising.

b Answer the following questions in complete sentences.

1. What is James Dyson famous for?
2. Why is he closing production plants in Britain?
3. What has happened to the manufacturing industries in developed countries.
4. What is the job situation like in Britain?
5. In which fields can jobs be kept in Britain?

c "Workers should accept worse conditions (wage, working hours, working conditions, no strikes) in order to save their jobs or to create new jobs." Do you agree? Give your comment.

Write a comment.

Follow these steps

		Example:
1.	**Write a general introduction to the topic, e.g. give reasons why the topic is of special importance today.**	Today the unemployment rate in many countries is high. So a lot of workers fear for their jobs, and the jobless are desperately looking for new jobs. Many of them are willing to accept lower pay and worse working conditions than before.
2.	**Collect ideas for arguments for and against the statement above and put them in a suitable order.**	Arguments for: – lower costs for companies – more competitive on international markets Arguments against: – lower standard of living
3.	**Then make complete sentences and decide which phrases may be suitable** **e.g.: Firstly/In addition/On the one hand/On the other hand/In contrast, ...**	On the one hand this brings many advantages to the companies. Firstly ...
4.	**Draw conclusions from the arguments above and state your point of view. Use these phrases:** **In conclusion/As a result/In my opinion/In my view/It is for this reason that ...**	In conclusion I would say that workers should/should not ...

d Translate lines 11 to 28.

Info-Box: How to write a comment

Remember:

1. Write a general introduction to the topic.
2. Collect ideas for arguments for and against the statement and put them in a suitable order.
3. Choose expressions to present your arguments and write complete sentences.
4. Draw your conclusions from the arguments given and state your personal point of view.

Extract 1

Looking for a new location

Imagine you work for Samsons Ltd, an international manufacturer of high class racing bicycles. They are very interested in finding a new site for a new factory and offices in England. Your company has looked at a lot of promotion literature for development areas in Britain.

Extract 2

Where on earth should we relocate?
The answer is easy: to the Black Country.

We're right in the centre of England which means there is direct access to London and the Channel Tunnel via the national motorway network. What else does the location offer? Plenty of skilled labour (after all we have represented the heart of Britain's ⁵ manufacturing base for more than 200 years). Thousands of square metres of land for offices and factories. The buildings which have already been built are of the highest standard and we have not forgotten to build large car parks! In addition, ¹⁰ we can provide all the back-up you need; from planning permission to expert help, even financial assistance. The Black Country – your future in Europe has never looked brighter.

For more information, ¹⁵
contact Linda Clement on **44 21 511 2000,
or write to her – Black Country Development Corporation, Black Country House, Rounds Green Road, Odbury, West Midlands B69 2DG, England.
http://www.bcde.gov.uk ²⁰
email: clement@blackcountry.co.uk

England's Largest County is Getting Bigger!

Large investments by private developers in the North's most attractive county allow us a wonderful opportunity to invite you to join our economic success. Fifteen new office and ⁵ business parks are being developed both in town centres and out of town. Offices with up to 25,000 square feet will soon be available, while offices up to 35,000 square feet can be built to your own requirements.
¹⁰ North Yorkshire has a growing population, top schools, colleges and universities, good housing and shopping facilities, excellent road and rail links (only 2 hours from London) and highly developed business contacts.

¹⁵ Write or phone today for details of current opportunities.

The Economic Development Centre,
North Yorkshire
County Council, County Hall,
²⁰ Northallerton, North Yorkshire DL7 8AD, England.
Telephone 0609 780780.
http://www.edcinfo.co.uk

a Read the two extracts above and do the following tasks.
1. Find out where exactly the two areas are.
2. Make a list of the key points in both of the extracts.
3. Find out from your key points
   – which points are mentioned in both texts.
   – which are only in one of the texts.
4. Give a short report about the two areas.
5. Discuss your results in class. Which area do you think is better for your company? Give reasons.
6. Write a letter to both areas stating your situation, and ask for more information.

b You are interested in finding out more about the two regions. Two colleagues have visited the areas. Listen to their reports and find out from their phone calls:
1. which towns they have visited.
2. where these towns are.

c Listen again and find out more about the following:
1. transport links
2. industry
3. price of land
4. housing
5. job situation
6. general impression

d Which town would you now choose for a new site for your company?
Work in groups and then write a report and give reasons for your decision.

Immigration in the United States

Two hundred years ago the U.S. had a population of about 4 million people. Today the population has risen to more than 280 million.

Immigrants – Where do they come from?

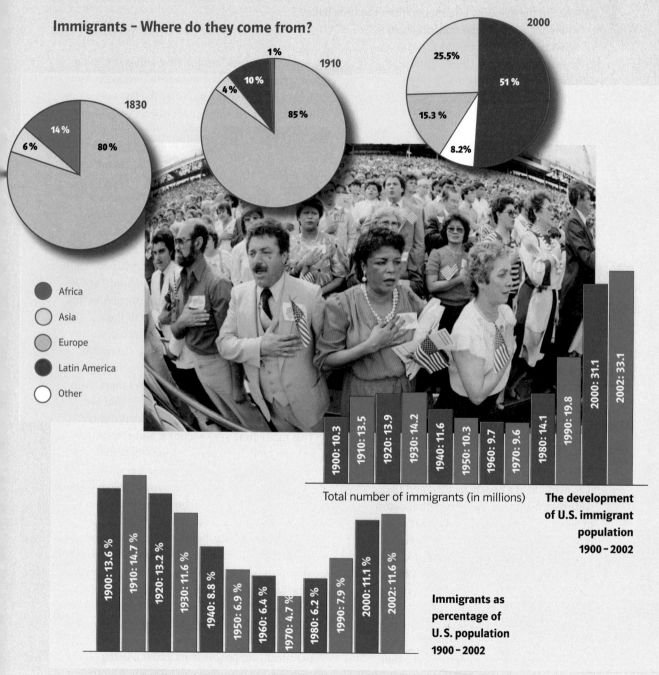

1830
14%
6%
80%

1910
1%
10%
4%
85%

2000
25.5%
51%
15.3%
8.2%

- Africa
- Asia
- Europe
- Latin America
- Other

Total number of immigrants (in millions)

1900: 10.3
1910: 13.5
1920: 13.9
1930: 14.2
1940: 11.6
1950: 10.3
1960: 9.7
1970: 9.6
1980: 14.1
1990: 19.8
2000: 31.1
2002: 33.1

The development of U.S. immigrant population 1900 – 2002

1900: 13.6 %
1910: 14.7 %
1920: 13.2 %
1930: 11.6 %
1940: 8.8 %
1950: 6.9 %
1960: 6.4 %
1970: 4.7 %
1980: 6.2 %
1990: 7.9 %
2000: 11.1 %
2002: 11.6 %

Immigrants as percentage of U.S. population 1900 – 2002

a Describe the development of immigration in the United States.

b Where have the different groups of immigrants come from over the years?

c What reasons have they had for coming? What do you think?

1 Two faces of America

a What do you think the title "Two faces of America" means?

b Find out the following information from the texts below:
1. where the people came from originally
2. when they arrived in the U.S.
3. where they live now
4. what they do in America
5. why they emigrated

Marek and Lisa Leschinski came to
Chicago from Poland with their two
sons seven years ago. They were fleeing
from nothing more than a middle-class
5 existence. Marek, now 32, was a technical
draughtsman in Warsaw. Lisa was a
receptionist in a hotel. "We had a small
apartment, jobs, a car and
everything we basically
needed," says Marek, "but
there were not really any
chances for more." After
three years of trying to get
a visa to the States, they
finally arrived in Chicago.
Marek first had to take a job as a machine
operator with wages of $310 a week, which
is not much when you have a family to
support. However, a year later he had more
20 than doubled his salary in another job. Lisa
was working in a cookie factory, and they
were saving most of the money that came
in. Soon they had saved enough for a down
payment on 'The European Cafe' on North
25 Lincoln Street, above which they live in a
5-room apartment. A year ago they bought
the 'Town Bakery' in a fashionable suburb
of Chicago. Marek says they earn $1500 a
week now. They have to work 16 hours a day,
30 doing everything from baking to making the
deliveries, but they are happier than they
have ever been before. As Marek puts it, "In
this country you have the chance – if you
work more, you can earn more." **236 words**

Growing up in Vietnam, June Yen learnt to be
an outsider. She is a so-called Amerasian. Her
father is an American soldier she has never met.
Her Vietnamese mother spent years explaining
to her why she   5
looked different
to her friends.
When she came
to the States years
ago she thought   10
she would finally
become integrated. She was wrong. "In Vietnam
they called me American," June explained, "here,
they don't know who I am and I still don't really
know where I belong." After arriving in America   15
she went to school in Atlanta. There she was put
into a class with children half her age because
her English was not good enough. This made
her feel like an outsider from the beginning.
To make matters worse one teacher there, who   20
had fought in the Vietnam war even told her,
"Why don't you go back to your own country?"
This made June very sceptical and even afraid
of her American teachers. June still cannot
speak or write English very well and she often   25
feels like a second-class person. After leaving
school without any real qualifications she got
a job in a Chinese restaurant. The pay was bad
and the hours long. Four years ago she met her
Vietnamese husband. A year later they moved to   30
Memphis where her husband found a new job.
June has given up work and now looks after their
two children at home. As June says "Emigration
to a new country takes a lot of courage and
determination. Arriving in a foreign country with 35
practically no possessions and not being able
to speak the language can be a very frightening
experience. I only hope my children will have a
better start in life than I did." **293 words**

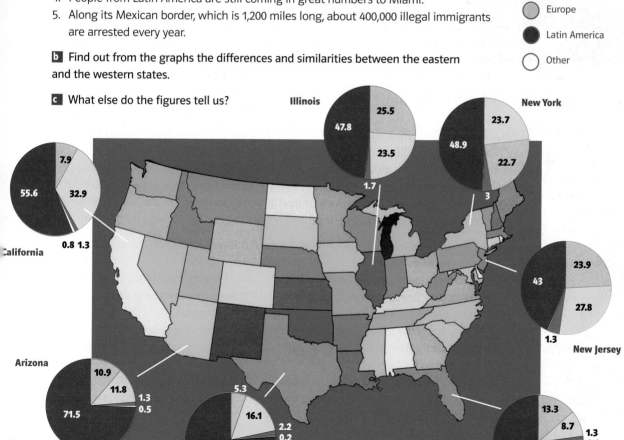

c Find out from the texts why the following statements are true.

1. Marek and Lisa were not poor immigrants.
2. It took 3 years before they could emigrate to America.
3. They started their own business in America.
4. The Leschinskis have found happiness in America.

5. June Yen had identity problems in Vietnam.
6. She had problems at the school in Atlanta.
7. She still feels like a second-class citizen.
8. Her children will hopefully have a happier childhood.

d Discuss the following quotations from the texts.

1. "In America you have the chance – if you work more, you can earn more."

2. "Emigration takes courage and determination."

2   American immigrants: who are they and where do they go?

a Link the five statements below with the states shown in the graph.

1. During the riots in L.A. in 1992 tension grew between the black community and the new immigrants. 2,000 Asian owned businesses were looted or damaged by fire.
2. More Poles live in Chicago than in any other city in the world except Warsaw. The city still attracts new Polish immigrants.
3. Ellis Island closed as a port of entry in 1954, but this city in the east still attracts more immigrants than any other city in America.
4. People from Latin America are still coming in great numbers to Miami.
5. Along its Mexican border, which is 1,200 miles long, about 400,000 illegal immigrants are arrested every year.

b Find out from the graphs the differences and similarities between the eastern and the western states.

c What else do the figures tell us?

Africa
Asia
Europe
Latin America
Other

Illinois
25.5
47.8
23.5
1.7

New York
23.7
48.9
22.7
3

California
7.9
55.6
32.9
0.8 1.3

New Jersey
23.9
43
27.8
1.3

Arizona
10.9
11.8
71.5
1.3
0.5

Texas
5.3
16.1
74.9
2.2
0.2

Florida
13.3
8.7
72.8
1.3
0.2

Foreign-born population in % (Census 2000)

1 California and the Chinese

The Californian population is a mixture of immigrants from many different nations **which includes** lots of Chinese. Most foreigners know the part of San Francisco **which is called** Chinatown.

Today Chinatown has not only a lot of fine restaurants **which have been built** for the tourists, but it is also a place where some Chinese people do not have enough to eat. In some areas there are families with four or five children **who live** in a single room. And so you find many families **who use** the same kitchen and bathroom. Today Chinatown is not only a tourist attraction but also a place with a lot of poverty. Meanwhile many young Chinese have left Chinatown for other places **which offer** better jobs. But most of the new immigrants **who come** from China cannot move because they do not know the language **which is spoken** outside the Chinese community. The older Chinese people **who have been** there for decades do not want to move to another place. They hold on to their old ways, and they do not often ask for help from outside the community.

■ Replace the words in bold type by a present participle (ing-form) or past participle (third form of the verb).

Example:

The Californian population is a mixture of immigrants from many different nations **including** lots of Chinese. Most foreigners know the part of San Francisco **called** Chinatown. Today Chinatown …

2 Native Americans in California

The American Indian was the first true Californian. The style of Indian art, music and clothing is part of the whole West, including California. But like other minorities, the Indians have had trouble in Californian society. In their case the problem is land. **As they believe** that they have been treated unfairly by the American politicians, many of them have become rather bitter. Others have started to

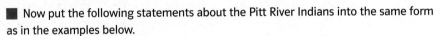

make their voices heard in various protest actions. One group includes the Pitt River Indians. **Before they started** their protest action, they talked to several reporters.

■ Now put the following statements about the Pitt River Indians into the same form as in the examples below.

1. When they realized how much gold there was on their land, the whites decided to take it away from the Indians.
2. As they knew the Indians had been treated badly, later governments gave them money for their land.
3. Because the Indians want their land back and not the money, they have decided to start a protest action.
4. After they have made their protest here, they are going to fly to Washington.
5. As they know how difficult it is to get a meeting with the President, they are prepared to wait as long as necessary.
6. Before they leave Washington the Indians will give a press conference.

Example:

Believing that they have been treated unfairly … **Before starting** their protest action …

3   A Mexican immigrant

A Mexican immigrant talks about his life in the U.S. during a break in his work.

■ Infinitive or ing-form? Fill in the correct form of the verb.

Example:

1. I'll never forget leaving my small Mexican hometown.
2. My mother told me: "Don't forget to write to us …

I'll never forget **1. (leave)** my small Mexican hometown. My mother told me:"Don't forget **2. (write)** to us when you're there. " I remember **3. (cross)** the border by night. I was afraid of **4. (be arrested)**, but I wanted **5. (change)** my life completely, so I decided **6. (take)** the chance. In the first town I stopped **7. (get)** some food. Inside the restaurant there was a sign **8. (say)** that they needed help in the kitchen. I remember **9. (ask)** the boss what he was prepared **10. (pay)**. It wasn't much, but **11. (need)** the money urgently I accepted it.
They made me **12. (do)** the dirty jobs. First I enjoyed **13. (work)** there because the other workers were friendly. But after **14. (stay)** there for six months I moved here to San Diego. I hope **15. (find)** my own apartment soon. I would like **16. (stay)** here forever. That's why I must remember **17. (phone)** the Housing Officer tomorrow. I used **18. (be)** a so-called illegal immigrant, but a couple of years ago I got a green card. Now I'm able **19. (live)** and work wherever I like. – Sorry, my break is over. I must stop **20. (talk)** now. I have **21. (get)** back to work again.

4   A German immigrant   Advanced

Ursula Zimmermann from Germany emigrated to America twenty years ago, but she has always kept in contact with her friends in Germany.

■ Translate the following part of one of her e-mails.

Vor einigen Monaten sah ich öfters drei junge Leute im Supermarkt. Ich erinnere mich, dass ich Herrn Cheng, den Leiter des Supermarktes, gefragt hatte, wer sie waren. Er erzählte mir, dass sie deutsche Studenten waren, die eine Reise von Kalifornien nach New York planten. Ich erinnere mich, dass ich sie eines Abends traf. Sie reparierten gerade ihr altes Auto. Ich hielt an, um mit ihnen zu reden. Es machte mir richtig Spaß, wieder Deutsch zu sprechen. Die jungen Leute freuten sich darauf, die USA zu durchqueren und die vielen Sehenswürdigkeiten zu sehen. Ich bot ihnen an, bei der Planung der Reise zu helfen.

Immigration and welfare

Together with corn and cars, immigration has been one of the main factors of American economic growth. The traditional theory is simple: new workers increase the supply of
5 goods and services with their labor and increase the demand for other goods and services by spending their wages. A circle of growth begins as a growing number of workers create a richer society for
15 each other. Two hundred years of U.S. history seem to confirm this theory. But there is a feeling today that immigration is not so good for the economy any more.

The polls show that many U.S. citizens are
20 worried that more immigrants will take jobs away from native-born workers. This can be true in times of high unemployment. In California, for example, a recent survey shows that the
25 population explosion between 1990 and 2000 was the result of a massive inflow of immigrants. With a jobless rate close to seven per cent (2003) many native-
30 born Americans are actually leaving to find work in other states. So we must see both sides: "The short-term costs of immigration are much higher
35 today," says Michael Boston, one of the leading American economists, "but in the long run, immigrants are still great news for our economy. Normally, new jobs are created through the immigrants' own work. The
40 immigrants' spending creates a demand for houses, food, etc. and their employers invest their growing profits in new machinery and jobs. That's how America got rich."

However, in the last few decades things have changed. In the early days of immigration public
45 education and some public health programs were the only services for those coming to New York or other Northeastern cities. One third of the new immigrants soon found out that America did not offer the opportunities they
50 were looking for and so they moved back home. Nowadays – even after the welfare reforms in 1996 which restricted help for immigrants – a lot of different welfare programs, from food stamps to unemployment benefit, help those who do
55 not succeed in finding work and even attract immigrants who would otherwise stay in their home countries. Furthermore, the level of skills of 90 per cent of the new immigrants is relatively low. And so are their earnings. As a result, state
60 governments spend between $11-22 billion to provide welfare to immigrants, and welfare costs are steadily climbing. Today welfare use by immigrants is 43 percent higher than by

native-born Americans and immigrants are still entering the United States in high numbers. In
65 many states immigration is said to be one of the main reasons for their financial problems and many experts believe that unless American immigration policies are changed there will be no end to the problem in the near future.
70

457 words

a Which of the following topics are mentioned in the text?
unemployment – transport – welfare costs – California – Texas – skills
– welfare use – environment

b Answer the following questions in complete sentences.
1. How can immigrants help the economy
   – as workers?
   – as consumers?
2. What are many people afraid of in a bad economic situation?
3. How has the welfare state developed since 1900?
4. How has the level of immigrants' skills changed in the last few
   decades?

c List the costs and the benefits of immigration according to the text.

d Find more arguments and state your point of view.

e Write a comment: Immigration helps the economy. Do you agree?

f Translate lines 44 to 70.

Follow these steps

1.	**Read the whole text first, even if you only have to translate part of it.** **Make sure you understand the unknown words.** **Use your dictionary.**	decade = Jahrzehnt, 10 Jahre
2.	**Translate the text into German in a way that you have a first draft. (word-by-word translation)**	Jedoch in den letzten Jahrzehnten haben sich die Dinge geändert.
3.	**Work through the text again. Compare the structure and the meaning of the English and the German sentence. Try to produce a suitable German final version.**	In den letzten Jahren hat sich jedoch die Situation geändert.

Info-Box: How to write a translation

Remember:

1. Read and try to understand the complete text.
2. Look up unknown words in your dictionary.
3. Make a first draft in a word-by-word translation.
4. Go through the text again and produce a final version in good German.

1 The new majority

The Californian lifestyle has grown out of many different cultures. People have been coming here from other American states and from foreign countries for a long time now. They have come to find better jobs, a better house, a better climate – in short a better way of life.

A Mom Chay Suth

B Santiago Rodriguez

C Lev Pischnik

 a Listen and put the photos into the correct order.

b Find out where these people came from.

c Find out where they live now in California.

d Listen again and find out the following information about the people:

	Marital Status	Language	Job in U.S./home country	Reasons for emigrating	Problems
Santiago					
Lev Pischnik					
Mom Chay Suth					

2 Minority groups

In many countries minority groups often face problems. Therefore some people are against immigration. On the other hand, immigration brings a lot of benefits to a country.

a Make a list of all the benefits you can think of in the following areas.

1. economy
2. employment
3. welfare
4. education
5. culture
6. language

b A local newspaper has just published a letter from someone wanting to stop immigration.
Write a letter to the editor of the newspaper, giving your arguments for immigration.

Sociology at work

Once upon a time there was a security guard and a worker in a factory. One day the worker came out of the factory carrying a cardboard box. "There is something funny here," thought the
5 guard. He opened the box, but there was nothing in the box except packing material. The next day the same thing happened, a cardboard box with packing material, a search and nothing found. Over the next few weeks the guard regularly

10 searched through the packing material, but he never found anything unusual. Finally, because it was driving him mad, the factory guard said to the worker, "Look. If I promise not to tell anybody, please would you tell me what you are stealing?"
15 "Cardboard boxes!" replied the worker.

Sometimes the most obvious things in life are those we overlook. Moreover, because everybody lives in society and experiences daily life, we seem to think that such experiences are so obvious that
20 they are not worth studying. But this is exactly what sociology is about. Its aim is to show how society forms our lives and our thinking. To find out more we often have to ask questions which people do not want to answer. However, in their
25 search for the truth sociologists have to use different methods when asking these questions.

Harald Newton, a sociologist from Colchester in England, realized this when he decided to interview farmers and farm workers for a survey on their opinions and attitudes to farm life.
30 When he interviewed the farmers, he played the role of a "serious" researcher – equipped with a briefcase, a printed questionnaire and adopting a formal manner. When interviewing the farm workers he soon found out that it was better
35 to leave this "equipment" at home. He had more success with the workers by appearing casual. Here he laughed and made jokes and simply wrote down his notes on a piece of paper.

In another case, Henry Turner, a sociologist
40 from Newcastle, decided to study a small group of adolescents from his home town. These young people were generally regarded as delinquents because they regularly stole car radios. Turner felt the best way to investigate
45 their delinquency was to try to see the world through their eyes. So he adopted a method of research called "participant observation" to find out the reasons for their behaviour. The problem here was to gain the young peoples'
50 acceptance. So Henry Turner spent two years with these young people. He went to their clubs, pubs and discos or just hung around street corners with them. Through his help and his advice with court cases he gradually became
55 accepted by the youngsters. In this way he could then carry out his research and find out the true reasons for their behaviour.

These two examples show us how important it is to choose the method of research carefully.
60 Usually surveys are preferred if the aim is to find out the opinions of a large number of people. On the other hand, when the sociologist wants to find out reasons for the behaviour of a smaller group, which may be unwilling to answer questions from
65 a stranger, he has to adopt alternative methods to come to a true picture.   **528 words**

Exam preparation

Comprehension questions

■ After you have read the text carefully, answer the following questions in your own words as far as possible.

1. How did the guard find out the truth?
2. How is sociology defined in the text?
3. How did Harald Newton differentiate when doing his survey?
4. Why did Henry Turner adopt a different method?
5. How did Henry Turner become an accepted member of the group?

Summary

■ Using your own words, give a summary of the text. It should be about 250 words long.

Vocabulary

1. Find synonyms in the text for the following words:
   a) look for
   b) clear
   c) purpose
   d) viewpoint
   e) young people
   f) criminals
   g) set of questions
   h) to study

2. Explain the following phrases in your own words:
   a) there is something funny here (line 4)
   b) everybody … experiences daily life (lines 17/18)
   c) adopting a formal manner (lines 33/34)
   d) to see the world through their eyes (lines 46/47)

Translation

■ Translate lines 40 to 58.

Comment

■ Comment on the following statement, using your own knowledge and ideas.
"When a sociologist becomes a fully accepted member of a group, he/she loses the ability to analyse the situation of that group in a clear and objective way."

Grammar revision

1 Mixed forms

■ Fill in the suitable form of the verbs in brackets.

Life without father

The decline of the traditional family (**1. be**) a worldwide trend. A new survey which (**2. publish**) last week says that one-parent homes (**3. become**) more popular all over the world. According to the survey the number of one-parent families (**4. rise**) steadily in every part of the world since 1970. Generally such a family (**5. consist**) of a mother with children. This usually (**6. mean**) poverty. Even married couples (**7. spend**) less time with their children than their parents (**8. do**). In 1976 for example, fewer than half the married women in the United States (**9. have**) jobs outside the home. By 1988 the figure (**10. go**) up to 60 per cent. And this trend (**11. continue**) up till now. So the development of social programmes (**12. seem**) to be necessary in order to help both two-parent families and single mothers and fathers.

Everyone (**13. know**) that Sweden (**14. have**) modern services for all families. But now the costs of all the social programmes (**15. destroy**) the Swedish welfare system. If the trend (**16. continue**), they (**17. have**) to pay 80 to 90 per cent taxes one day. On the other hand the survey mentions Brazil where about 200,000 children (**18. live**) on the streets. In the first three months of this year about 300 young people (**19. be killed**) in Rio de Janeiro. This number (**20. rise**) since last year. The problems in Sweden or Brazil (**21. not mean**) that we should give up hope. But time (**22. run**) out.

2 Infinitive or "ing"-form?

■ Fill in the infinitive with or without "to" or a suitable "ing"-form.

How young people in Europe see themselves

They love the way Italian men look and Spanish women make them (**1. feel**) weak at the knees. They prefer British TV and they like (**2. drive**) a German car. Of course, (**3. buy**) French clothes is best, and we are not surprised (**4. hear**) that young Europeans also prefer (**5. eat**) French food. It may not be (**6. surprise**), but it is true. At least, this is what an MTV survey on young people (**7. live**) in Europe found out. The image is more or less realistic.

After (**8. interview**) 3,300 young adults, the result was that most young Europeans saw themselves as responsible, intelligent and optimistic. More than half believe themselves (**9. be**) better off than their parents. The largest group (**10. support**) the European Union were the Italians with 90 per cent of the interviewed people. When it comes to social attitudes some national differences seem (**11. remain**).

Young Spaniards (**12. look**) for a happier life should travel north into France where the young – although (**13. suffer**) from some problems – seem (**14. lead**) more carefree lives.

Many young people in all European countries are afraid of (**15. be**) attacked or even killed on the streets. Others are concerned about (**16. lose**) their jobs.

Although many of them do not want (**17. see**) violence[*] on TV, nothing can keep them from (**18. spend**) two and a half hours (**19. watch**) TV. When not (**20. sit**) in front of the box, they love (**21. listen**) to the radio or recorded music. These three activities take up seven hours a day on average. How can Europe's youth find time (**22. do**) anything else?

violence – Gewalt

Methods of research

A sociologist chooses the method which seems most fitting to the circumstances and the aims of the research. Below you can read some definitions of different kinds of methods.

a Match the definitions with the terms in the box.
1. …is used to study smaller groups from within. Simply asking them questions would not uncover the true reasons for their behaviour.
2. …is often chosen to find out about groups of people over a number of years and to note changes in their viewpoints.
3. …means pretending to be a member of a group. This method is often used in research of gangs or criminals.
4. …means asking a representative sample of people to find out about certain opinions at the exact time of the survey.

> Cross-section survey – Longitudinal survey – Participant observation – Covert/Secret participant observation

b Which method of research is best?
Read the following case reports and say which methods of research were used. Give reasons.
1. We wanted to find out the current political views of the whole British population. Names were chosen from lists of all the voters in Britain. Twenty-two addresses were selected at random in 114 districts. This gave us 2,508 addresses. Interviewers then went to these houses to ask our selected questions.
2. It was when I was working as a social worker in Manchester that I first met "The Boys". I got on well with them and was very interested in finding out more about them – especially about their theft behaviour and sexual exploits. Once accepted by a few of "The Boys", I was able to explain my situation to them and then move slowly into a wider acceptance. In this way I could carry out my research.
3. I decided to study my own colleagues in the police force to show the way that the police force really works. However, many of my colleagues were strongly against my research, so I had to do it in secret.
4. In order to show that delinquents really are different from other youngsters, they must be studied from an early age, using regular interviews. My study was based on 411 boys. They represented an unselected sample of schoolboys living in a traditional working class area of London. They were intensively studied from eight to ten years and interviewed regularly up until the age of nineteen.

c Which type of research would you use if you were studying
1. the Mafia?
2. students' attitudes towards teachers in your own college?
3. the behaviour of a group of young people at a disco?
4. the attitudes of the population in your country on the punishment for juvenile delinquents?
Give reasons for your choices and mention some of the difficulties you might have in your research.

"It wasn't like that in my day"

Recent newspaper reports have been full of complaints about the declining standards of teenage behaviour. A lot of people say that young people are suffering from a loss of values.

5 However, according to a study by Leslie Francis from the University of Wales, many young people are just confused about what is right or wrong. A survey of 14,000 schoolchildren aged 13 to 15 found that 17 % believe there is nothing wrong
10 in playing truant from school. 16 % think that travelling on public transport without a ticket is not wrong; 6 % feel there is nothing wrong with shoplifting; and only 29 % said that they had never stolen anything. Although ideas about right
15 and wrong or good or bad depend on people's viewpoint, sociologists can judge a society's morals by using crime levels as indicators. They can also interview people to find out their opinions on issues such as smoking, drinking and
20 drug taking.

But was it better in the past? Were young people less immoral and less violent than they are today? According to Dr Henry Henrick, a British sociologist at Oxford University, young people
25 tend to develop the values of the society in which they grow up. Moreover, links between social poverty and crime are well known. One survey of Newcastle's young people found that 60 % of

boys and 9 % of girls from "deprived families" eventually became criminal. This survey suggests
30 that poverty has a negative effect on the parent's ability to educate their children in a socially acceptable way. Another factor which leads to juvenile delinquency is unemployment. The British Youth Council has recently published
35 figures which show that unemployment is running at 16 % for the under-25s. Income support for most 16- and 17-year-olds has been abolished and the government's promise to provide youth training places for every teenager
40 remains unfulfilled. What is worse, long-term unemployment is linked with suicide. In the last ten years the suicide rate among the under-25s has risen by 30 %. Alcohol and drug taking is also growing. It has been proven that the typical young
45 person who has been unemployed for a longer period of time is likely to fall victim to a wide variety of accidents and crimes.

In his book "Hooligans: a report of respectable fears", Geoffrey Pearson argues that adults have
50 always had fears and prejudices with the so-called young rebels. According to him, because society always looks at its past days through rose-tinted glasses, it suffers from historical amnesia. In other words, when adults look at young people's morals,
55 they always maintain that they were better in the good old days.

Such forgetfulness about past times can lead to moral panic in which adults are deeply shocked by children's behaviour and as a result start to
60 blame individuals instead of looking to wider causes.

Young people will always create their own style, but do their morals and behaviour really change from one generation to the next? It is the job of
65 sociologists to analyse situations and to suggest help. All of us, as members of society, have then the duty to try and find possible solutions to the problems which young people face.   **532 words**

The Guardian (adapted)

Exam preparation

Comprehension questions

■ After you have read the text carefully, answer the following questions in your own words as far as possible.

1. Which crimes does the author mention in the text? Describe these crimes in your own words.
2. How can sociologists find out about what people believe is right or wrong?
3. How are poverty and crime connected?
4. How does the sex of a child affect his/her chances of becoming delinquent?
5. How does long-term unemployment affect young people?
6. Why, according to Geoffrey Pearson, do adults believe that young people were 'better' in the past?

Summary

■ Using your own words, give a summary of the text. It should be about 250 words long.

Vocabulary

1. Find the verbs which correspond to the following nouns taken from the text:
   a) complaint (line 2)
   b) behaviour (line 3)
   c) indicator (line 17)
   d) (un)employment (line 34)
   e) forgetfulness (line 58)
   f) solution (line 68)

2. Explain the following in your own words:
   a) to play truant (line 10)
   b) in a socially acceptable way (lines 32/33)
   c) juvenile delinquency (line 34)
   d) youth training places (line 40)
   e) the good old days (line 57)

Translation

■ Translate lines 63 to 69.

Comment

■ Comment on the following statement, using your own knowledge and ideas.
"Young people today do not know the difference between what is right or what is wrong."

Grammar revision

1 Mixed forms

■ Fill in the suitable form of the verbs in brackets.

A boy and his gun

In Omaha nowadays even young people (**1. own**) weapons. Doug, who (**2. be**) 15, (**3. get**) his first gun last year. After a classmate (**4. give**) him the number of a dealer in town, Doug (**5. take**) his older brother's pick-up truck, which (**6. give**) him the right image. He then (**7. buy**) a gun for just $25. "If you (**8. have**) a gun, people (**9. respect**) you," he says. The next evening while his parents (**10. watch**) TV, Dough (**11. go**) into the garage and (**12. look**) at the gun closely. He soon (**13. find out**) that (**14. fire**) the gun for the first time was more difficult than (**15. buy**) it. But then he (**16. get**) used to it. In the last few months he (**17. do**) nine drive-by shootings at cars and houses. Bonnie Elseman, a single mother in the neighbourhood says: "I (**18. live**) in this area all my life. But now the boys (**19. shoot**) at each other just for fun. I (**20. know**) Doug for a long time. He (**21. be**) such a nice child when he (**22. be**) younger. But when they (**23. kick**) him out of school he suddenly (**24. become**) totally different. Maybe if he (**25. find**) work after school, he (**26. make**) it. But if he (**27. go**) on like this, he (**28. end**) up in prison."

2 Reported speech

■ Change the following statements by Mrs Turner, a neighbour of Bonnie Elseman, into reported speech. Use different reporting verbs. Start the sentences with "Mrs Turner …".

A neighbour's view

Some weeks ago Mrs Turner told a reporter:

1. "I have known Dough for a long time.
2. He lives not far away from where I live.
3. He was a nice boy when he was younger.
4. But some years ago things changed.
5. Since then he has been hanging around the streets.
6. He never works.
7. He steals what he needs.
8. I don't know how this will end.
9. I'm afraid for my children when I see him passing by.
10. We all know that he is carrying a gun.
11. Guns must be banned.
12. We can't do a lot about crime here.
13. We are organizing self-help groups.
14. We hope that the politicians will do something about the situation."

1 A case study: Death on the streets

In this interview a young boy (15 years old) says why he started joyriding:

"When I was 14 I got a Saturday morning job at a scrap yard. I started playing about with old cars. I knew how to drive because I had watched my dad. Well, one Saturday evening we didn't have much to do – there's never much to do in our town. My mates suggested going on a joyride, just for a bit of fun. They knew I could drive a bit. So we broke into this car and off we went down the motorway. My mates told me to drive faster and faster. It's difficult to describe the feeling you get. I suppose it's about being in control of so much power. Just like in the movies or on TV adverts. I didn't really think about the risk we were taking. Then we got caught by the police. That's when my real problems started …"

a Now discuss this case study in class. In your discussion you should try to find reasons for and solutions to the problem.

b Write a report on the results of your discussion.

2 Labelling and the sad story of boy B

The labelling theory is not so much based on what the individual does, but more on the reactions of others.

■ With the help of the cartoons below try to explain the meaning of the term "labelling".

Growing up on welfare

The stereotype of the American poor is "black and lazy". That is why many middle-class Americans believe that their tax-money is being wasted on welfare payments. They insist that a lot of these
5 payments go to lazy black women who are only interested in having sex without birth control and also do not want to get married. Rosemary L. Bray, a black woman from Illinois, tries to explain what living on welfare really means by telling us her
10 own childhood experiences.

"I know what it means to be poor. And I know that the welfare system leaves people on the edge of survival. I know because I have been there. My parents came to Chicago in 1980. My mother got
15 a part-time job in a restaurant. Father worked at whatever came to hand – from selling junk at open air markets to selling hamburgers on the street.

When I was born, he made my mother quit her job. They had, like most American couples, their 20 own American dream – a husband who goes to work, a wife at home and a family of smiling children. But, as it is true for so many African-American couples, their dream was an illusion. After being married for several years my mother 25 realized that my father was a gambler and an alcoholic. One day he didn't return home and he has not been back since. After discussing her case with the social workers, she decided to sign up for AFDC*. The welfare payments for the rent and 30 for all other expenses, by any standards, were not really sufficient. There were times when we hardly had a loaf of bread. So what did it take to survive? It took the kindness of friends and strangers, the charity of the churches, low expectations, 35 deprivation and a lot of patience.

What really made our lives work was my mother's genius at "making do". Shopping for food was done at the cheapest stores. Clothes were bought at charity second hand stores or at street markets. 40 However Mama's biggest worry was that we children should grow up uneducated. So she sent us to a church-run private school. When one social worker asked her how she could afford to send us there, she declared "My kids need 45 an education" and told him to mind his own business. She reminded us again and again that every book, every test, every page of homework was in fact a ticket out and away from the life we were leading at that time. 50

We lived on welfare for 18 years. In the meantime Mama has died and we children are all tax-paying working adults. When I read articles about the abuse of the welfare system in America I get angry. Most of them are full of lies and prejudices. Of 55 course, some women are lazy and misuse the system. But the vast majority of welfare recipients are honest and hard-working. And life on the welfare is no picnic. **496 words**

AFDC = Aid for Families with Dependent Children

Exam preparation

Comprehension questions

■ After you have read the text carefully, answer the following questions in your own words as far as possible.

1. Which prejudices are mentioned in the text?
2. Why was the "American dream" an illusion for the Bray family?
3. In what way was education an important factor for Rosemary's mother?
4. How did the family manage on the welfare payments?
5. Why is Rosemary still angry?

Summary

■ Using your own words, give a summary of the text. It should be about 250 words long.

Vocabulary

1. Find the antonyms to these words taken from the text:
   a) poor (line 1)
   b) part-time (line 15)
   c) illusion (line 24)
   d) cheapest (line 39)
   e) private school (line 43)
   f) lie (line 55)
   g) majority (line 57)
   h) hard-working (line 58)

2. Explain the following in your own words:
   a) living on welfare (line 9)
   b) the edge of survival (lines 12/13)
   c) making do (line 38)
   d) a ticket out and away from the life we were leading at that time (lines 49/50)
   e) welfare is no picnic (line 59)

Translation

■ Translate lines 51 to 59.

Comment

■ Comment on the following statement, using your own knowledge and ideas.
"Welfare payments should be kept low so that the recipients adopt more responsibility for their own lives."

Grammar revision

1 Mixed forms

■ Fill in the suitable form of the verbs in brackets.

Welfare for the rich

He (**1. pay**) into Social Security since 1938, one year after workers (**2. begin**) (**3. contribute**) to President Roosevelt's new social programme – and he still (**4. pay**) today. At the age of 80 years Harlow Savage still (**5. walk**) to his office every workday morning – at his own company. Everybody (**6. believe**) that Savage (**7. earn**) his retirement benefits*, but he himself (**8. not see**) it that way. On the one hand he still (**9. receive**) a salary of more than $100,000 and (**10. have to**) pay Social Security contributions for that, but on the other hand he (**11. get**) a monthly Social Security check of $3,000. After he (**12. reach**) the age of 65, Savage (**13. receive**) retirement benefits like all other workers. After a few years he (**14. get**) all the money he (**15. pay**) into the system. And since then they (**16. pay**) him extra money. "Every month they (**17. take**) the money from the younger and lower-paid workers and (**18. give**) it to people like me," Savage says. But things (**19. change**) right now. A CNN survey last week (**20. find**) out that a majority of Americans (**21. believe**) in (**22. cut**) the payments to high-income Americans. If the government (**23. cut**) these payments, they (**24. save**) more than $40 billion every year. Harlow Savage's granddaughter Amanda says: "I (**25. not think**) that I (**26. be able**) (**27. live**) half as well as my grandfather or father." She (**28. return**) to college next year but she already (**29. hear**) from friends that even after college she only (**30. get**) a low-paid service job if she (**31. be**) lucky.

retirement benefits – Rente

2 Adjective or Adverb?

■ Fill in the correct form of the words in brackets.

Information for single parents

Please read this information on child support. It will (**1. probable**) be (**2. helpful**). A (**3. new**) system of help for children was introduced in 1993. In order to receive help (**4. usual**) both parents must live in Great Britain or Northern Ireland. An absent* parent has to pay (**5. regular**) for his/her children. This payment is (**6. automatical**) checked every two years by the Child Support Agency. The payment depends on the parent's (**7. regular**) income after taxes. If an absent parent does not pay, the agency which is (**8. responsible**) for the child will pay until it finally gets the money back from the parent. It may be (**9. possible**) for the absent parent to make an arrangement with the agency. (**10. Normal**) no one needs to pay more than 30 per cent of his income.

absent – abwesend

1 The cycle of deprivation and poverty

a After you have studied the diagram below, complete it with suitable words from the box.

children born
in poor **❶**

A deprived
childhood

Materially
Poor housing: damp,
cold houses in poor
❷ neighbourhoods.
Inadequate food
and **❸**

Culturally
No encouragement or help
from **❹** with school work. Few
books at home. **❺** family life.
The gang or **❻** becomes very
important.

People get used to poverty
and don't see any **❾** to their
problems. Emphasis is on now
rather than **❿** planning.

Poverty

Poor
school **❼**

Unemployment
or **❽** jobs

inner-city – clothing – parents – peer group – solutions – families – future – marks –
long-term – inferiority – husbands – educational – wishes – poorly-paid – unstable

b Now describe the diagram in your own words.

2 Voluntary organisations

■ Look at the cartoon on the right
and discuss the problem which is
shown in it.

"Does society care about black kids?"

Let me introduce myself. I am an ordinary mother of three and I live in East London. Five years ago I took a decision. I decided to send my children to a "Saturday school". Every week, for two hours, my
5   children receive that little bit of extra tuition that will help them to get the best out of their "normal" school.

There are about 50 Saturday schools around the country and they are all run by black parents who

10 are convinced that their children need more help than the normal schools provide. Now our schools are in danger. The local governments are threatening to close them down. The authorities say that we do not follow the rules which regulate
15 safety, pupil-teacher ratios and insurance cover. All the teachers at the Saturday schools teach for free and the schools are run by volunteers. It would be so unfair if we have to close. Moreover, it will confirm the fear that many of us have – that
20 society does not care about black kids.

My mother came to Britain from the West Indies in the sixties and she used to tell us "in order to get on in this world you have to be ten times better than your white counterparts". I, too, have told my children the same. I am sorry to say this,   25 but I am convinced that black children are not getting the best education in the normal schools. Personal experience has shown me that there is a lot of racism in the schools. I have seen many cases where black children are not encouraged by   30 their (white) teachers to reach their full potential. This was one reason why I sent my children to a Saturday school.

We, West Indians, know that we are not a race of under-achievers, but the statistics tell a   35 different story. According to the latest statistics, pupils from the West Indian families do badly in British schools – a situation which frightens me because I want my children to do well at school. Saturday school is a way of checking my children's   40 performance at their ordinary school. Moreover, it is a way of giving them extra help. Another important advantage is that they are taught there by black teachers. This is something they do not normally experience at their state school. These   45 teachers are really interested in the future of black children and they do not suffer from the inability to look beyond the colour of the child's skin. They can help the children and they do not have the preconceived idea that these children are not able   50 to reach a higher standard.

Most parents of my generation had their early education in the West Indies, arrived here aged 9 or 10 and did well in primary school, but fell behind at secondary school. Our parents did not   55 realize the problem because they never criticized the teachers and simply accepted the school system. Now we understand the system and are not afraid to criticize teachers or racism in schools. Maybe with the help of Saturday schools   60 and open-minded teachers we will be able to show society that black children can do well at school. Please save our Saturday schools!

533 words

Exam preparation

Comprehension questions

◼ After you have read the text carefully, answer the following questions in your own words as far as possible.

1. Why did Ms McTaggert decide to send her children to a Saturday school?
2. Where can you find such schools and how are they organized?
3. Why did Ms McTaggert write this article in the newspaper?
4. In what way, in Ms McTaggert's opinion, are the teachers at the Saturday school good for her children?
5. Why, according to Maureen McTaggert, did the parents of her generation not do anything about the problems at school?

Summary

◼ Using your own words, give a summary of the text. It should be about 250 words long.

Vocabulary

1. Find synonyms in the text for the following words:
   a) normal
   b) teaching
   c) figures
   d) benefit
   e) first school
   f) aid

2. Explain the following in your own words:
   a) pupil-teacher ratio (line 15)
   b) racism in the schools (line 29)
   c) West Indians (line 34)
   d) under-achievers (line 35)
   e) preconceived idea (line 50)
   f) primary/secondary school (lines 54/55)

Translation

◼ Translate lines 52 to 63.

Comment

◼ Using your own knowledge and ideas, give examples of where you can find racial discrimination in our society and suggest solutions to the problem.

Grammar revision

1 Mixed forms

■ Fill in the suitable form of the verbs in brackets.

Hot lines

The telephone never **(1. stop)** **(2. ring)** in the office of the Association for Immigrant Rights in Los Angeles. "At what hospital **(3. happen)** that?" David Soldan, who **(4. work)** there three times a week, **(5. want)** **(6. know)**. A moment later another complaint: "The police **(7. take)** my car yesterday because I **(8. not have)** my green card with me."

In the last two weeks hot lines in some big Californian cities **(9. receive)** thousands of calls from such people **(10. report)** acts of discrimination.

A Mexican-American mother **(11. call)** some days ago after the hospital staff **(12. leave)** her sick two-year old child **(13. wait)** at hospital for five hours and then they **(14. send)** the child away after a short examination. Later the hospital **(15. accept)** the seriously ill child. But while the mother **(16. sit)** by her child's bed, they **(17. ask)** for her immigration papers.

The situation **(18. become)** worse for both legal and illegal immigrants in the last few years. "Nobody **(19. know)** how this situation **(20. develop)** in the future," a black nurse from Woodland Hills **(21. tell)** me last night. "Last Monday when I **(22. go)** past a high school which I **(23. pass)** for 10 years without any trouble they **(24. start)** to throw stones at me. Sometimes I just **(25. no know)** what **(26. do)**. Life **(27. get)** harder every day. If the situation **(28. not improve)**, I **(29. give)** up my job and **(30. move)** away from here."

2 Conditionals

■ Complete the following if-sentences in the correct tense.

Two politicians are talking about immigration

R. Thompson: "I believe that if the American immigrants from Europe **(1. give)** up, things **(2. develop)** very differently. The US **(3. not become)** so powerful, if there **(4. not be)** so many people who had wanted to be free and independent."

P. McDonald: "That may be true, but things have changed. If we **(5. allow)** simply everybody into the country today there **(6. be)** a lot of problems in the future."

R. Thompson: "That's why we must help the Third World countries. If the developing countries **(7. be)** richer, a lot of immigrants **(8. stay)** home. The problems **(9. continue)** if we **(10. not change)** anything."

P. McDonald: "You know most illegal immigrants have come here for economic reasons. We are going to do something about that. We **(11. save)** a lot of social costs if we **(12. send)** them home."

R. Thompson: "But remember the immigrants who come here for political reasons. You realize, don't you, that they **(13. risk)** their lives if they **(14. stay)** home."

Ethnic minorities – School and work

a First read the statements below which were made by some children of ethnic minorities in British schools.

1. *"Our teachers just believe
   we are slow learners."*
   John, 16, West Indian,
   born in London.

2. *"They always tell us we
   should speak properly."*
   Marie, 17, West Indian,
   born in Birmingham.

3. *"In the history lessons
   all the 'heroes' are white."*
   Minati, 17, Indian, born
   in Dehli.

4. *"In music and literature we
   only study Western culture."*
   George, 15, Hong Kong Chinese,
   born in Manchester.

5. *"I get very bored at school.
   What has school got to do
   with my life?"*
   Kim, 15, Hong Kong Chinese,
   born in Hong Kong.

6. *"I'm the only pupil from
   Pakistan. It's not easy for
   me to make friends."*
   Faruk, 16, Pakistani, born in Lahore.

b What do these statements tell us about life in school for pupils of ethnic minorities.
Think about
1. cultural background
2. language
3. attitudes of teachers and classmates

c Discuss the diagram on employment of ethnic minorities in Britain according to the statistics made in 2000. What are the most outstanding differences?

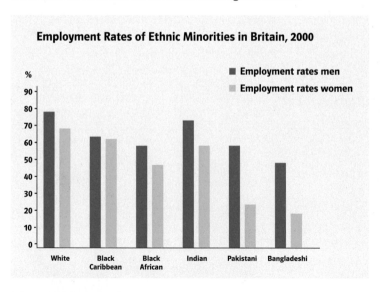

d Try to find out corresponding figures for your town/region/country and compare them with the above diagram.

Freizeit

The British on holiday

Before the Second World War, amazing as it seems today, only about a quarter of the population of the British Isles ever went away on holiday at all. During the one week of the year when most
5 working people had their official annual holiday they stayed at home, frequently very near the factory where they worked. Very often the simple opportunity to stay in bed for an hour or two longer on a weekday morning meant a holiday
10 in itself. 'Going away' meant at best a day trip to a seaside resort. Even though Britain is a small island where no inland town is more than a few hours' journey from the coast, and a country with a strong sea-going history, many working-class
15 people went through their lives never setting eyes on the sea.
The social revolution which has taken place in Britain since 1945 is nowhere more evident than in British attitudes to holidays and leisure. The
20 two weeks holiday at a local seaside resort became a British institution. With the opening up of mass tourism the 'average Brit' started to discover the 'Continent'. Just how quickly the British changed their holiday habits surprised everyone
25 concerned. And it took some time for the truth to sink in: that very little had changed. The average British holidaymaker continued to want what he had always wanted: a seaside resort, improved and modernized of course, but populated mainly

by his fellow countrymen, where English is spoken 30 and the food is familiar. In other words the same holiday but in the sun.
Interest in foreign travel for its own sake is still negligible. Small groups of educated travellers continue to seek art and beauty on holiday, 35 spending hours in museums, looking for rare wild flowers in the mountains of northern Greece, standing in front of stained glass windows, but for the mass of holidaymakers culture of any kind rarely plays a role at all. 40
What the average tourist wants is sun and sand, alcohol and sex. Many of them who have been to Spain many times would have difficulty telling you anything about the country beyond the small area between their hotel and the nearest 45 beach.
However, the number of people who try to avoid mass tourism is increasing. Many take their cars to explore parts of Europe beyond the reach of the package holiday. Inland Spain, the mountain 50 villages of Italy and the deep south of Greece have been the favourite areas. And even some motorists are prepared to tackle a journey from Britain to Turkey. In the old days the same people would have hesitated to drive from London 55 to Edinburgh. With the growth of the car ferry services and the building of the Eurotunnel, the English Channel is now the busiest stretch of water in the world. **471 words**

Exam preparation

Comprehension questions

■ After you have read the text carefully, answer the following questions in your own words as far as possible.

1. Why did most people in Britain before 1939 stay at home for their holidays?
2. What does a holiday mean for the majority of British people nowadays?
3. How do people spend their holidays who do not want the so-called package holidays?

Summary

■ Using your own words, give a summary of the text. It should be about 250 words long.

Vocabulary

1. Find synonyms in the text for the following words:
   a) yearly
   b) chance
   c) coastal
   d) clear
   e) tourists
   f) car drivers

2. Explain the following in your own words:
   a) mass tourism (lines 21/22)
   b) package holiday (line 50)
   c) the food is familiar (line 31)
   d) car ferry services (lines 56/57)
   e) the Eurotunnel (line 57)

Translation

■ Translate lines 17 to 32.

Comment

■ Comment on the following statement, using your own knowledge and ideas.
"It is our jobs which influence our leisure choices most."

Grammar revision

1 Mixed forms

■ Fill in the suitable form of the verbs in brackets.

European tourism fights a crisis

The European Commission **(1. publish)** a green paper on tourism last week which **(2. deal)** with the development of tourism in the EU. According to the latest figures from the World Tourism Organisation, Europe's share of international visitors **(3. drop)** from 73 per cent in the 1960s to 63 per cent in the 1990s and **(4. fall)** to 51 per cent by 2010. Last year the number of tourists in East Asia **(5. go)** up by 7 per cent, in America by 4 per cent, but in Europe and Africa the number **(6. remain)** almost constant.

Although tourism **(7. be)** a major factor in a lot of European countries for many years, the European Commission only just **(8. realize)** that it is also responsible for this sector. Until now tourism **(9. create)** a lot of jobs for the young and poorly qualified. If the negative trend in European tourism **(10. go)** on, this **(11. mean)** more unemployment, of course.

"From the beginning of next year when we **(12. hold)** the EU presidency, we **(13. do)** everything in our power **(14. increase)** interest in the tourist industry," one EU official **(15. announce)** yesterday.

2 Passive

■ Rewrite the following sentences in the passive form.

Tourism – what can be done?
1. The European Commission published a document on tourism some days ago.
2. We are losing tourists to Asia and America.
3. Unfortunately, the EU has not supported tourism for a long time.
4. We must run promotion actions to attract visitors.
5. The European Commission will give EU money to certain regions.
6. In Germany we have organized tourism along regional lines.
7. "We do not require changes in the German tourist industry," a German official says.
8. The members of the EU commission feel that they should fight the problems of unemployment in the tourist industry.

The influences on leisure patterns

Our choice of leisure pursuits is influenced by a number of social factors. The most important ones are our social class, our age group and our sex.

a Compare the following four people.
Write about what you think their leisure activities might be, considering the factors mentioned above. Give reasons for your choices.

1. Graham Lane
56, lorry driver, married, 2 children aged 23 and 20

2. Lisa Gates
27, managing director of own firm, married, no children

3. Robert Lee
19, unemployed, single

4. Rose Jenkins
30, single parent, 3 children, part-time secretary

b The chart below describes what British people often do in their spare time according to a recent survey. Discuss the results of the chart. Try to think of reasons for the differences.

Leisure activities (Average minutes spent per person per day)

	male	female
socializing	51	62
entertainment/culture	6	6
resting/time out	18	25
sports/outdoor activities	18	11
hobbies/games	15	12
TV/Video/DVD	161	137
Reading	28	28
computing	11	4

c Do you think our leisure pursuits will change in the future? Why/why not?

The missing

Every year around 100,000 children run away. Many are escaping abuse or trouble at home, but some just go.

Sarah Turner held a poster of her missing 14-year-old daughter up to the face of a teenage girl of similar age, living on the streets of South London. The girl, a crack addict, read how Ruth, a bright and attractive schoolgirl, had disappeared outside her local library – leaving her parents unable to

imagine why she should do so. As the girl read, tears rolled down her cheeks. Then she shook her head and said that she was sorry but she had not seen Ruth. "I'm sure she cried because she recognised so much of her own story in Ruth's," says Sarah Turner.

Until Ruth disappeared Mrs Turner had been unfamiliar with the world of life on the streets. But after Ruth went missing last month, the police reported a sighting of her in the central London area. So Mrs Turner began to search every street and every corner. She became well-acquainted with the area's outdoor population. "The police told me that looking for runaways like Ruth is like looking for a needle in a haystack," she says. "I knew that if I wanted her back, I would have to find her myself and find her quickly before something terrible happened to her." She searched day and night, while her husband Paul and her elder daughter Joanna waited by the phone at home.

This was not the first time Ruth had run away, but it was the longest she had ever been missing. For a few years, she had left home from time to time, first only for a few hours, later staying away overnight. Although she often stayed away from the exclusive girls' school she attended, Ruth seemed able to keep up with her work. "All she said, each time she returned," says Sarah Turner, "was that she had sat on a bus and waited to see where she would end up. It didn't matter to her." The lack of explanation for her flights has been one of the hardest things for her parents. There has not been a single accusation in a moment of anger. All her mother knows for certain is that Ruth suffers from low self-esteem and seems unhappy at school. "She doesn't have a lot of friends and I think she feels isolated. She thinks differently to other kids, and from a young age, she was always asking questions which have no answers like: *Why did the universe start?* Maybe she's frightened of something."

Ruth is one of about 100,000 under-16s who go missing every year. One in three boys and one in five girls are under 11 when they first run away. From the age of 14 upwards, girls are twice as likely to run away as boys. 45% of children in care run away compared with 9.5% of those who live with their families.

Happily, Ruth turned up safe and well after 10 days away. When the police collected her from a homeless project where she had sought help, the officers said that they were convinced that she had not been abused in any way and that she had not taken drugs. But Ruth has refused to see her family and chosen instead to go into foster care. Social workers have told her family that they cannot see her at present. For her parents this is a painful time as they wait for social services to permit a meeting, for her mother in particular. She says: "I just miss her so much and want her to come home again."

590 words

The Guardian (adapted)

Exam preparation

Comprehension questions

■ After you have read the text carefully, answer the following questions in your own words as far as possible.

1. Why did Sarah Turner search the streets of London?
2. What was Mrs Turner afraid of?
3. Why may Ruth have left home?
4. What children are most likely to run away?
5. Why – do you think – did Ruth not want to return?

Summary

■ Using your own words, give a summary of the text. It should be about 250 words long.

Vocabulary

1. Look in the text to find synonyms for these words:
   a) run away
   b) problems
   c) intelligent
   d) good-looking
   e) go to (school)
   f) come back
   g) 20 percent
   h) two times
   i) sure

2. Explain the following:
   a) abuse (line 2)
   b) live on the streets (line 6)
   c) addict (line 7)
   d) runaway(s) (line 23)
   e) like looking for a needle in a haystack (line 24)
   f) go missing (lines 52/53)
   g) homeless (line 61)
   h) foster care (lines 65/66)
   i) social worker (line 66)

Translation

■ Translate lines 4 to 15.

Comment

■ Comment on the following statement, using your own knowledge and ideas.
"Most parents can't help their teenage children because they just don't understand their problems."

More help needed for disabled children

Over the last three decades the number of children suffering from cerebral palsy (CP) has tripled, according to a new report. Cerebral palsy is a condition caused by failure of part of the brain
5 to develop either before birth, at birth or in early childhood. It affects the child's ability to control its muscles and can vary from being hardly noticeable to being extremely severe. No two people are affected in the same way.

10 Medical advances, however, mean that babies born with cerebral palsy now have a better chance of surviving. Nevertheless, SCOPE, a charity for people with CP, say that too little is done to help CP sufferers. SCOPE make several
15 suggestions which in their opinion could improve the situation. For instance, they believe that if the health and social services worked together with the schools, it would mean that the children could get the special equipment which they really need to lead a normal life. SCOPE maintain that at the 20 moment many requests for wheelchairs, house adjustments and speech aids are not fulfilled because these requests fall between different government departments.

A typical example of this bureaucracy is the case 25 of Beth Miller, a 7-year-old CP sufferer. Beth finds it very difficult to walk, dress and eat by herself. Nevertheless the 7-year-old from Epsom near London is determined to lead a life which is as normal as possible. With the help from a full-time 30 carer she is able to go to a normal primary school where she has made many friends. However, Beth's mother says that Beth's life would be much easier if she were given better equipment without the long delays and the governmental 35 red tape. For example, the voice computer she has is very slow and causes a lot of problems for Beth at school. She will probably have to wait 18 months before she can get a better one. As already mentioned, Beth has problems with walking. She 40 can take two or three steps on her own, but then she needs the help of a walking frame. An electric wheelchair would help her a lot outdoors. But electric wheelchairs are not available for children under 12 because the social services department 45 does not accept that children under this age should go out on their own.

And even if Beth could get an electric wheelchair for outdoors, she would not be allowed to use it as she does not have a wheelchair for indoors. 50 The reason why she does not have a wheelchair for indoors is simple – she can manage quite easily with her walking frame! A governmental department spokesperson said that they would like to offer a more flexible approach: "We know that 55 the population of disabled children has grown over the last 10 years and we would like to adapt to the changes that have taken place. It is essential that the social and health departments work together with the schools to meet current needs." **492 words**

Comprehension questions

■ After you have read the text carefully, answer the following questions in your own words as far as possible.
1. How is CP caused and which symptoms does it produce?
2. What do SCOPE criticize?
3. What physical problems does Beth have?
4. How could her life be made easier for her?
5. Why can't Beth get the help she needs at the moment?

Summary

■ Using your own words, give a summary of the text. It should be about 250 words long.

Vocabulary

1. Look in the text to find the opposites for these words:
    a) worse
    b) death
    c) more difficult
    d) outdoors
    e) adults
    f) unimportant

2. Explain the following:
    a) charity (line 13)
    b) social services (line 17)
    c) speech aids (line 22)
    d) full-time carer (lines 30/31)
    e) walking frame (line 42)
    f) wheelchair (line 43)

Translation

■ Translate lines 25 to 47.

Comment

■ Comment on the following statement, using your own knowledge and ideas.
"It is essential that we should all work together to meet the needs of disabled people in our society."

Ecstasy – The dangerous "high"

It is midnight at a club in London. Lights flash, loud music plays, young people dance wildly to the beat. Outside there is a poster banning the use of Ecstasy. But few seem to notice it. Most
5 of the teenagers inside the club have taken the drug, despite all the warnings about its dangers. For many teenagers, going to a club or a rave means taking "E". Those who use it say it makes them feel optimistic and warm about everything
10 and everyone they see. One teenager describes it like this: "You don't feel cold, you don't feel pain. Everything is beautiful and you can dance all night."
Ecstasy is taken by about 5 million young people
15 in Britain. The so-called "love-drug" started off in the United States, where it was often used by rich Yuppies as an expensive way of getting high. Nowadays Ecstasy is Europe's most popular drug for the 15 – 25 age group. Like all drugs,
20 Ecstasy can be very dangerous. Over the last five years over 150 people have died after taking the drug. Death is caused when organs fail due to dehydration. Ecstasy raises the body temperature, and hours of wild dancing without enough to
25 drink make it even more dangerous. The drug

is often mixed with other ingredients in tablets: heroin, aspirin and dog-worm tablets have all been found in Ecstasy tablets which leads to high risks when taking the drug. Moreover, Ecstasy has long-term negative effects. Doctors believe it 30 causes serious depressions in later life and may lead to permanent brain damage.
Most young people know about the risks involved. So why do they still take Ecstasy? Like most things that are dangerous, but also pleasurable – alcohol 35 and smoking included – people tend to ignore the risks and concentrate on the fun. Furthermore, Ecstasy is regarded as an acceptable, even glamorous drug, unlike hard drugs such as heroin and cocaine. Drug counsellors, however, 40 see nothing glamorous about "E". They see it as a dangerous way of trying to escape from life's problems. Often it is taken by unemployed teenagers as an escape from poor housing and the hopelessness of not being able to find a job. 45 The case of Leah Betts, an 18-year-old British girl, who died after taking Ecstasy, shocked many people in Britain this year. Leah was a typical "nice" young girl from a good home, who knew all about the risks involved. This case shows us 50 all how difficult it is to convince young people that Ecstasy is very dangerous. Many parents will now worry even more when their teenage children go 55 out to parties and clubs. Others will hope that the shock of this latest Ecstasy death will be enough to persuade their kids that it is not worth risking death 60 for a few hours of feeling good.

468 words

Comprehension questions

■ After you have read the text carefully, answer the following questions in your own words as far as possible.

1. Why do many teenagers take Ecstasy?
2. Why have some people died after taking the drug?
3. What other negative effects can the drug have?
4. Why do people take the drug although they know about the risks involved?
5. How do drug counsellors see the situation?
6. What does the death of Leah Betts demonstrate?

Summary

■ Using your own words, give a summary of the text. It should be about 250 words long.

Vocabulary

1. Look in the text to find verbs for the following nouns:
   a) description
   b) use
   c) feeling
   d) death
   e) mixture
   f) cause
   g) knowledge
   h) hope

2. Explain the following:
   a) dehydration (line 23)
   b) ingredients (line 26)
   c) glamorous drug (line 39)
   d) drug counsellors (line 40)
   e) unemployed teenagers (lines 43/44)

Translation

■ Translate lines 46 to 61.

Comment

■ Using your own knowledge and ideas, write a comment on the following statement.
"The reports about the deaths of teenagers like Leah Betts will persuade young people not to take drugs like Ecstasy."

Do TV and computer games make young people violent?

Every time there is a school shooting – usually in the U.S., but sometimes in Europe – the same questions are asked. Did the killer watch too much violence on TV? Did he play too many violent computer games?

5 After 30 years of research into the question, many scientists, psychologists and psychiatrists are quite convinced that there is a link between violence in the media and violence in real life.

One of the latest studies, published earlier this year, 10 found that teenagers who watched more than one hour of television a day – not just violent pro- grammes, but anything, were four times more likely to be violent in later life than the ones who watched less than one hour. Of the ones who watched more 15 than 3 hours, 28.8 per cent later commited crimes, got into fights or showed other aggressive behaviour. This research was carried out at Columbia University in New York and studied the viewing habits and behaviour of 707 people for 17 years.

20 Another study showed that if the amount of television young people watch is reduced then the amount of violence is also reduced. Children at a school in San Jose, California were given lessons in media aware- ness and were asked to watch only seven hours of 25 television a week for several months. The study found that there was a 25 per cent decrease in violence at the school.

Many parents are understandably worried by these statistics and 30 the fact that the technology is becoming more and more complex. Cable and satellite TV offer a huge variety of programmes and games for example, and films can also be 35 downloaded from the internet. They cannot themselves monitor all this and want politicians to take action. Many other people however, still do not believe in the link between 40 media violence and violence in real life. Despite the debate on violence, children still watch an average of 3 hours of television per day.

TV and movie producers argue that some children may watch violence on the screen because they tend 45 to be violent anyway, and not the other way around. Or that although millions of young people watch murder and bloodshed in the media, only a few ever become violent or kill in real life.

As a student at Columbine High School in Littleton, 50 Colorado, the scene of one massacre in which 13 were killed, said in an interview, "If the media were the cause, every one of the 1,850 students at Columbine would be a killer because the students all watch the same movies and TV programmes, listen to the same 55 music and play the same video and computer games." The debate on the link between media and violence is sure to continue. Meanwhile, American TV and also TV companies around the world have been trying to reduce the amount of violence they show. 60 They are using 'watershed hours' to regulate the times they show certain programmes. In this way, programmes, which may not be suitable for children, are shown later in the evening. They are also planning technological aids for the future such as the v-chip. 65 This could flash information about the content of programmes, block out certain programmes or allow parents to check what their children have been watching.

511 words

Comprehension questions

■ After you have read the text carefully, answer the following questions in your own words as far as possible.

1. What links are often made between violence in the media and violence in real life?
2. What arguments support the view that watching television increases the probability of violent behaviour?
3. How do parents react to these statistics?
4. What are the arguments which suggest the media does not influence the amount of violence in real life?
5. What measures could be used to reduce the danger that violence in the media may cause violence in real life?

Summary

■ Using your own words, give a summary of the text. It should be about 250 words long.

Vocabulary

1. Explain the following:
   a) psychiatrist (line 6)
   b) viewing habits (line 18)
   c) media awareness (lines 23/24)
   d) cable and satellite TV (line 32)
   e) massacre (line 51)
   f) watershed hours (line 61)

2. Look in the text to find words which mean the opposite of the following:
   a) uncertain
   b) earliest
   c) more
   d) increase (n)
   e) simple
   f) a lot

Translation

■ Translate lines 50 to 69.

Comment

■ Write a letter to the editor of the newspaper in which this article appeared, giving your views and comments on the issues it discusses.

Maytree Day Nursery School
kindergarten

Dear Parents

Your children can come to our nursery school as soon as they have reached their first birthday. We can take a maximum of 30 children in each morning or afternoon session. The general aim of our nursery school is to help children to develop and to become confident. When they leave us, we hope they will be ready to move on to full-time primary school education. The children are all treated as individuals and are encouraged to explore their own personalities. We also try to help them develop various skills while growing and learning at their own pace.

Moreover, our nursery school has good links with the local primary school. For example, the book "Letterland", which is used at the primary school to teach the alphabet, is introduced in our sessions. Many of our children also attend "story-time" which is a session we hold after nursery school on Thursdays in the reception class at the primary school. This is especially helpful for those children preparing to start primary school. We also offer a number of special events during the year such as the Christmas play or educational visits from people like health visitors, road safety officers and primary school teachers. Most of these events are linked with the local primary school.

■ Our nursery school has five main areas. For the younger children, the "Toddler Room" provides a warm, safe and caring environment in which the younger children can both develop as individuals and also start to explore other areas within the nursery.

■ The "Main Room" incorporates a craft and messy area where children can take part in a number of creative activities, such as working with sand, water, clay, paint and paper. In the room there is also a stimulating "home corner", which is ideal for the development of imaginative role play.

■ The cosy "Quiet Room" provides a more peaceful atmosphere, where we encourage interaction between younger and older children. Some of the activities provided there include playing with floor and tabletop toys, reading and looking at picture books, playing musical instruments, singing, drawing or just talking.

■ Overlooking our lovely garden we have the "Learning Station" which is situated in a large airy room. It has been especially designed for older children where they can experience a number of pre-reading and -writing possibilities. Here they can develop their concentration in preparation for primary school life.

■ We also have a "Dining Room" where we provide food and drinks. At a minimal cost we can give your child three meals a day. The food of course is chosen from a nutritionally balanced menu. Moreover, tea and coffee for parents and helpers is always available.

- Our nursery school is open from 8 a.m. to 4 p.m. Monday to Friday.
- We are fully registered with the Social Services.
- Our team of 2 nursery school teachers and 2 nursery school assistants are NNEB qualified and highly experienced.
- We also encourage children's mums and dads and child carers to join in some of our sessions.

All in all we are here for your child's enjoyment and needs together with your peace of mind.

For further information

contact Anna Radford on Woodbury 232183
NNEB – National Nursery Education Board
www.maytreenursery.sch.uk

514 words

Exam preparation

Comprehension questions

■ After you have read the text carefully, answer the following questions in your own words as far as possible.
1. What are the main aims of this nursery school?
2. How does the nursery school co-operate with the local primary school?
3. What is the difference between the "Quiet Room" and the "Learning Station"?
4. What special sessions are provided?
5. Which of the features mentioned in the brochure, do you think, will give parents "peace of mind"?

Summary

■ Using your own words, give a summary of the text. It should be about 250 words long.

Vocabulary

1. Explain the following:
   a) learning at their own pace (line 11)
   b) preparing to start … school (line 20)
   c) educational visits (line 22)
   d) creative activities (lines 37/38)
   e) imaginative role play (lines 41/42)
   f) nutritionally balanced menu (line 68)

2. Look in the text to find verbs for these nouns:
   a) treat
   b) encouragement
   c) introduction
   d) development
   e) song
   f) design
   g) choice
   h) qualification

Translation

■ Translate lines 26 to 42.

Comment

■ You are interested in an exchange visit between the nursery school teachers from Maytree Day Nursery School and your own nursery school teachers. Write a letter to Anna Radford, explaining the situation. Try to describe your nursery school in an interesting way.

Abbildungsnachweis

Titelseite: Tischfußball: Getty Images RF (Photodisc Rot/RF), München; Highway: Corbis (ML Sinibaldi), Düsseldorf
S. 9: oben, v. li. n. re.: MSI/BULLS; Corbis (Spiegel), Düsseldorf; Corbis (Woodcock; Reflections Photolibrary/CORBI), Düsseldorf; Mitte, v. li. n. re.: Siemens AG, Berlin; Corbis Digital Stock (RF/CORBIS), London; Siemens AG, Berlin; unten, v. li. n. re.: Corbis (Lewine), Düsseldorf; IBM Deutschland GmbH, Stuttgart; Getty Images (EyeWire), München
S. 10: www.britainonview.com, London
S. 11: Corbis (Ronnie Kaufman), Düsseldorf
S. 12: oben: MEV, Augsburg; unten: Elmar Feuerbach, Remshalden
S. 13: MEV, Augsburg
S. 14: Wolfram Büchel, Remshalden
S. 16: www.britainonview.com, London; Fabrikarbeiter: Corbis (Robert Essel NYC), Düsseldorf
S. 18: Getty Images, München
S. 19: Elmar Feuerbach, Remshalden
S. 20: IBM Deutschland GmbH, Stuttgart
S. 21: Mauritius, Mittenwald
S. 23: MEV, Augsburg; Frau mit Kind: Getty Images, München; älterer Mann: Henry Zeidler, Leipzig
S. 25: Alamy Images (RF), Oxfordshire
S. 26: MEV, Augsburg
S. 27: MEV, Augsburg
S. 28: MEV, Augsburg
S. 29: oben: Getty Images, München; unten: Corbis (Tim Page), Düsseldorf
S. 30: Corbis (Ben Wood), Düsseldorf
S. 31: MEV, Augsburg
S. 32: MEV, Augsburg; Krone: Getty Images (Ryan McVay), München; Parlament: www.britainonview.com, London
S. 33: oben li.: Corbis (Fleming), Düsseldorf; oben Mi.: IBM Deutschland GmbH (Edmondson), Stuttgart; Mitte: Siemens AG, Berlin; unten li.: Corbis (Edmondson), Düsseldorf; unten re.: Siemens AG, Berlin
S. 34: Corbis (C. Moore), Düsseldorf
S. 35: li.: IBM Deutschland GmbH, Stuttgart; Mi. u. re.: MEV, Augsburg
S. 36: IBM Deutschland GmbH, Stuttgart
S. 37: MEV, Augsburg
S. 38: Kessler-Medien, Saarbrücken
S. 40: oben: MEV, Augsburg; unten: Corbis (Randy Faris), Düsseldorf
S. 41: Corbis (Robert Landau), Düsseldorf
S. 42: Alamy Images (David Gould / Alamy), Oxfordshire
S. 43: Corbis (Roger Ressmeyer), Düsseldorf
S. 44: oben, v. li. n. re.: Corbis (FORESTIER YVES/CORBIS SYGMA), Düsseldorf; www.britainonview.com, London; MEV, Augsburg; www.britainonview.com, London; unten, v. li. n. re.: Corbis (Gabe Palmer), Düsseldorf; Corbis (LWA-Dann Tardif/CORBIS), Düsseldorf; Corbis (Richard T. Nowitz), Düsseldorf; Corbis (Benjamin Rondel), Düsseldorf
S. 45: Corbis (RF), Düsseldorf
S. 46: Pauline Ashworth, Stuttgart
S. 47: oben, v. li. n. re.: Getty Images, München; Corbis (Nick Hawkes), Düsseldorf; unten, v. li. n. re.: Alamy Images (David Crausby / Alamy), Oxfordshire; Siemens AG, Berlin; Corbis (Alan Schein Photography/CORBIS), Düsseldorf; TransportEnergy, London
S. 48: Highways Agency, London
S. 49: Getty Images, München
S. 51: v. oben n. unten: Corbis (Premium Stock/CORBIS), Düsseldorf; MEV, Augsburg; TransportEnergy, London; Corbis (Jeremy Horner), Düsseldorf
S. 53: Corbis (Annie Griffiths Belt), Düsseldorf
S. 54: BMW AG, München
S. 57: MEV, Augsburg
S. 58: Getty Images, München

S. 61: MEV, Augsburg
S. 62: oben: Getty Images (Glen Allison), München; unten li.: Corbis Digital Stock, London; unten re.: UTC Fuel Cells
S. 64: Fibrowatt Ltd, London
S. 65: oben: ullstein bild, Berlin; unten: Corbis (Ray Juno), Düsseldorf
S. 66: v. oben n. unten: Siemens AG, Berlin; IBM, Stuttgart; DaimlerChrysler AG, Stuttgart; MEV, Augsburg; IBM, Stuttgart
S. 67: Audi, Ingolstadt; Auspuff: Mauritius (Stock Image), Mittenwald
S. 68: Audi, Ingolstadt
S. 69: MEV, Augsburg
S. 71: Elmar Feuerbach, Remshalden
S. 73: oben, v. li. n. re.: Red Door VR, Leeds; Getty Images (B.C. Moller), München; Mitte, v. li. n. re.: The Homes of Football (Stuart Clarke), The Lake District; University of Leeds; Leeds Bradford International Airport, Leeds; unten, v. li. n. re.: reproduced courtesy of Leeds City Council; www.britainonview.com, London; Red Door VR, Leeds
S. 74: Klett-Archiv, Stuttgart
S. 75: www.graeme-peacock.com, Newcastle upon Tyne
S. 76: MEV, Augsburg
S. 77: oben: Getty Images RF, München; li.: MEV, Augsburg; re.: Creativ Collection Verlag GmbH, Freiburg; unten: Getty Images, München
S. 78: Corbis (Michel Setboun), Düsseldorf
S. 80: Corbis Digital Stock (RF/CORBIS), London
S. 81: Corbis (Bettmann/CORBIS), Düsseldorf
S. 82: li.: Getty Images (McVay), München; re.: Corbis (Strauss/Curtis/CORBIS), Düsseldorf
S. 83: Corbis Digital Stock (RF), London
S. 84: oben: Corbis (Dave G. Houser/CORBIS), Düsseldorf; unten: Corbis Digital Stock (RF), London
S. 85: oben: Getty Images RF (A Carpenter), München; unten: Corbis (Strauss/Curtis/CORBIS), Düsseldorf
S. 86: oben: Corbis (Bettmann/CORBIS), Düsseldorf; unten: Getty Images, München
S. 88: v. li. n. re.: Geoatlas, Hendaye; Corbis (David H. Wells/CORBIS), Düsseldorf; Steve Skjold / Alamy; Corbis (Randy Duchaine/CORBIS), Düsseldorf
S. 89: oben, li. u. Mitte: Getty Images, München; oben, re.: Alamy Images, Oxfordshire; Mitte: Corbis, Düsseldorf; unten: Getty Images RF (RF), München
S. 90: Getty Images RF (Photodisc Grün), München
S. 94: Mauritius (Pöhlmann), Mittenwald
S. 98: Getty Images RF (Photodisc Rot), München
S. 102: Alamy Images (Janine Wiedel), Oxfordshire
S. 105: li., v. oben n. unten: Getty Images (Stone/Philip Lee Harvey), München; Corbis (C/B Productions), Düsseldorf; Corbis (Brian A. Vikander), Düsseldorf; re., v. oben n. unten: Corbis (Walter Hodges), Düsseldorf; Corbis (Randy Faris), Düsseldorf; Getty Images (Taxi/Seth Kushner), München
S. 106: oben: Corbis (RF), Düsseldorf; unten: Corbis (Dave Bartruff), Düsseldorf
S. 109: v. li. n. re.: Getty Images (Stone/Walter Hodges), München; Alamy Images (ImageState/RF), Oxfordshire; Alamy Images (Image Source/RF), Oxfordshire; Alamy Images (Comstock Images/RF), Oxfordshire
S. 110: Alamy Images (Nordicphotos), Oxfordshire
S. 112, 114, 116: Corbis, Düsseldorf
S. 118: Corbis, Düsseldorf; li. unten u. re. Mitte: Getty Images RF (RF), München
S. 199: Klett-Archiv, Stuttgart
S. 200: Klett-Archiv, Stuttgart

In einigen Fällen ist es uns trotz intensiver Bemühungen nicht gelungen, die Rechteinhaber zu ermitteln. Wir bitten diese, sich mit dem Verlag in Verbindung zu setzen.

Indefinite article (Unbestimmter Artikel)

Form

a	college student university	vor **gesprochenen** Konsonanten
an	interview address hour	vor **gesprochenen** Vokalen

Verwendung

I have bought **a** book for you.	für zählbare Begriffe in der Einzahl
He is **a** teacher.	vor Berufsbezeichnungen

Definite article (Bestimmter Artikel)

Form

the	course language European	vor **gesprochenen** Konsonanten Aussprache [ðɛ]
the	engineer office hour	vor **gesprochenen** Vokalen Aussprache [ðiː]

Verwendung

the people of London **the** life of Lucy Jordan **the** University of Manchester	bei Substantiven (Personen, Dingen, Abstrakta), wenn sie näher bestimmt sind oder werden
the Americans	für die Gesamtheit von Personen
the United States	für Ländernamen im Plural
the Thames, **the** North Sea	für Flüsse und Meere
the Browns	für Eigennamen im Plural
On their tour they visited **the** church.	für die konkrete Bedeutung als Gebäude

Verwendung ohne Artikel

Der Artikel wird abweichend vom Deutschen **nicht** verwendet:	
nature, life, time, people	für abstrakte Begriffe und Sammelbezeichnungen, wenn sie nicht näher bestimmt sind oder werden
Trafalgar Square, Buckingham Palace	für Ortsbezeichnungen
Switzerland, Normandy, Lake Windermere	für Länder, Berge und Seen im Singular
church, school, college When does church begin?	für Gebäudebezeichnungen, wenn die normale Nutzung gemeint ist
Americans	für einzelne Angehörige einer Personengruppe

Plural (Mehrzahl)

Form

student college	students colleges	Die meisten Nomen bilden den Plural durch Anhängen von -s.
university city	universities cities	Konsonant + y wird zu -ies.
address match	addresses matches	Nach Zischlauten (z. B. s, ss, ch, sh) wird -es angehängt.
man woman child life	**men** **women** **children** **lives**	Einige Nomen haben unregelmäßige Pluralformen.

Verwendung

information, weather, nature, knowledge, work, furniture	Einige Nomen treten nur im Singular auf.
trousers, jeans, glasses, clothes, thanks	Einige Nomen treten nur im Plural auf.
news, the United States, the United Nations, economics, mathematics, electronics No news **is** good news.	Einige Nomen treten nur in der Pluralform auf, das Verb steht jedoch im Singular.

!

Some important prepositions

Zeitliche Präpositionen

on 20th September **on** Saturday **on** weekdays	**at** six o'clock **at** the age of 16 **at** night **at** noon **at** midnight	**by** day
		twelve minutes **to** five
in 1992 **in** the morning **in** the evening		a quarter **past** six

Präpositionen der Art und Weise

go **by** bus, car, bike
go **on** foot

Räumliche Präpositionen

go **to** the cinema go **to** college I've been **to** Scotland
at home **at** school **at** the supermarket

Possessive case (Genitiv)

's-Genitiv

Verwendung bei Personen, Tieren, Zeiten

Henry**'s** exam the baker**'s** (shop)	Nomen im Singular + **'s**
his parents**'** computer shop the Greens**'** house	Nomen im Plural + **'**
people**'s** faces children**'s** books	bei Nomen im Plural **ohne** s Anhängung von **'s**
today**'s** newspaper two weeks**'** pay	Bei Zeiten gelten die gleichen Regeln.

of-Genitiv

Verwendung bei Sachen

the title **of** the book the price **of** the computers	Der *of*-Genitiv wird im Singular und im Plural verwendet.

Comparison of adjectives (Steigerung von Adjektiven)

Form

cheap small	cheap**er** small**er**	cheap**est** small**est**	Steigerung der kurzen Adjektive mit -er und -est
nice	nic**er**	nic**est**	stummes -e entfällt
heavy	heav**ier**	heav**iest**	-y wird zu -ier und -iest
big	bi**gg**er	bi**gg**est	Nach kurzen Vokalen wird der Endkonsonant verdoppelt.
good bad little	**better** **worse** **less**	**best** **worst** **least**	Einige Adjektive haben unregelmäßige Steigerungsformen.
careful difficult	**more** careful **more** difficult	**most** careful **most** difficult	Alle dreisilbigen und mehrsilbigen Adjektive und alle zweisilbigen Adjektive, die nicht auf -er, -le, -y, -ow enden, werden mit *more* und *most* gesteigert.
careful difficult	**less** careful **less** difficult	**least** careful **least** difficult	Eine Verminderung der Adjektive ist mit *less* und *least* möglich.

Verwendung

In town centres walking is often **as fast as** going by car.	Gleichheiten werden mit *as … as* ausgedrückt.
Travelling by plane is **faster than** travelling by train. Travelling by car is **more expensive than** walking.	Komparative werden mit … *than* gebildet.
A bicycle is **not so expensive as** (isn't as expensive as) a car. A bicycle is **less expensive than** a car.	Eine andere Form Ungleichheit auszudrücken, ist *not so … as* oder umgangssprachlich *not as … as*. Wie im Deutschen kann man auch „weniger als" verwenden.
The Concorde was **the fastest** airliner from Paris to New York.	Der Superlativ wird nur benutzt, wenn mehr als zwei Dinge miteinander verglichen werden.

Adjective and adverb (Adjektiv und Adverb)

Form

Adjective	Adverb	
cheap	cheap**ly**	Das Adverb wird gebildet aus Adjektiv + -ly.
lazy	laz**ily**	-y wird zu -ily
horrible	horrib**ly**	-le wird zu -ly
economic	economi**cally**	-ic wird zu -ically
fast	**fast**	Einige Adverbien bilden unregelmäßige Formen.
good	**well**	

Adjective	Adverb	Adverb	
late	**late** (spät)	**lately** (in letzter Zeit)	Einige Adverbien bilden mehrere Formen.
hard	**hard** (hart)	**hardly** (kaum)	
near	**near** (nah)	**nearly** (beinahe)	

!

Verwendung

There are many **new computers** on the market. **They** are still **expensive**.	Adjektive beziehen sich auf Nomen oder Pronomen.
We can't **control** the technology **exactly**. Comics are **really popular** with children. Modern computers work **extremely quickly**. **Fortunately, she e-mailed the information to me in time.**	Adverbien beziehen sich auf – Verben – Adjektive – Adverbien – ganze Sätze
He **felt nervous** about his new job.	Nach Verben, die einen Zustand darstellen (z.B. *feel, be, become, get, seem, appear, keep*) folgt ein Adjektiv.

!

Word order with adverbs and adverbials (Wortstellung bei Adverbien und adverbialen Bestimmungen)

Die Stellung der Adverbien und adverbialen Bestimmungen (a. B.) ist im Englischen sehr flexibel. Folgende Stellungen sind allerdings üblich:	
At nine o'clock he caught the bus **to work**.	Adverbien/a. B. der Zeit stehen am Anfang oder Ende des Satzes. Adverbien/a. B. des Ortes stehen in der Regel am Ende des Satzes.
Mr Woods **always** travels to work by train. The train arrives **punctually**.	Adverbien/a.B. der Häufigkeit stehen vor dem (Haupt-)Verb. Adverbien/a. B. der Art und Weise stehen in der Regel nach dem Verb (den Verben).
The bus drove **slowly** through **London during the rush hour**.	Treten mehrere Adverbien/a.B. zur gleichen Zeit auf, gilt die Regel: Art und Weise vor Ort und Zeit.

Some or any?

Verwendung

I need **some** help with this program. **Some** newspapers in Britain only appear on Sundays.	in Aussagesätzen vor unbestimmten Mengen (etwas) oder Anzahlen (einige)
They didn't make **any** money with the new campaign. Some TV stations do not show **any** adverts.	in verneinten Sätzen vor unbestimmten Mengen oder Anzahlen (kein oder keine)
Have they done **any** research on the new product? Have you got **any** ideas for a new logo?	in Fragesätzen vor unbestimmten Mengen (etwas) oder Anzahlen (welche?)
Would you like me to show you **some** examples?	in Fragesätzen, wenn sie eine Aufforderung, Bitte oder ein Angebot enthalten
We never needed **any** electronic devices in the past.	nach Wörtern mit negativer Bedeutung

Some/any + -one/-body/-thing/-where

Somebody wants to see you. We haven't been **anywhere** this weekend. Have you got **anything** to say?	Die Regeln zum Gebrauch von *some* und *any* gelten auch für diese Formen.

Much – many – a lot of

Form

much a lot of	viel	nicht zählbar
many a lot of	viele	zählbar

Verwendung

He spends **a lot of** time practising his communication skills. **A lot of** (many) people have computers in their homes.	In Aussagesätzen wird in der Regel *a lot of* bevorzugt.
I don't have **a lot of/much** money to spend on computers. There aren't **a lot of/many** experts on the staff.	In verneinten Sätzen kann man beide Formen gebrauchen.
How **much** money do you earn? How **many** adverts did they show?	Nach *how* müssen *much* oder *many* stehen.

Little/a little – few/a few

Form

We had **little** help during our training. John had only **a little** time to explain.	wenig ein bisschen	unzählbar
Few computers never break down. There are **a few** good adverts on TV.	wenige ein paar	zählbar

Modal auxiliaries (Modale Hilfsverben)

Form

Modale Form	Ersatzform	Bedeutung
must	**have to**	müssen
can	**be able to**	können
can	**be allowed to**	dürfen
mustn't **can't**	**not be allowed to**	nicht dürfen
can't	**not be able to**	nicht können
needn't	**not have to**	nicht brauchen/nicht müssen

Verwendung

Cars **must/have to** stop at red lights. You **needn't/don't have to** pay in that car park. John **can't/isn't able to** find a parking space.	In der Gegenwart kann entweder die modale oder die Ersatzform benutzt werden.
We **had to** turn right at the traffic lights. He **didn't have to** wait as the lights were green. Jane **couldn't/wasn't allowed to** leave her car outside the house, as there was a "No Parking" sign.	Mit Ausnahme von *could* oder *couldn't* können die modalen Hilfsverben keine anderen Zeiten bilden. Für die anderen Zeiten werden die Ersatzformen verwendet.

Defining relative clauses (Notwendige Relativsätze)

Verwendung

Ein Relativsatz ist notwendig, wenn die darin enthaltene Information nötig ist, um zu erkennen, welche Person oder Sache gemeint ist.	
The man **who/that** is getting on the bus is on his way to the office.	Bei Personen werden die Relativpronomen *who* oder *that* verwendet.
The bus **which/that** is waiting at the traffic lights is going to London.	Bei Sachen wird *which* oder *that* verwendet.
He greeted the man (**who**) he saw on the platform. He read the paper (**which**) he had bought that morning.	Wenn das Relativpronomen Objekt des Satzes ist, kann es weggelassen werden.

Non-defining relative clauses (Nicht notwendige Relativsätze)

Verwendung

Ein Relativsatz ist nicht notwendig, wenn die darin enthaltene Information nicht nötig ist, um zu erkennen, welche Person oder Sache gemeint ist.	
Henry's wife, **who is 58**, was waiting for him at the station.	Ein Relativsatz wird durch Kommas vom Hauptsatz getrennt.
The train, **which was an Intercity**, left punctually.	*that* darf hier nicht verwendet werden.
Henry, **who I met at the station**, is retiring next week.	Wenn das Relativpronomen Objekt eines Relativsatzes ist, darf es nicht weggelassen werden.

The Tenses (Die Zeiten)

Present simple

Form

I/you/we/they he/she/it	**live** **lives**	in Leeds.	Aussage
I/you/we/they he/she/it	**do not (don't) live** **does not (doesn't) live**	in Birmingham.	Verneinung

Do **Does**	I/you/we/they he/she/it	**(not)**	**live**	in Liverpool?	(verneinte) Frage
Where **Why**	**do** you **does** she	**live?** **smoke?**			

Who **How many students**	**likes** **live**	basketball? at home?	Ist das Fragewort Subjekt oder Teil des Subjekts, wird *do/does* nicht verwendet.

Besonderheiten bei der Schreibung der s-Endung

go, do watch, kiss carry, try	go**es**, do**es** watch**es**, kiss**es** carr**ies**, tr**ies**

Verwendung

She **has** a brother.	bei einem Dauerzustand
She **(usually) goes** to college by bus. He **(often) helps** at home.	bei regelmäßigen oder wiederholten Handlungen (oft mit Häufigkeitsadverbien wie *usually, normally, often, sometimes, never, always*)
She **doesn't smoke**.	bei Gewohnheiten
He **has** a flat in Mayfield. I **think** that this **is** a good idea.	bei bestimmten Verben, wenn sie einen Zustand beschreiben, z.B. *be, have, look, think, see, know, like, want*
The train **arrives** at 8 o'clock tomorrow morning.	bei Fahrplänen und Veranstaltungsprogrammen (mit Zukunftsbezug)

Present continuous

Form

I you/we/they he/she/it	**am** **are** **is**	**(not)**	**reading** a book.	Aussage und Verneinung

Kurzform der Verneinung: aren't, isn't

Am **Are** **Is**	I you/we/they he/she/it	**(not)**	**reading** a magazine?	Frage und verneinte Frage

Besonderheiten bei der Schreibung

come, take sit, run	coming, taking si**tt**ing, ru**nn**ing

Verwendung

They **are talking** about their courses.	bei Handlungen, die im Moment des Sprechens stattfinden
She **is studying** for her exam this year.	bei Handlungen, die vorübergehend stattfinden, nicht aber unbedingt im Augenblick
She **is having** a good time. A lot of people **are thinking** about their future.	bei bestimmten Verben (siehe *present simple*), wenn sie eine vorübergehende Handlung und keinen Zustand beschreiben
I **am meeting** him tomorrow.	bei zukünftigen Handlungen (mit Zeitbestimmung)
Some students **are always complaining**.	zur gefühlsbetonten Darstellung von Handlungen in Verbindung mit *always*

Past simple

Form

She You	work**ed** need**ed**	in Glasgow a new car.	last year.	Aussagen Grundform + -ed (Infinitiv)

Besonderheiten

move try stop go meet	mov**ed** tr**ied** sto**pped** **went** **met**	stummes -e entfällt Konsonant + y wird zu ie Lautverdopplung unregelmäßige Verben haben besondere Formen für das *simple past* dabei wird die 2. Form verwendet

He We	**did not** **(didn't)**	**need** **lose**	special software. the money.	Verneinung

Did	you they	**(not)**	**move** **live**	to Glasgow? in Birmingham? more than	(verneinte) Frage
	it		**take**	6 months?	
Why did	he	**(not)**	**stop**	in Liverpool?	

Verwendung

Jane **moved** to Glasgow 7 years ago. First she **worked** for a computer company.	bei Handlungen zu einem bestimmten Zeitpunkt oder in einem abgeschlossenen Zeitraum in der Vergangenheit (oft mit einer Zeitbestimmung wie z. B. *yesterday, last year, in 1988, … ago, from … until*)

Past continuous

Form

I/He/She/It	**was**	**(not)** **(wasn't)**	**standing**	on the platform.	(verneinte) Aussage
We/You/They	**were**	**(not)** **(weren't)**			

Verwendung

As/while he **was driving** to the airport, it started to rain. A lot of passengers **were waiting** at the counter when Jason went into the bank.	für eine Handlung, die schon im Gange war, als eine neue Handlung eintrat
! While I **was reading** a book, my friend **was writing** a letter.	Bei gleichzeitigem Verlauf zweier Handlungen steht die Verlaufsform in beiden Fällen.
! What **did** you **do** when Susan **came** in? When she **came** in I **put** down my newspaper and talked to her.	Für Handlungen, die nacheinander stattfanden, wird in beiden Fällen *past simple* benutzt

Present perfect simple

Form

I/You/We/They	**have**	**(not)** **(haven't)**	**had** a car for three years.	(verneinte) Aussage *have/has* + 3. Form
He/She/It	**has**	**(not)** **(hasn't)**	**sold** 20 million CDs. **been** to Scotland.	

Have	I/you/we/they	**(not)**	**made** a loss? **taken** a photo? **been** here?	(verneinte) Frage
Has	he/she/it			

Verwendung

I **have repaired** the car.	bei Handlungen in der Vergangenheit ohne Zeitangabe – das Ergebnis ist oft wichtiger als die Zeitangabe
They **have sold** 50,000 cars **up till now**.	mit Zeitbestimmungen, die einen Zeitraum beschreiben, der noch andauert, z.B. *today, this week, so far, in the last ten years*
He has **already paid** the bill.	mit bestimmten Adverbien wie z.B. *ever, never, always, yet, just, already*
How long have you **known** about this book? The Browns **have lived** there **for** 3 years. We **have lived** here **since** 1986.	bei nicht abgeschlossenen Zuständen mit *how long, since* und *for* – *since* bezieht sich dabei auf einen Zeitpunkt, *for* auf einen Zeitraum

Present perfect continuous

Form

I/you/we/they	**have**	**been standing.**	Present simple von *have* + *been* + -ing-Form

Verwendung

How long have you been waiting? I've been waiting – for half an hour. – since ten o'clock.	bei Handlungen, die in der Vergangenheit begannen und noch andauern – meist in Verbindung mit *how long, since, for*

Past perfect simple

Form

I/You/He/She/ It/We/They	**had**	**(not)** **(hadn't)**	**travelled** to Paris.	(verneinte) Aussage

Verwendung

After he **had arrived** at the hotel, he went to his room. When I arrived at the station, the ticket office **had** already **closed**.	für Handlungen oder Zustände, die vor einem Zeitpunkt in der Vergangenheit abgeschlossen waren

Future with 'going to'

Form

I	am ('m)	(not)	going to watch TV.	(verneinte) Aussage
He/She/It	is ('s)			
We/You/They	are ('re)			

Am	I	going to have	a cup of coffee?	Frage
Is	he/she/it			
Are	we/you/they			

Verwendung

She **is going to answer** the phone.	bei Absichten und Vorhaben
That fax machine **is going to break** down.	bei Vorhersagen, die aufgrund bereits bekannter Fakten oder bisheriger Erfahrungen sicher oder logischerweise in Erfüllung gehen müssen

Future with 'will'

Form

I/You	will	use alternative energy.	Aussage
He/She/It			
We/They	will not (won't)	waste water.	Verneinung

Will	I/you	use talking computers?	Frage
	he/she/it		
	we/they		

Verwendung

Computers **will probably do** most of the work.	bei Vorhersagen mit *suppose/expect* und *probably*
Just a minute, **I'll help** you with your shopping.	bei Entscheidungen, die im Moment des Sprechens getroffen werden
I'll phone you tomorrow, I promise.	bei Versprechen
Will you **make** some coffee, please.	um eine Bitte auszudrücken

Question tags (Frageanhängsel)

Form

Aussagesatz	Frageanhängsel	
You can drive,	**can't you?**	Das Hilfsverb wird in dem Frageanhängsel wiederholt.
Pollution is increasing,	**isn't it?**	Ist der Aussagesatz positiv, so wird das Frageanhängsel verneint.
Trams will improve our public transport service,	**won't they?**	
Statistics aren't always correct,	**are they?**	Ist der Aussagesatz verneint, so wird das Frageanhängsel bejaht.
You mustn't drive over 70 mph on motorways,	**must you?**	
We enjoyed the journey,	**didn't we?**	Wenn der Aussagesatz kein Hilfsverb enthält, wird das Frageanhängsel mit *to do* in der Zeit des Aussagesatzes gebildet.
She usually goes to Britain,	**doesn't she?**	

Verwendung

	Frageanhängsel werden verwendet:
Air travel is really comfortable, **isn't it?**	beim Wunsch nach Bestätigung
You didn't walk here, **did you?**	bei Überraschung
Oh, it's not another traffic jam, **is it?**	bei Verärgerung
Well, that's a really new idea, **isn't it?**	bei ironischen Aussagen

Reported speech (Indirekte Rede)

Form

Aussagen

	Die Zeitformen ändern sich:
"We are protesting about pollution." Harry said they **were protesting** about pollution. "He doesn't buy cans." June told me he **didn't buy** cans.	*Present tenses* werden zu *past tenses*.
"Watsons opened four supermarkets in 1995." Fred pointed out that Watsons **had opened** four supermarkets in 1995. "They have started a bus service." He added that they **had started** a bus service.	*Simple past* und *present perfect* werden zu *past perfect*.
"There will be more 'green' products." Sue went on to say that there **would be** more 'green' products.	*will* wird zu *would*.
"I can save more energy." Harry told me that **he** could save more energy.	Die Pronomen werden angepasst.
"We are meeting the town planner tomorrow." Sue added that they were meeting the town planner **the next day**. "I bought the car three days ago." He said that he had bought the car **three days before**.	Orts- (z. B. *here* wird zu *there*) und Zeitbestimmungen werden angepasst.

Fragen

	Bei Fragen wird die Wortstellung geändert.
"What are you doing about waste?" **They asked what we were doing** about waste. "When did you introduce bicycle routes?" **We wanted to know when they had introduced** bicycle routes.	

Verwendung

Indirekte Rede wird benutzt, wenn berichtet werden soll, was jemand gesagt oder gefragt hat.

Conditionals (Bedingungssätze)

Form

Type 1

If-Satz	Hauptsatz	
If **we fit** a shower,	**we will** save water.	*Present simple* wird für das Verb im If-Satz, Futur mit *will* für das Verb im Hauptsatz verwendet.

Type 2

If-Satz	Hauptsatz	
If the government **developed** solar energy,	there **would be** less pollution.	*Past simple* wird für das Verb im If-Satz, *Conditional I* für das Verb im Hauptsatz verwendet.
If I **were** Environment Minister,	I **could** put my ideas about energy into practice.	*could* oder *might* sind Alternativen zu *would* im Hauptsatz.

Type 3

If-Satz	Hauptsatz	
If Tom and Kate **had insulated** their roof years ago,	they **would have saved** a lot of money.	*Past perfect* wird für das Verb im If-Satz, *Conditional II* für das Verb im Hauptsatz verwendet.

Verwendung

Type 1 wird gebraucht, wenn die Voraussetzungen für die Erfüllung der Bedingung schon existieren und es deswegen wahrscheinlich ist, dass die Handlung im If-Satz in Erfüllung gehen wird (wir planen, eine Dusche einzubauen).

Type 2 wird gebraucht, wenn
a) wir nicht erwarten, dass die Handlung im If-Satz eintreten wird. Wir stellen uns die Situation rein theoretisch vor.
b) die Handlung im If-Satz gar nicht eintreten kann, weil sie in Gegensatz zu den Tatsachen steht (ich bin nicht der Umweltminister).

Type 3 wird gebraucht, wenn die Handlung im If-Satz nicht eintreten kann, weil sie in der Vergangenheit liegt. Es kann an der Situation nichts mehr geändert werden.

Passive voice (Passiv)

Form

The robots **are equipped** with sensors. This motor **was not made** in Great Britain. **Will** the new car **be sold** in Japan?	Form von *be* in der jeweiligen Zeit + Partizip Perfekt (3. Form) des Verbs
Now the wheels **can be fitted**. The car **must be tested** first.	auch mit Hilfsverben

Verwendung

These cars **were made** in Germany. The handbook **is written** in English.		hauptsächlich in der Schriftsprache, wenn der Ausführende unbekannt, unwichtig oder selbstverständlich ist
This information **is checked by** the central computer.		Wenn der Ausführende allerdings genannt werden soll, dann benutzt man die Präposition *by* *(by-agent)*.
It is said **It is reported** **It is believed** **It is supposed**	that computers will become even more important in the future.	bei Verben des Meinens und Berichtens
He is said to be rich.		
English **is spoken** here. = Man spricht Englisch. We **will be told** the result later = Man wird uns später das Ergebnis sagen.		im Deutschen wird ein Aktivsatz mit ‚man' bevorzugt

Infinitive (Infinitiv)

Verwendung
ohne *to*

We **must write** a report about our trip to England.	nach den meisten Hilfsverben
Our new teachers **make us work** very hard, but on Friday they **let us go** home early.	nach *make* und *let* + direktem Objekt

mit *to*

The teacher **asked me to show** my photos of Newcastle. She **told them to wait** outside for a moment.	nach bestimmten Verben (*ask/tell/advise/expect* etc.)
This is not **easy to understand**. I am **surprised to hear** that.	nach Adjektiven
I do not know **what to do**. I soon found out **where to go**.	nach Fragewörtern

Gerund (Gerundium)

Verwendung

Drinking and **driving** is dangerous.	als Subjekt
I **enjoy swimming**.	als Objekt nach Verben ohne Präpositionen, wenn eine allgemeingültige Situation beschrieben wird: z. B. *enjoy/like/dislike/hate/stop/start/avoid/ suggest/mind/love/recommend/prefer*
I **look forward to seeing** you again. He is **tired of waiting** here. They saw the **danger of destroying** the environment.	nach Verben/Adjektiven/Substantiven mit Präpositionen
He has helped me a lot **by giving** me that map of Newcastle. The child crossed the road **without looking**.	nach Präpositionen mit adverbialer Bedeutung, z. B. *by/without/instead of*
Normally I enjoy swimming but today I **would prefer to play** tennis. I remember learning those rules. = Ich erinnere mich daran, dass ich die Regeln gelernt habe. I must remember to learn these rules. = Ich muss daran denken, diese Regeln zu lernen.	aber kein Gerundium, wenn es sich um eine Ausnahmesituation handelt (oft mit *would*) oder wenn die Bedeutung es nicht zulässt, z. B. bei *stop/start/remember*

Participle (Partizip)

Form

Das Partizip besteht aus zwei Formen

waiting/going/watching	Partizip Präsens
waited/gone/watched	Partizip Perfekt

Verwendung

The weather forecast for the **coming** week … The weather in New York last week was rather **mixed**.	als Adjektiv
You can find several families **living** in one flat. There are a lot of restaurants there especially **built** for the tourists.	anstatt von Relativsätzen
After talking to the press they started their demonstration. **Having discussed** the problem with the President personally, they flew home to California.	als Verkürzung von Adverbialsätzen (*after/before/because/while* etc.)

AE = American English
BE = British English

Unit 1

Starter

BTEC National Diploma [ˌbiːtiːiːˈsiː ˌnæʃənl dɪˈpləʊmə]	etwa: Fachhochschulreifeprüfung
business studies [ˈbɪznɪs ˌstʌdɪz]	etwa: Fachbereich Wirtschaft
certificate [səˈtɪfɪkət]	Zeugnis
comprehensive school [kɒmprɪˈhensɪv ˌskuːl]	Gesamtschule
engineering studies [ˌendʒɪˈnɪərɪŋ ˌstʌdɪz]	etwa: Fachbereich Technik
GCSE [ˌdʒiːsiːesˈiː] = General Certificate of Secondary Education [ˌdʒenərəl səˈtɪfɪkət əʌ ˌsekəndrɪ ˌedʒʊˈkeɪʃn]	etwa: Fachoberschulreife
public service [ˌpʌblɪk ˈsɜːvɪs]	öffentlicher Dienst
social studies [ˈsəʊʃl ˌstʌdɪz]	Sozialwissenschaften
studies [ˈstʌdɪz]	Kurs, Studium

A1

accountancy [əˈkaʊntənsɪ]	Rechnungswesen
application [ˌæplɪˈkeɪʃn]	Anwendung
bus pass [ˈbʌs ˌpɑːs]	Busausweis
CAD [ˌsiːeɪˈdiː] (Computer Aided Design) [kəmˈpjuːtər ˌeɪdɪd dɪˈzaɪn]	Computerunterstützte Zeichnung
CAM [ˌsiːeɪˈem] (Computer Aided Manufacturing) [kəmˈpjuːtər ˌeɪdɪd ˌmænjəˈfæktʃərɪŋ]	Computerunterstützte Fertigung
civil engineering [ˈsɪvl ˌendʒɪˈnɪərɪŋ]	Bauwesen
control [kənˈtrəʊl]	Kontrolle, hier: Regeltechnik
electrical engineering [ɪˈlektrɪkl ˌendʒɪˈnɪərɪŋ]	Elektrotechnik
equipment [ɪˈkwɪpmənt]	Ausrüstung
finance [ˈfaɪnæns]	Finanzwesen
full-time [ˌfʊl ˈtaɪm]	Vollzeit
general science [ˌdʒenərəl ˈsaɪəns]	allgemeine Naturwissenschaften
grant [ɡrɑːnt]	Zuschuss, Bafög
health care [ˈhelθ ˌkeə]	Gesundheitsfürsorge
industrial [ɪnˈdʌstrɪəl]	industriell

instrumentation [ˌɪnstrəmenˈteɪʃn]	Messtechnik
level [ˈlevl]	Stufe, Niveau
mechanical engineering [məˈkænɪkl ˌendʒɪˈnɪərɪŋ]	Maschinenbau
office skills [ˈɒfɪs ˌskɪlz]	Bürofertigkeiten
paragraph [ˈpærəɡrɑːf]	Absatz
part-time [ˌpɑːt ˈtaɪm]	Teilzeit
principle [ˈprɪnsəpl]	Grundsatz, Prinzip
psychology [saɪˈkɒlədʒɪ]	Psychologie
qualification [ˌkwɒlɪfɪˈkeɪʃn]	Qualifikation, Befähigung
to run courses [rʌn ˈkɔːsɪz]	Kurse anbieten
sociology [ˌsəʊʃɪˈɒlədʒɪ]	Soziologie
statistics [stəˈtɪstɪks]	Statistik

A2

bedsitter [bedˈsɪtə]	Einzimmerwohnung
beginner [bɪˈɡɪnə]	Anfänger(in)
campus [ˈkæmpəs]	Campus, Universitätsgelände
coach [kəʊtʃ]	Trainer(in)
dialogue [ˈdaɪəlɒɡ]	Dialog
female [ˈfiːmeɪl]	weiblich
formula [ˈfɔːmjələ]	Formel
information sheet [ˌɪnfəˈmeɪʃn ˌʃiːt]	Informationsblatt
long time no see [lɒŋ ˌtaɪm nəʊ ˈsiː]	lange nicht gesehen
male [meɪl]	männlich
packing [ˈpækɪŋ]	Verpackung
pocket money [ˈpɒkɪt ˌmʌnɪ]	Taschengeld
to rush [rʌʃ]	eilen
social studies [ˈsəʊʃl ˌstʌdɪz]	Sozialwissenschaften

C1

adventure [ədˈventʃə]	Abenteuer
as well as [əz ˈwel əz]	sowie
to be into [biː ˈɪntuː]	Fan von etwas sein
biscuit [ˈbɪskɪt]	Keks
bold type [ˌbəʊld ˈtaɪp]	Fettdruck
to broaden the mind [ˌbrɔːdn ðə ˈmaɪnd]	den Horizont erweitern
comment [ˈkɒment]	Bemerkung, Kommentar
to cope [kəʊp] (with)	mit etwas klarkommen
district [ˈdɪstrɪkt]	Bezirk, Gegend
exchange [ɪksˈtʃeɪndʒ]	Austausch
to get on like a house on fire [ɡet ˈɒn laɪk əˌhaʊs ɒn ˈfaɪə]	sich sehr gut verstehen

to get to know [get_tʊ 'nəʊ] — kennen lernen

head of department [ˌhed_əv dɪ'pɑːtmənt] — hier: Fachbereichsleiter

heavy metal [ˌhevɪ 'metl] — Heavy Metal (harte Rockmusik)

host [həʊst] — Gastgeber(in)

joint [dʒɔɪnt] — gemeinsam

metal ['metl] — Metall

moor [mɔːr] — Moor

organizer ['ɔːgənaɪzə] — Veranstalter(in)

project ['prɒdʒekt] — Projekt

to put (s.o./sth.) to the test [ˌpʊt_tʊ ðə 'test] — (jmdn./etwas) auf die Probe stellen

remark [rɪ'mɑːk] — Bemerkung

sights [saɪts] — Sehenswürdigkeiten

smoker ['sməʊkə] — Raucher(in)

staffroom ['stɑːfruːm] — Lehrerzimmer

workshop ['wɜːkʃɒp] — Werkstatt

C2

can't stand [kɑːnt_'stænd] — nicht ausstehen können

informal [ɪn'fɔːml] — informell

to look like ['lʊk laɪk] — aussehen wie

personality [ˌpɜːsə'nælətɪ] — Persönlichkeit

scheme [skiːm] — Projekt, Plan, Programm

Yours [jɔːz] — Dein(e)

D1

a bit [ə bɪt] — ein bisschen

enthusiastic [ɪn,θjuːzɪ'æstɪk] — begeistert

for instance [fər_'ɪnstəns] — beispielsweise

hard-working [ˌhɑːd'wɜːkɪŋ] — fleißig

in my view [ɪn_'maɪ ˌvjuː] — meiner Ansicht nach

locals ['ləʊklz] — Einwohner

phrase [freɪz] — Ausdruck

Unit 2

Starter

active ['æktɪv] — aktiv

advertising manager ['ædvətaɪzɪŋ ˌmænɪdʒə] — Werbeleiter(in)

creative [kriː'eɪtɪv] — kreativ

dancer ['dɑːnsə] — Tänzer(in)

to discover [dɪ'skʌvə] — entdecken

flight attendant ['flaɪt_ə,tendənt] — Flugbegleiter(in)

hairdresser ['heə,dresə] — Friseur(in)

independent [ˌɪndɪ'pendənt] — unabhängig

logical ['lɒdʒɪkl] — logisch

mark [mɑːk] — Zensur, Note

novel ['nɒvl] — Roman

office worker ['ɒfɪs ,wɜːkə] — Büroangestellte(r)

officer ['ɒfɪsə] — Beamte(r), Offizier(in)

on your own [ˌɒn_jər_'əʊn] — allein

per [pə] — pro

practical ['præktɪkl] — praktisch

puzzle ['pʌzl] — Rätsel

salesman/saleswoman ['seɪlzmən /'seɪlz,wʊmən] — Verkäufer(in)

singer ['sɪŋə] — Sänger(in)

specialist ['speʃəlɪst] — Spezialist(in)

sportsman ['spɔːtsmən] — Sportler

sportswoman ['spɔːts,wʊmən] — Sportlerin

suggestion [sə'dʒestʃn] — Vorschlag

suitable ['sjuːtəbl] — geeignet

tourist guide ['tʊərɪst ,gaɪd] — Fremdenführer(in)

well-paid [ˌwel 'peɪd] — gut bezahlt

to work out [wɜːk_'aʊt] — herausfinden, ausarbeiten, lösen

A1

to adapt [ə'dæpt] — bearbeiten

adjective ['ædʒɪktɪv] — Adjektiv

alive [ə'laɪv] — lebend, lebendig, aktiv

degree [dɪ'griː] — akad. Grad (z.B. B.A., M.A.)

enormous [ɪ'nɔːməs] — gewaltig, enorm

to expand [ɪk'spænd] — ausdehnen

fortune ['fɔːtʃuːn] — Glück, Reichtum

to graduate ['grædʒʊeɪt] — Studium beenden, einen akad. Grad erwerben

in the meantime [ɪn ðə 'miːntaɪm] — in der Zwischenzeit

moreover [mɔː'rəʊvə] — überdies, außerdem

natural ['nætʃərəl] — natürlich

noun [naʊn] — Substantiv

risk [rɪsk] — Risiko

sales [seɪlz] — Verkaufszahlen

self-employed [ˌselfɪm'plɔɪd] — selbstständig

to service ['sɜːvɪs] — (Auto, Maschine etc.) warten

to sum up [sʌm 'ʌp] — zusammenfassen

to a great extent [tʊ_ə ,greɪt_ɪk'stent] — in großem Umfang

turnover ['tɜːn,əʊvə] — Umsatz

unlimited (company) [ʌn,lɪmɪtɪd 'kʌmpənɪ] — Gesellschaft mit unbeschränkter Haftung

wage [weɪdʒ] — Lohn

A2

to afford [ə'fɔːd] — sich leisten

to close down [kləʊz 'daʊn] — schließen, zumachen (z.B. Firma)

equipment [ɪ'kwɪpmənt] — Ausrüstung

income ['ɪŋkʌm] — Einkommen

to link [lɪŋk] — verbinden
listener ['lɪsnə] — Zuhörer(in)
main [meɪn] — Haupt-
to make up one's mind [ˌmeɪk ˌʌp wʌnz ˈmaɪnd] — sich entschließen
market development [ˌmɑːkɪt dɪˈveləpmənt] — Marktentwicklung
photographer [fəˈtɒgrəfə] — Fotograf(in)
to record [rɪˈkɔːd] — aufnehmen (Ton, Video etc.)
to start up (business) [stɑːt ˌʌp ˈbɪznɪs] — (Geschäft) anfangen
tense [tens] — Zeitform
thought [θɔːt] — Gedanke
video production [ˈvɪdɪəʊ prəˌdʌkʃn] — Videoproduktion
wedding [ˈwedɪŋ] — Hochzeit

C1

amount [əˈmaʊnt] — Betrag, Menge
attitude [ˈætɪtjuːd] — Haltung, Einstellung
average [ˈævərɪdʒ] — Durchschnitt
Bank Holiday [ˌbæŋk ˈhɒlɪdeɪ] — (öffentlicher) Feiertag
benefit [ˈbenɪfɪt] — Zuwendung, soziale Leistung
to carry out [ˌkærɪ ˈaʊt] — ausführen
condition [kənˈdɪʃn] — Bedingung
Dutch [dʌtʃ] — niederländisch; Niederländer(in)
employee [ɪmˈplɔiːː] — Arbeitnehmer(in), Angestellte(r)
except [ɪkˈsept] — außer
to get on with [get ˈɒn wɪð] — auskommen mit
to have in common [hæv ɪn ˈkɒmən] — gemeinsam haben
to identify [aɪˈdentɪfaɪ] — identifizieren
in general [ɪn ˈdʒenərəl] — im Allgemeinen
satisfaction [ˌsætɪsˈfækʃn] — Zufriedenheit
satisfied [ˈsætɪsfaɪd] — zufrieden
sick leave [ˈsɪk ˌliːv] — krankheitsbedingte Abwesenheit
survey [ˈsɜːveɪ] — Untersuchung, Umfrage
underpaid [ˌʌndəˈpeɪd] — unterbezahlt
to vary [ˈveərɪ] — sich ändern, unterschiedlich sein
working class [ˌwɜːkɪŋ ˈklɑːs] — Arbeiterklasse
working hours [ˈwɜːkɪŋ ˌaʊəz] — Arbeitszeit
workmate [ˈwɜːkmeɪt] — Arbeitskollege, -kollegin

C2

in order to [ɪn ˈɔːdə tuː] — um zu
secure [sɪˈkjʊə] — sicher
would like [wʊd ˈlaɪk] — würde(n) gerne

D

aged … [eɪdʒd] — … Jahre alt
applicant [ˈæplɪkənt] — Bewerber(in)
application [ˌæplɪˈkeɪʃn] — Bewerbung
to apply [əˈplaɪ] — sich bewerben
assistant [əˈsɪstənt] — Assistent(in)
candidate [ˈkændɪdət] — Kandidat(in), Bewerber(in)
to care for [keə fɔː] — sich um etw. kümmern
childcare assistant [ˈtʃaɪldkeər əˌsɪstənt] — Kinderpfleger(in)
CV = curriculum vitae [ˌsiːˈviː] [kəˌrɪkjələm ˈviːtaɪ] — Lebenslauf
data [ˈdeɪtə] — Daten
Dear Madam [dɪə ˈmædəm] — Sehr geehrte Dame
Dear Sir [dɪə ˈsɜː] — Sehr geehrter Herr
to enclose [ɪnˈkləʊz] — beilegen (als Anlage)
essential [ɪˈsenʃl] — wesentlich
export assistant [ˈekspɔːt əˌsɪstənt] — etwa: Außenhandels-kaufmann, -frau
foreign [ˈfɒrən] — ausländisch
leading [ˈliːdɪŋ] — führend
to look forward to (-ing) [lʊk ˈfɔːwəd tuː] — sich freuen auf (Schlussformel im Geschäftsbrief)
nationality [ˌnæʃəˈnælətɪ] — Nationalität
overseas [ˌəʊvəˈsiːz] — in Übersee
reference [ˈrefrəns] — Referenz
to require [rɪˈkwaɪə] — benötigen, erfordern
responsible [rɪˈspɒnsəbl] — verantwortlich
salary [ˈsælərɪ] — Gehalt
sales department [ˈseɪls dɪˌpɑːtmənt] — Verkaufsabteilung
similar [ˈsɪmələ] — ähnlich
step [step] — Schritt, Stufe
task [tɑːsk] — Aufgabe
vacancy [ˈveɪkənsɪ] — freie Stelle
willing [ˈwɪlɪŋ] — bereit
with reference to [wɪð ˈrefrəns tuː] — mit Bezug auf
Yours faithfully [jɔːz ˈfeɪθfʊlɪ] — Mit freundlichen Grüßen, Hochachtungsvoll
Yours sincerely [jɔːz sɪnˈsɪəlɪ] — Mit freundlichen Grüßen

Unit 3

Starter

capital city [ˌkæpɪtl ˈsɪtɪ] — Hauptstadt
citizen [ˈsɪtɪzn] — Bürger(in)
European Commission [ˌjʊərəpɪən kəˈmɪʃn] — Europäische Kommission
European Union [ˌjʊərəpɪən ˈjuːnjən] — Europäische Union (die EG wurde im November 1993 in EU umbenannt)

143

A1

bureaucracy [bjʊ'rɒkrəsɪ]	Bürokratie
discount ['dɪskaʊnt]	Rabatt
economics [ˌiːkə'nɒmɪks]	Wirtschaft(swissenschaft)
entrance exam ['entrəns ˌɪgˌzæm]	Aufnahmeprüfung
to fill in [fɪl_'ɪn]	ausfüllen
to insure [ɪn'ʃʊə]	versichern
to know by name [nəʊ baɪ 'neɪm]	mit Namen kennen
lecture ['lektʃə]	Vorlesung
Poland ['pəʊlənd]	Polen
Polish ['pəʊlɪʃ]	polnisch
to reserve [rɪ'zɜːv]	reservieren
seminar ['semɪnɑː]	Seminar
to take a (language) test [teɪk_ə 'test]	einen Test machen, an einer (Sprach-) Prüfung teilnehmen
Warsaw ['wɔːsɔː]	Warschau
youth hostel ['juːθ ˌhɒstl]	Jugendherberge

A2

Belgium ['beldʒəm]	Belgien
column ['kɒləm]	Spalte
to come into operation ['kʌm_ˌɪntʊ_ˌɒpə'reɪʃn]	in Kraft treten
community [kə'mjuːnətɪ]	Gemeinschaft
currency ['kʌrənsɪ]	Währung
democratic [ˌdemə'krætɪk]	demokratisch
Denmark ['denmɑːk]	Dänemark
election [ɪ'lekʃn]	Wahl
factor ['fæktə]	Faktor
Germany ['dʒɜːmənɪ]	Deutschland
Great Britain [ˌgreɪt_'brɪtn]	Großbritannien
Greece [griːs]	Griechenland
Ireland ['aɪələnd]	Irland
Italy ['ɪtəlɪ]	Italien
Luxembourg ['lʌksəmbɜːg]	Luxemburg
(the) Netherlands [ðə 'neðələndz]	Niederlande
parliament ['pɑːləmənt]	Parlament
past tense [ˌpɑːst_'tens]	Vergangenheitsform
peaceful ['piːsfʊl]	friedlich
political [pə'lɪtɪkl]	politisch
process ['prəʊses]	Vorgang, Prozess
single ['sɪŋgl]	einzig, hier: einheitlich
to slow down [sləʊ 'daʊn]	verlangsamen
Spain [speɪn]	Spanien
state [steɪt]	Staat
treaty ['triːtɪ]	Vertrag
unity ['juːnətɪ]	Einheit
wealthy ['welθɪ]	wohlhabend

C1

to afford [ə'fɔːd]	sich leisten
Baltic ['bɔːltɪk]	baltisch; Ostsee
boundary ['baʊndərɪ]	Grenze
communist era ['kɒmjənɪst ˌɪərə]	kommunistisches Zeitalter
cosmopolitan [ˌkɒsmə'pɒlɪtn]	kosmopolitisch
countryside ['kʌntrɪsaɪd]	Land, Landschaft
disappearance [ˌdɪsə'pɪərəns]	Verschwinden
diversity [daɪ'vɜːsətɪ]	Vielfalt, Verschiedenheit
Estonia [es'təʊnɪə]	Estland
glass-walled [ˌglɑːs'wɔːld]	mit Wänden aus Glas
gradually ['grædʒʊəlɪ]	allmählich
high-speed [ˌhaɪ'spiːd]	Hochgeschwindigkeits-
huge [hjuːdʒ]	riesig
individually [ˌɪndɪ'vɪdʒʊəlɪ]	einzeln
leadership ['liːdəʃɪp]	Führung, Leitung
to link; link [lɪŋk]	verbinden; Verbindung
low-cost [ˌləʊ'kɒst]	preiswert
mayor [meə]	Bürgermeister(in)
millennium [mɪ'lenɪəm]	Jahrtausend
Millennium Wheel [mɪ'lenɪəm ˌwiːl]	Millennium-Riesenrad
neglect [nɪ'glekt]	Vernachlässigung
permanent ['pɜːmənənt]	ständig, permanent, dauerhaft
Prague [prɑːg]	Prag
to realise/realize ['rɪəlaɪz]	feststellen, erkennen, bemerken
run-down [ˌrʌn'daʊn]	heruntergekommen
strength [streŋkθ]	Stärke
sunchair ['sʌnˌtʃeə]	Liegestuhl
trading centre ['treɪdɪŋ ˌsentə]	Handelszentrum
to turn into [tɜːn_'ɪntuː]	verwandeln
view [vjuː]	Blick, Ansicht

C2

above [ə'bʌv]	oben
domestic trip [dəˌmestɪk 'trɪp]	Inlandsausflug
holidaymaker ['hɒlɪdeɪˌmeɪkə]	Urlauber(in)
holidaymaking ['hɒlɪdeɪˌmeɪkɪŋ]	in den Urlaub fahren
least [liːst]	am wenigsten
outbound ['aʊtbaʊnd]	ins Ausland
rate [reɪt]	Quote, Prozentsatz
United Kingdom [juːˌnaɪtɪd 'kɪŋdəm]	Vereinigtes Königreich

D1

conservative [kən'sɜːvətɪv]	konservativ
constituency [kən'stɪtjʊənsɪ]	Wahlkreis
democrat ['deməkræt]	Demokrat(in)
former ['fɔːmə]	ehemalig
labour ['leɪbə]	Arbeit
voter ['vəʊtə]	Wähler(in)
voting system ['vəʊtɪŋ ˌsɪstəm]	Wahlsystem

D2

to appoint [ə'pɔɪnt]	ernennen, bestimmen
cabinet ['kæbɪnət]	Kabinett
to delay [dɪ'leɪ]	verschieben, aufschieben
diagram ['daɪəgræm]	Diagramm
to elect [ɪ'lekt]	wählen
hereditary peers [hɪˌredɪtərɪ 'pɪəz]	Peer mit vererbtem Adelstitel
House of Commons [ˌhaʊs_əv 'kɒmənz]	Unterhaus
House of Lords [ˌhaʊs_əv 'lɔːdz]	Oberhaus
Law Lord ['lɔː ˌlɔːd]	Mitglied des Oberhauses mit besonderer Verantwortung in Rechtsfragen
legislation [ˌledʒɪs'leɪʃn]	Gesetzgebung
life peers [ˌlaɪf 'pɪəz]	Peer auf Lebenszeit
on recommendation [ɒn ˌrekəmen'deɪʃn]	auf Empfehlung
previous ['priːvɪəs]	vorhergehend, früher
prime minister [ˌpraɪm_'mɪnɪstə]	Premierminister(in)
sovereign ['sɒvrɪn]	Souverän, Herrscher(in)
to vote; vote [vəʊt]	wählen; Stimme

Unit 4

Starter

communications [kəˌmjuːnɪ'keɪʃnz]	Telekommunikation, Kommunikationswege
device [dɪ'vaɪs]	Gerät

A1

actual ['æktʃʊəl]	tatsächlich
apparatus [ˌæpə'reɪtəs]	Gerät
appliance [ə'plaɪəns]	Gerät
to call up [kɔːl_'ʌp]	anrufen, aufrufen
to combine [kəm'baɪn]	verbinden, vereinigen
complex ['kɒmpleks]	komplex, kompliziert
complicated ['kɒmplɪkeɪtɪd]	kompliziert
consumer [kən'sjuːmə]	Verbraucher(in)

to crash [kræʃ]	zusammenbrechen
data ['deɪtə]	Daten
digital ['dɪdʒɪtl]	digital
document ['dɒkjʊmənt]	Dokument, Unterlage
easy-to-use [ˌiːzɪ tʊ_'juːz]	einfach zu bedienen
electronic [ˌɪlek'trɒnɪk]	elektronisch
multi- ['mʌltɪ]	Mehr-, Viel-
network ['netwɜːk]	Netzwerk
paradise ['pærədaɪs]	Paradies
poverty ['pɒvətɪ]	Armut
screen [skriːn]	Bildschirm, Leinwand
to store [stɔː]	speichern
transmission [trænz'mɪʃn]	Übertragung
to transmit [trænz'mɪt]	senden
TV set [ˌtiː'viː ˌset]	Fernsehgerät
user ['juːzə]	Benutzer(in)
user-friendly [ˌjuːzə'frendlɪ]	benutzerfreundlich
virtual ['vɜːtʃʊəl]	virtuell
wireless ['waɪələs]	drahtlos

A2

access ['ækses]	Zugang
bar graph ['bɑːgrɑːf]	Säulendiagramm
broadband ['brɔːdbænd]	Breitband
figure ['fɪgə]	Zahl, Figur
graph [grɑːf]	Diagramm, Schaubild
household ['haʊshəʊld]	Haushalt
mobile phone [ˌməʊbaɪl 'fəʊn]	Handy
percentage [pə'sentɪdʒ]	prozentualer Anteil

C

according to [ə'kɔːdɪŋ_tuː]	(seiner/ihrer) Meinung nach, laut
advertiser ['ædvəˌtaɪzə]	Inserent(in), Auftraggeber(in) von Werbesendungen
airtime ['eətaɪm]	Sendezeit
background ['bækgraʊnd]	Hintergrund
best known [ˌbest_'nəʊn]	bekannteste(r, s)
campaign [kæm'peɪn]	Kampagne, Werbefeldzug
commercial [kə'mɜːʃl]	Werbespot
to decrease [dɪ'kriːs]	abnehmen, vermindern
expenditure [ɪk'spendɪtʃə]	Ausgabe(n), Aufwand
to fail [feɪl]	scheitern
habit ['hæbɪt]	Gewohnheit
logo ['ləʊgəʊ]	Logo, (Firmen-)Emblem
on the one hand [ɒn_ðə 'wʌn_ˌhænd]	auf der einen Seite
outdoor [ˌaʊt'dɔː]	draußen, im Freien
to overestimate [ˌəʊvər'estɪmeɪt]	überschätzen
per head [pə 'hed]	pro Kopf
pleased [pliːzd]	zufrieden, erfreut
to recognize ['rekəgnaɪz]	(wieder)erkennen

remote control [rɪˌməʊt_kənˈtrəʊl] — Fernbedienung
share [ʃeə] — Anteil
to switch [swɪtʃ] — umschalten, schalten
tennis serve [ˈtenɪs ˌsɜːv] — Aufschlag (Tennis)
value [ˈvæljuː] — Wert
viewer [ˈvjʊə] — Zuschauer(in)
viewpoint [ˈvjuːpɔɪnt] — Standpunkt
whereas [weəˈræz] — während
worldwide [ˌwɜːldˈwaɪd] — weltweit

D1

polite [pəˈlaɪt] — höflich
superb [sjuːˈpɜːb] — erstklassig
superfast [ˌsjuːpəˈfɑːst] — sehr schnell

D2

advert [ˈædvɜːt] — Kurzform von "advertisement" = Werbeanzeige
to aim (at) [eɪm] — zielen (auf)
to associate [əˈsəʊʃɪeɪt] — assoziieren, in Verbindung bringen
brand name [ˈbrænd_ˌneɪm] — Markenname
lifestyle [ˈlaɪfstaɪl] — Lebensstil
to refer to [rɪˈfɜː tuː] — sich beziehen auf
slogan [ˈsləʊgn] — Slogan, Werbespruch
target group [ˈtɑːgɪt_ˌgruːp] — Zielgruppe

Unit 5

Starter

to reduce [rɪdjuːs] — verringern, senken
view [vjuː] — Sicht, Ansicht, Aussicht

A1

congested [kənˈdʒestɪd] — überfüllt, verstopft
congestion [kənˈdʒestʃn] — Stau
day by day [ˌdeɪ baɪ ˈdeɪ] — Tag für Tag
fumes [fjuːmz] — Rauch, Dämpfe, Abgase
to get used to [get ˈjuːst_tuː] — sich gewöhnen an
innovation [ˌɪnəˈveɪʃn] — Neuerung
to look into [lʊk_ˈɪntuː] — untersuchen, prüfen
major [ˈmeɪdʒə] — bedeutend, Haupt-
motorway [ˈməʊtəweɪ] — Autobahn
navigation system [ˌnævɪˈgeɪʃn ˌsɪstəm] — Navigationssystem
overcrowded [ˌəʊvəˈkraʊdɪd] — überfüllt
rush-hour [ˈrʌʃˌaʊə] — Hauptverkehrszeit
technological [ˌteknəˈlɒdʒɪkl] — technologisch, technisch

traffic jam [ˈtræfɪk ˌdʒæm] — Verkehrsstau
tram [træm] — Straßenbahn

A2

accent [ˈæksənt] — Akzent
additional [əˈdɪʃənl] — zusätzlich
aid [eɪd] — Hilfe, Hilfsmittel
audio [ˈɔːdɪəʊ] — audio, Hör-
available [əˈveɪləbl] — verfügbar, vorhanden
to avoid [əˈvɔɪd] — vermeiden
button [ˈbʌtn] — Knopf
command [kəˈmɑːnd] — Befehl
destination [ˌdestɪˈneɪʃn] — Reiseziel, Zielort
display [dɪˈspleɪ] — Anzeige
diversion [daɪˈvɜːʃn] — Umleitung
due to [djuː tuː] — aufgrund von
to enter [ˈentə] — eingeben (Daten)
to equip [ɪˈkwɪp] — ausrüsten
feature [ˈfiːtʃə] — Merkmal, Bestandteil
fog [fɒg] — Nebel
glance [glɑːns] — Blick
GPS (Global Positioning System) [ˌdʒiːpiːˈes] [ˌgləʊbl pəˈzɪʃənɪŋ ˌsɪstəm] — GPS-Navigationssystem
to guide [gaɪd] — leiten, führen
to install [ɪnˈstɔːl] — einbauen
interval [ˈɪntəvl] — Abstand
location [ləʊˈkeɪʃn] — Lage, Standort
to monitor [ˈmɒnɪtə] — überwachen
network [ˈnetwɜːk] — Netz
to obtain [ɒbˈteɪn] — bekommen, erhalten
petrol station [ˈpetrl ˌsteɪʃn] — Tankstelle
to pinpoint [ˈpɪnpɔɪnt] — genau anzeigen, genau bestimmen
to programme [ˈprəʊgræm] — programmieren
to recalculate [ˌriːˈkælkjəleɪt] — neu berechnen
to reduce [rɪˈdʒuːs] — verringern, senken
to regulate [ˈregjəleɪt] — regulieren
to rely on [rɪˈlaɪ_ɒn] — sich verlassen auf
to rewrite [ˌriːˈraɪt] — neu schreiben, umschreiben
road works [ˈrəʊdˌwɜːks] — Straßenbauarbeiten
to run out of sth. [rʌn_ˈaʊt_əv ˌsʌmθɪŋ] — ausgehen, etwas nicht mehr haben
satellite [ˈsætəlaɪt] — Satellit
sensor [ˈsensə] — Sensor, Fühler
slow moving traffic [ˈsləʊˌmuːvɪŋ ˈtræfɪk] — zäh fließender Verkehr
steering wheel [ˈstɪərɪŋ_ˌwiːl] — Lenkrad
suburban [səˈbɜːbn] — Vorort-
to suggest [səˈdʒest] — vorschlagen
to take care [teɪk_ˈkeə] — aufpassen
touch [tʌtʃ] — Berührung

traffic flow ['træfɪk ˌfləʊ]   Verkehrsfluss
traffic jam   Verkehrsstau
  ['træfɪk ˌdʒæm]
to transmit [trænz'mɪt]   übermitteln
user ['juːzə]   Benutzer(in)
voice recognition   Spracherkennung
  ['vɔɪs ˌrekəg'nɪʃn]
to worry ['wʌrɪ]   sich sorgen, sich
          beunruhigen

C1

attractive   reizvoll, anziehend,
  [ə'træktɪv]   attraktiv
commuter [kə'mjuːtə]   Pendler(in)
convenient [kən'viːnɪənt]   günstig, praktisch
crazy ['kreɪzɪ]   verrückt
ecological   ökologisch,
  [ˌiːkə'lɒdʒɪkl]   umweltfreundlich
electrically-driven   elektrisch angetrieben
  [ɪˌlektrɪklɪ 'drɪvən]
environmentalist   Umweltschützer(in)
  [ɪnˌvaɪrən'mentəlɪst]
to estimate ['estɪmeɪt]   schätzen
expert ['ekspɜːt]   Experte, Expertin
to face sth.   mit etw. konfrontiert sein
  ['feɪsˌsʌmθɪŋ]
fixed-route [ˌfɪkst'ruːt]   schienengebunden
flexible ['fleksɪbl]   flexibel
freedom ['friːdəm]   Freiheit
to get rid of [get 'rɪdˌəv]   loswerden, abschaffen
heading ['hedɪŋ]   Überschrift
individual [ˌɪndɪ'vɪdʒʊəl]   individuell
in favour of   zugunsten von
  [ɪn 'feɪvərˌəv]
inner ['ɪnə]   Innen-, inner-
to make sense   einen Sinn ergeben
  [meɪk 'sens]
medium-sized   mittelgroß
  [ˌmiːdjəm 'saɪzd]
peak time ['piːk ˌtaɪm]   Hauptverkehrszeit
planner ['plænə]   Planer(in)
progress ['prəʊgres]   Fortschritt
to provide   sorgen für, liefern,
  [prə'vaɪd]   bereitstellen
to put into practice   in die Praxis umsetzen,
  [ˌpʊtˌɪntʊ 'præktɪs]   realisieren
rail [reɪl]   Schiene
sort [sɔːt]   Art, Sorte
thanks to ['θæŋks tuː]   dank
tramway ['træmweɪ]   Straßenbahngleis
underground   Untergrund, U-Bahn
  ['ʌndəgraʊnd]
unpopular [ˌʌn'pɒpjʊlə]   unpopulär

C2

definite ['defɪnɪt]   eindeutig, bestimmt
to suffer ['sʌfə]   leiden

D1

motorist ['məʊtərɪst]   Autofahrer(in)

D2

base   Basis, Stützpunkt,
  [beɪs]   Ausgangspunkt
by rail [baɪ 'reɪl]   mit der Bahn
coaching days   Postkutschenzeit
  ['kəʊtʃɪŋ ˌdeɪz]
to concentrate on   sich konzentrieren auf
  ['kɒnsəntreɪtˌɒn]
continental [ˌkɒntɪ'nentl]   kontinental
crossroads ['krɒsrəʊdz]   Kreuzung
intercontinental   interkontinental
  [ˌɪntəkɒntɪ'nentl]
on top of [ɒn 'tɒpˌəv]   zusätzlich zu
to operate ['ɒpəreɪt]   verkehren, bedienen
promotion [prə'məʊʃn]   Werbung, Beförderung
town hall [ˌtaʊn 'hɔːl]   Rathaus
via ['vaɪə]   über

Unit 6

Starter

chart [tʃɑːt]   Tabelle, Schaubild
composting ['kɒmpɒstɪŋ]   Kompostierung
energy recovery   Energierückgewinnung
  ['enədʒɪ rɪˌkʌvərɪ]
landfill ['lændfɪl]   Mülldeponie
plastic ['plæstɪk]   Kunststoff, Plastik
recovery [rɪ'kʌvərɪ]   Wiedergewinnung
ton [tʌn]   Tonne
waste [weɪst]   Müll, Abfall

A1

acid rain [ˌæsɪdˌ'reɪn]   saurer Regen
advertising campaign   Werbekampagne
  ['ædvətaɪzɪŋˌkæmˌpeɪn]
at all costs [ətˌɔːl 'kɒsts]   um jeden Preis
bulb [bʌlb]   (Glüh)birne
conscious ['kɒnʃəs]   bewusst
consumer [kən'sjuːmə]   Verbraucher(in)
consumption   Verbrauch
  [kən'sʌmpʃn]
to contribute   beitragen
  [kən'trɪbjuːt]
contribution   Beitrag
  [ˌkɒntrɪ'bjuːʃn]
disposal [dɪs'pəʊsl]   Beseitigung, Entsorgung
emission [ɪ'mɪʃn]   Emission, Ausstoß
emphasis ['emfəsɪs]   Betonung
to emphasize ['emfəsaɪz]   betonen
environmental   Umwelt-
  [ɪnˌvaɪrən'mentl]

environmentalist [ɪn,vaɪrən'mentəlɪst] — Umweltschützer(in)

in conclusion [ɪn_kən'klu:ʒn] — abschließend

to influence ['ɪnfluəns] — beeinflussen

to insulate ['ɪnsjəleɪt] — isolieren

insulation [,ɪnsjə'leɪʃn] — Isolierung

lighting ['laɪtɪŋ] — Beleuchtung

to manufacture [,mænjə'fæktʃə] — herstellen

manufacturer [,mænjə'fæktʃərə] — Hersteller(in)

– to meet the growing demand [,mi:t_ðə_,grəʊɪŋ_dɪ'mɑːnd] — der wachsenden Nachfrage gerecht werden

non-returnable [,nɒnrɪ't3:nəbl] — Einweg-

once again [wʌns_ə'gen] — noch einmal

ozone hole ['əʊzəʊn_,həʊl] — Ozonloch

packaging ['pækɪdʒɪŋ] — Verpackung

power station ['paʊə_,steɪʃn] — Kraftwerk, Elektrizitätswerk

range [reɪndʒ] — Sortiment, Umfang, Reichweite

reaction [rɪ'ækʃn] — Reaktion

recyclable [,riː'saɪkləbl] — wiederverwertbar

reduction [rɪ'dʌkʃn] — Verminderung

to refuse [rɪ'fjuːz] — ablehnen, sich weigern

responsibility [rɪ,spɒnsə'bɪlətɪ] — Verantwortung

retailer ['riːteɪlə] — Einzelhändler(in)

returnable [rɪ't3:nəbl] — Mehrweg-

rubbish ['rʌbɪʃ] — Abfall, Müll

so-called [,səʊ'kɔːld] — so genannt

to turn to ['t3:n tu:] — sich zuwenden

wasteful ['weɪstfʊl] — verschwenderisch

A2

additional [ə'dɪʃənl] — zusätzlich

all over the world [ɔːl_,əʊvə ðə 'w3:ld] — in der ganzen Welt

CFC [,siː:ef'siː] — FCKW (Fluorchlorkohlen-wasserstoff)

chemist ['kemɪst] — Chemiker(in)

convinced [kən'vɪnst] — überzeugt

direct speech [daɪ,rekt 'spiːtʃ] — direkte Rede

disagreement [,dɪsə'griːmənt] — abweichende Meinung, Meinungsverschiedenheit

elsewhere [,els'weə] — woanders

fuel [fjʊəl] — Brennstoff, Kraftstoff

furthermore ['f3:ðəmɔː] — außerdem, ferner

improvement [ɪm'pruːvmənt] — Verbesserung

to maintain [meɪn'teɪn] — behaupten

moreover [mɔː'rəʊvə] — überdies, zudem, ferner

ought to ['ɔːt_tuː] — sollte(n)

to take the view [teɪk_ðə 'vjuː] — der Ansicht sein

C

(not) any more [nɒt / ,eni_'mɔː] — nicht länger

approach [ə'prəʊtʃ] — Ansatz, Annäherung

to attack [ə'tæk] — in Angriff nehmen, angreifen

card [kɑːd] — Karte

to code; code [kəʊd] — kodieren; Kode

to come true [kʌm 'truː] — wahr werden

dealer ['diːlə] — Händler(in)

to dismantle [dɪs'mæntl] — zerlegen, demontieren

to dump; dump [dʌmp] — (Müll) abladen; Müllkippe

Friends of the Earth [,frendz_əv_ðɪ_'3:θ] — Name einer Umwelt-schutzorganisation

to get rid of [get 'rɪd_əv] — loswerden

left [left] — übrig

to melt [melt] — schmelzen

over and over again [,əʊvər_ən_,əʊvər_ə'gen] — immer wieder

paraphrase ['pærəfreɪz] — Umschreibung

precise [prɪ'saɪs] — genau

raw [rɔː] — Roh-, roh

to re-use [,riː'juːz] — wiederverwenden

to recycle [,riː'saɪkl] — wiederverwerten

scrap [skræp] — Schrott, Fetzen

to separate ['sepəreɪt] — trennen

to shift [ʃɪft] — verlagern

to substitute; substitute ['sʌbstɪtjuːt] — ersetzen; Ersatz

supplier [sə'plaɪə] — Lieferant(in)

to take to pieces [,teɪk tu 'piːsɪz] — zerlegen

unknown [,ʌn'nəʊn] — unbekannt

unlikely [ʌn'laɪklɪ] — unwahrscheinlich

waste management ['weɪst_,mænɪdʒmənt] — Abfallentsorgung

D1

countryside ['kʌntrɪsaɪd] — Landschaft

to create [kriː'eɪt] — schaffen, verursachen

deposit [dɪ'pɒzɪt] — Lagerstätte, Guthaben

ecology [ɪ'kɒlədʒɪ] — Ökologie

fear [fɪə] — Furcht

mining ['maɪnɪŋ] — Bergbau

nature ['neɪtʃə] — Natur

ore [ɔː] — Erz

recording [rɪ'kɔːdɪŋ] — Aufnahme

summary ['sʌmərɪ] — Zusammenfassung

technologist [tek'nɒlədʒɪst] — Techniker(in)

zinc [zɪŋk] — Zink

D2

attraction [ə'trækʃn] — Anziehungskraft

coastal ['kəʊstl] — Küsten-

concerned [kən's3:nd] — betroffen, interessiert

housing estate ['haʊzɪŋ ˌɪˌsteɪt] — Siedlung

issue ['ɪʃuː] — Thema, Frage

major road [ˌmeɪdʒə ˈrəʊd] — Hauptstraße

MP (Member of Parliament) [ˌem'piː] [ˌmembər ˌəv 'pɑːləmənt] — Mitglied des Parlaments

primary school ['praɪmərɪ ˌskuːl] — Grundschule

public library [ˌpʌblɪk 'laɪbrərɪ] — Stadtbücherei

reported speech [rɪˌpɔːtɪd 'spiːtʃ] — indirekte Rede

role [rəʊl] — Rolle

seaside resort ['siːsaɪd rɪˌzɔːt] — Seebad

surface ['sɜːfɪs] — Oberfläche

tax [tæks] — Steuer

unemployed [ˌʌnɪm'plɔɪd] — arbeitslos

source [sɔːs] — Quelle

standard of living [ˌstændəd ˌəv 'lɪvɪŋ] — Lebensstandard

to take action [teɪk 'ækʃn] — etwas unternehmen

total ['təʊtl] — gesamt

to transfer [træns'fɜː] — übertragen

trillion ['trɪljən] — Trillion (AE: Billion)

wealth [welθ] — Reichtum

what … like? [wɒt … 'laɪk] — wie (ist er/sie/es) …?

Unit 7

Starter

fast running [ˌfɑːst 'rʌnɪŋ] — schnell fließend

machinery [mə'ʃiːnərɪ] — Maschinen

peat bog ['piːt ˌbɒg] — Torfmoor

resources [rɪ'sɔːsɪz] [rɪ'zɔːsɪz] — Boden-, Naturschätze, Mittel

A1

antonym ['æntənɪm] — Antonym, Wort mit gegensätzlicher Bedeutung

availability [əˌveɪlə'bɪlətɪ] — Vorhandensein, Verfügbarkeit

billion ['bɪljən] — Billion, (AE: Milliarde)

citizen ['sɪtɪzn] — Bürger(in)

developing country [dɪˌveləpɪŋ ˈkʌntrɪ] — Entwicklungsland

fossil fuels [ˌfɒsl 'fjʊəlz] — fossile Brennstoffe

geographical [ˌdʒɪə'græfɪkl] — geografisch

global warming [ˌgləʊbl 'wɔːmɪŋ] — weltweiter Temperaturanstieg

to harm [hɑːm] — schädigen

impression [ɪm'preʃn] — Eindruck

industrialized [ɪn'dʌstrɪəlaɪzd] — industrialisiert

mankind [mæn'kaɪnd] — Menschheit

plentiful ['plentɪfʊl] — reichlich, häufig

plenty ['plentɪ] — viel, eine Menge

to predict [prɪ'dɪkt] — vorhersagen

secure [sɪ'kjʊə] — sicher

significant [sɪg'nɪfɪkənt] — bedeutend, bedeutsam

slight [slaɪt] — leicht, schwach, gering

solar power [ˌsəʊlə 'paʊə] — Sonnenenergie

A2

BTU British Thermal Unit [ˌbiːtiːˈjuː] [ˌbrɪtɪʃ ˌθɜːml 'juːnɪt] — BTU = brit. Wärmeeinheit

constant ['kɒnstənt] — ständig, gleichbleibend

to drop [drɒp] — fallen, fallen lassen

gradual ['grædʒʊəl] — allmählich, sanft (ansteigen/abfallen)

graph [grɑːf] — Schaubild, mathematische Kurve

projection [prə'dʒekʃn] — Prognose, Projektion

sharp [ʃɑːp] — scharf, deutlich, steil

stable ['steɪbl] — stabil, dauerhaft

steady ['stedɪ] — stabil, gleichbleibend

substantial [səb'stænʃl] — beträchtlich, erheblich

temperature ['temprətʃə] — Temperatur

C

to argue ['ɑːgjuː] — behaupten

as a result [əz ˌə rɪ'zʌlt] — folglich

beer [bɪə] — Bier

cable ['keɪbl] — Kabel

cell [sel] — Zelle

consequently ['kɒnsɪkwəntlɪ] — folglich

to dig up [dɪg ˌ'ʌp] — (aus)graben

domestic [də'mestɪk] — häuslich

e.g. [ˌiː'dʒiː] [fər ˌɪg'zɑːmpl] — z.B. (zum Beispiel)

fossil fuels [ˌfɒsl 'fjʊəlz] — fossile Brennstoffe

fuel cell ['fjʊəl ˌsel] — Brennstoffzelle

to generate ['dʒenəreɪt] — erzeugen

grid [grɪd] — Versorgungsnetz

highway ['haɪweɪ] — Landstraße

hydro ['haɪdrəʊ] — Wasser-

hydrogen-based [ˌhaɪdrədʒn'beɪst] — auf Wasserstoffbasis arbeitend

in the mid [ɪn ˌðə 'mɪd] — in der Mitte von, Mitte der …

introductory [ˌɪntrə'dʌktərɪ] — einleitend

to join [dʒɔɪn] — sich anschließen

key point ['kiː ˌpɔɪnt] — springender Punkt

to light (lit, lit) [laɪt lɪt lɪt] — anzünden, (be)leuchten

maintenance ['meɪntənəns] — Wartung, Instandhaltung

maker ['meɪkə] — Hersteller(in)

off-the-grid
[ˌɒf_ðə ˈɡrɪd]
nicht an das Versorgungs-
netz angeschlossen

panel [ˈpænl]
Schalttafel

photovoltaic (pv)
[ˌfəʊtəʊvɒlˈteɪɪk]
[ˌpiːˈviː]
fotoelektrisch

powered [ˈpaʊəd]
angetrieben, betrieben

power line [ˈpaʊə laɪn]
(Stark-)Stromleitung

power plant
[ˈpaʊə ˌplɑːnt]
Kraftwerk

power station
[ˈpaʊə ˌsteɪʃn]
Kraftwerk

renewable energy
[rɪˌnjuːəbl ˈenədʒi]
erneuerbare Energie

research [ˈriːsɜːtʃ]
Forschung

scientist [ˈsaɪəntɪst]
Wissenschaftler(in)

shower [ˈʃaʊə]
Dusche

to state
[steɪt]
darlegen, vortragen,
nennen

subject matter
[ˈsʌbdʒɪkt ˌmætə]
Stoff, Inhalt

to supply [səˈplaɪ]
versorgen

traditional [trəˈdɪʃənl]
traditionell, herkömmlich

yearly [ˈjɪəli]
jährlich

D1

agricultural
[ˌæɡrɪˈkʌltʃərəl]
landwirtschaftlich

biomass [ˈbaɪəʊmæs]
Biomasse

conversation
[ˌkɒnvəˈseɪʃn]
Unterhaltung, Gespräch

conveyor [kənˈveɪə]
Förderband

delivery hall
[dɪˈlɪvri ˌhɔːl]
An-/Auslieferungshalle

fertilizer [ˈfɜːtəlaɪzə]
Dünger

to fix [fɪks]
vorhaben, organisieren

furnace [ˈfɜːnɪs]
Ofen

generator [ˈdʒenəreɪtə]
Generator, Lichtmaschine

litter [ˈlɪtə]
Streu, Stroh

manure [məˈnjʊə]
Dung

megawatt [ˈmeɡəwɒt]
Megawatt

neat
[niːt]
ordentlich, gelungen,
schlau

output [ˈaʊtpʊt]
(Produktions-)Leistung

pit [pɪt]
Grube

poultry [ˈpəʊltri]
Geflügel

steam [stiːm]
Dampf

storage [ˈstɔːrɪdʒ]
Lagerung, Aufbewahrung

straight in [streɪt_ˈɪn]
direkt hinein

to tip [tɪp]
kippen

turbine [ˈtɜːbaɪn]
Turbine

D2

ash [æʃ]
Asche

conveyor belt
[kənˈveɪə ˌbelt]
Förderband, Fließband

employee [ɪmˈplɔɪiː]
Angestellte(r)

greenhouse [ˈɡriːnhaʊs]
Treibhaus, Gewächshaus

manpower [ˈmænˌpaʊə]
Arbeitskraft

Unit 8

A1

again and again
[əˌɡen_ən_əˈɡen]
immer wieder

all kind(s) of
[ɔːl ˈkaɪndz_əv]
alle Arten von, alle
möglichen

to automate [ˈɔːtəmeɪt]
automatisieren

automatic [ˌɔːtəˈmætɪk]
automatisch

available [əˈveɪləbl]
verfügbar, vorhanden

CAD [ˌsiːeɪˈdiː]
(Computer
Aided Design)
[kəmˈpjuːtər_
ˌeɪdɪd_dɪˈzaɪn]
Computerunterstützte
Zeichnung

CAM [ˌsiː eɪˈem]
(Computer Aided
Manufacturing)
[kəmˈpjuːtər_ˌeɪdɪd
mænjəˈfæktʃərɪŋ]
Computerunterstützte
Fertigung

civilized [ˈsɪvɪlaɪzd]
zivilisiert

CIM [ˌsiː aɪˈem]
(Computer Integrated
Manufacturing)
[kəmˈpjuːtər_ˌɪntɪɡreɪtɪd
mænjəˈfæktʃərɪŋ]
Computerintegrierte
Fertigung

designer [dɪˈzaɪnə]
Zeichner(in), Designer(in)

economical [ˌiːkəˈnɒmɪkl]
sparsam, wirtschaftlich

to equip [ɪˈkwɪp]
ausrüsten

etc. (et cetera)
[ˌiː tiːˈsiː] [ɪtˈsetərə]
und so weiter

fault [fɔːlt]
Fehler, Schuld, Mangel

feedback [ˈfiːdbæk]
Rückmeldung, Feedback

latest [ˈleɪtɪst]
der, die, das Neueste

to link together
[lɪŋk_təˈɡeðə]
miteinander verbinden

particular [pəˈtɪkjələ]
besondere(r,s)

productivity
[ˌprɒdʌkˈtɪvəti]
Produktivität,
Leistungsfähigkeit

research department
[ˈriːsɜːtʃ dɪˌpɑːtmənt]
Forschungsabteilung

robot
[ˈrəʊbɒt]
Roboter, vollautomatische
Vorrichtung

sensor [ˈsensə]
Fühler, Sensor

shop floor [ˌʃɒp_ˈflɔː]
Produktionsstätte, -halle

to simulate [ˈsɪmjəleɪt]
simulieren

term [tɜːm]
Ausdruck, Wort

to touch; touch [tʌtʃ]
berühren; Berührung

unsuitable [ʌnˈsjuːtəbl]
unpassend, ungeeignet

A2

to assemble [əˈsembl]
zusammenbauen

bumper [ˈbʌmpə]
Stoßstange

car body [ˈkɑː ˌbɒdi]
Karosserie

dashboard [ˈdæʃˌbɔːd]
Armaturenbrett

to dip [dɪp]
(in Farbe) eintauchen

engine [ˈendʒɪn]
Motor

exhaust pipe
[ɪɡˈzɔːst_ˌpaɪp]
Auspuffrohr

to fit [fɪt]	einbauen, anbringen
headlight ['hedlaɪt]	Scheinwerfer
to spray [spreɪ]	sprühen, spritzen
to weld [weld]	schweißen
windscreen ['wɪnd,skriːn]	Windschutzscheibe

C1

to arrange [ə'reɪndʒ]	aufstellen, planen, veranlassen
arrangement [ə'reɪndʒmənt]	Vereinbarung, Arrangement
customer-orientated [,kʌstəmər 'ɔːriənteɪtɪd]	kundenorientiert
decision-making process [dɪ'sɪʒn ,meɪkɪŋ ,prəʊses]	Entscheidungsprozess
to dominate ['dɒmɪneɪt]	beherrschen, dominieren
flexibility [,fleksə'bɪlətɪ]	Flexibilität
inflexible [ɪn'fleksəbl]	unflexibel
Japanese [,dʒæpə'niːz]	japanisch; Japaner(in)
lean management [,liːn 'mænɪdʒmənt]	„schlankes" Management
monotonous [mə'nɒtənəs]	eintönig, monoton
opportunity [ɒpə'tjuːnətɪ]	Gelegenheit, Möglichkeit
to perform [pə'fɔːm]	ausführen, vollbringen
personnel [,pɜːsə'nel]	Personal
repetitive [rɪ'petətɪv]	(sich) wiederholend, eintönig
to replace [rɪ'pleɪs]	ersetzen
schedule ['ʃedjuːl]	(Zeit-, Fahr-)Plan, Programm
style [staɪl]	Stil, Art
to suit [sjuːt]	passen
task [tɑːsk]	Aufgabe
team work ['tiːmwɜːk]	Teamarbeit
union ['juːnjən]	Gewerkschaft
unit ['juːnɪt]	Einheit, Gruppe

C2

DVD [,diːviː'diː] (recorder)	DVD-Rekorder (-Aufnahmegerät)
infinitive [ɪn'fɪnətɪv]	Infinitiv, Grundform
to insert [ɪn'sɜːt]	einlegen (Diskette, Kassette)
modal ['məʊdl]	Hilfsverb
model ['mɒdl]	Modell
passive ['pæsɪv]	Passiv
to press [pres]	drücken
to record [rɪ'kɔːd]	aufnehmen
recording instruction [rɪ'kɔːdɪŋ ɪn,strʌkʃn]	Aufnahmeanleitung
to select [sə'lekt]	auswählen
to switch on [swɪtʃ 'ɒn]	anstellen

D1

handbook ['hændbʊk]	Handbuch
installation [,ɪnstə'leɪʃn]	Installation, Anschluss
to print [prɪnt]	drucken
printer ['prɪntə]	Drucker
resolution [,rezə'luːʃn]	Auflösung

D2

cartridge ['kɑːtrɪdʒ]	Kassette, Patrone
connector [kə'nektə]	Verbindungselement, Stecker
cover ['kʌvə]	Abdeckung
ink [ɪŋk]	Tinte
ink jet printer ['ɪŋkdʒet ,prɪntə]	Tintenstrahldrucker
interface ['ɪntəfeɪs]	Schnittstelle
to make sure [meɪk 'ʃʊə]	sich überzeugen
to mix up [mɪks 'ʌp]	vertauschen
to remove [rɪ'muːv]	entfernen
to screw; screw [skruː]	schrauben; Schraube
to snap [snæp]	einrasten
to take off [teɪk 'ɒf]	abnehmen
tape [teɪp]	Band, Klebestreifen
to tighten ['taɪtn]	(fest) anziehen, verschärfen

Unit 9

Starter

financial services [faɪ,nənʃl 'sɜːvɪsɪz]	Finanzdienstleistungen
legal services [,liːgl 'sɜːvɪsɪz]	Rechtsberatungen, -dienstleistungen
printing ['prɪntɪŋ]	Druckwesen
publishing ['pʌblɪʃɪŋ]	Verlagswesen

A1

shipbuilding ['ʃɪp,bɪldɪŋ]	Schiffbau
shipyard ['ʃɪpjɑːd]	Werft
steel [stiːl]	Stahl

A2

to achieve [ə'tʃiːv]	erreichen, erzielen
arms [ɑːmz]	Waffen
to be located [biː ləʊ'keɪtɪd]	sich befinden, liegen
broadband ['brɔːdbænd]	Breitband
corporation [,kɔːpə'reɪʃn]	Gesellschaft, Körperschaft
coverage ['kʌvərɪdʒ]	hier: Ausstattung
data processing ['deɪtə ,prəʊsesɪŋ]	Datenverarbeitung
decade ['dekeɪd]	Jahrzehnt, Dekade
entrepreneurship [,ɒntrəprə'nɜːʃɪp]	Unternehmertum, unternehmerische Vorhaben

former ['fɔːmə] — früher
innovation [ˌɪnəˈveɪʃn] — Innovation, Neuerung
large-scale [ˌlɑːdʒˈskeɪl] — groß angelegt, in großem Umfang
to let [let] — vermieten
light industry [ˌlaɪt ˈɪndʌstrɪ] — Leichtindustrie
managing director [ˌmænɪdʒɪŋ_daɪˈrektə] — Geschäftsführer(in)
to occupy [ˈɒkjəpaɪ] — einnehmen, besetzen, beschäftigen
official [əˈfɪʃl] — offiziell; Beamte(r), Funktionär(in)
outstanding [ˌaʊtˈstændɪŋ] — hervorragend, außergewöhnlich
to provide [prəˈvaɪd] — bereitstellen
range [reɪndʒ] — Reihe, Auswahl
scheme [skiːm] — Plan, Programm, Projekt
site [saɪt] — Grundstück, Sitz, Standort
square [skweə] — Quadrat
to take over [teɪk_ˈəʊvə] — übernehmen
wired [ˈwaɪəd] — verkabelt

C

to account for [əˈkaʊnt fɔː] — beitragen
to add [æd] — hinzufügen
to announce [əˈnaʊns] — bekannt geben
annual output [ˌænjʊəl_ˈaʊtpʊt] — Jahresproduktion
appeal [əˈpiːl] — Anziehungskraft
assembly line [əˈsemblɪ ˌlaɪn] — Fließband
average increase [ˌævərɪdʒ_ˈɪnkriːs] — durchschnittlicher Anstieg
bagless [ˈbægləs] — hier: ohne Staubsaugerbeutel
by contrast [baɪ ˈkɒntrɑːst] — im Gegensatz
call centre [ˈkɔːl ˌsentə] — Callcenter, telefon. Auskunftsdienst
to contrast [kənˈtrɑːst] — vergleichen
desperately [ˈdespərətlɪ] — verzweifelt
economical [ˌiːkəˈnɒmɪkl] — wirtschaftlich, sparsam
to eliminate [ɪˈlɪmɪneɪt] — beseitigen, entfernen
estimated value [ˌestɪmeɪtɪd ˈvæljuː] — geschätzter Wert
icon [ˈaɪkən] — Idol, Ikone
innovative [ˈɪnəvətɪv] [ɪˈnɒvətɪv] — innovativ
inventor [ɪnˈventə] — Erfinder(in)
labour market [ˈleɪbə ˌmɑːkɪt] — Arbeitsmarkt
law of economics [ˌlɔːr_əv_iːkəˈnɒmɪks] — Wirtschaftsgesetz
low interest rate [ˌləʊ_ˈɪntrəst_ˌreɪt] — niedrige Zinsrate
Malaysia [məˈleɪzə] — Malaysia
move [muːv] — Umzug
plant [plɑːnt] — Werk

to prosper [ˈprɒspə] — gedeihen
recession [rɪˈseʃn] — Flaute
to record [rɪˈkɔːd] — verzeichnen
to roar away [rɔːr_əˈweɪ] — "wegdonnern"
sales [seɪlz] — Absätze
service industry [ˈsɜːvɪs ˌɪndʌstrɪ] — Dienstleistungsbranche
to shift [ʃɪft] — verschieben, verlagern
shopkeeper [ˈʃɒpˌkiːpə] — Ladenbesitzer(in)
shopper [ˈʃɒpə] — Käufer(in)
spending power [ˈspendɪŋ ˌpaʊə] — Kaufkraft
strike [straɪk] — Streik
to struggle with [ˈstrʌgl wɪð] — kämpfen mit
to survive [səˈvaɪv] — überleben
to tend [tend] — neigen
to turn into [tɜːn_ˈɪntuː] — umwandeln in
two-speed [ˌtuːˈspiːd] — mit zwei Geschwindigkeiten
unemployment rate [ˌʌnɪmˈplɔɪmənt ˌreɪt] — Arbeitslosenquote
vacuum cleaner [ˈvækjuːm ˌkliːnə] — Staubsauger

D

access [ˈækses] — Zugang, Zutritt
after all [ˌɑːftər_ˈɔːl] — schließlich
assistance [əˈsɪstəns] — Hilfe
back-up [ˈbækʌp] — Unterstützung
bright [braɪt] — hell, strahlend
car park [ˈkɑːpɑːk] — Parkplatz
council [ˈkaʊnsl] — (Stadt-, Grafschafts-)Rat
county [ˈkaʊntɪ] — Grafschaft, Bezirk
current [ˈkʌrənt] — aktuell, gegenwärtig
developer [dɪˈveləpə] — Entwickler(in), Bauunternehmer(in)
extract [ˈekstrækt] — Auszug, Extrakt
facility [fəˈsɪlətɪ] — Einrichtung, Möglichkeit
high class [ˌhaɪˈklɑːs] — hochwertig, erstklassig
housing [ˈhaʊzɪŋ] — Unterkunft, Wohnungen
link [lɪŋk] — Verbindung
literature [ˈlɪtrətʃə] — Literatur, Informationsmaterial
location [ləʊˈkeɪʃn] — Lage, Standort
out of town [ˌaʊt_əv ˈtaʊn] — außerhalb der Stadt
permission [pəˈmɪʃn] — Erlaubnis
phone call [ˈfəʊnkɔːl] — Anruf
promotion literature [prəˈməʊʃn ˌlɪtrətʃə] — Werbematerial
racing bicycle [ˈreɪsɪŋ ˌbaɪsɪkl] — Rennrad
region [ˈriːdʒn] — Gebiet, Bezirk
to relocate [ˌriːləʊˈkeɪt] — (Geschäftssitz) verlegen
to represent [ˌreprɪˈzent] — darstellen, stehen für
requirement [rɪˈkwaɪəmənt] — Bedarf, Erfordernis
shopping [ˈʃɒpɪŋ] — Einkauf(en)

skilled [skɪld] — qualifiziert, ausgebildet
standard ['stændəd] — Niveau, Standard, Maßstab
up to [ʌp̮ 'tuː] — bis zu

Unit 10

Starter

immigration [ˌɪmɪ'greɪʃn] — Einwanderung

A1

Amerasian [ˌæmər'eɪʒn] — amerikanisch-asiatisch
childhood ['tʃaɪldhʊd] — Kindheit
Chinese [tʃaɪ'niːz] — Chinese, Chinesin; chinesisch
cookie ['kʊkɪ] — Keks, Plätzchen
courage ['kʌrɪdʒ] — Mut
determination [dɪˌtɜːmɪ'neɪʃn] — Entschlossenheit, Bestimmung
down payment [ˌdaʊn̮ 'peɪmənt] — Anzahlung
draughtsman ['drɑːftsmən] — Zeichner(in)
to emigrate ['emɪgreɪt] — auswandern
emigration [ˌemɪ'greɪʃn] — Auswanderung
existence [ɪg'zɪstəns] — Existenz, Dasein
fashionable ['fæʃnəbl] — modisch
to flee [fliː] — fliehen, flüchten
to frighten ['fraɪtən] — erschrecken, Angst machen
to grow up [grəʊ̮ 'ʌp] — aufwachsen
happiness ['hæpɪnəs] — Glück, Heiterkeit, Zufriedenheit
hopeful ['həʊpfʊl] — zuversichtlich, vielversprechend
identity [aɪ'dentətɪ] — Identität, Übereinstimmung
to integrate ['ɪntɪgreɪt] — integrieren
to make matters worse [meɪk ˌmætəz̮ 'wɜːs] — zu allem Unglück
operator ['ɒpəreɪtə] — (Maschinen-)Bediener(in), Telefonvermittler(in)
original [ə'rɪdʒənl] — ursprünglich, originell
outsider [ˌaʊt'saɪdə] — Außenseiter(in)
possession [pə'zeʃn] — Besitz
quotation [kwəʊ'teɪʃn] — Zitat, Kostenvoranschlag
sceptical ['skeptɪkl] — skeptisch
soldier ['səʊldʒə] — Soldat(in)
title ['taɪtl] — Titel
Vietnamese [ˌvjetnə'miːz] — Vietnamese, Vietnamesin; vietnamesisch
visa ['viːzə] — Visum

A2

to arrest; arrest [ə'rest] — verhaften; Verhaftung
Asian ['eɪʒn] — Asiat(in); asiatisch

community [kə'mjuːnətɪ] — Bevölkerungsgruppe, Gemeinde
illegal [ɪ'liːgl] — illegal, gesetzlich unzulässig
Latin America [ˌlætɪn̮ ə'merɪkə] — Lateinamerika
to loot [luːt] — plündern
Mexican ['meksɪkən] — Mexikaner(in); mexikanisch
Pole [pəʊl] — Pole, Polin
Polish ['pəʊlɪʃ] — polnisch
riot ['raɪət] — Aufruhr, Krawall
tension ['tenʃn] — Spannung

C

circle ['sɜːkl] — Kreis, Kreislauf
to confirm [kən'fɜːm] — bestätigen
corn [kɔːn] — Getreide, Mais, Korn
draft [drɑːft] — Entwurf, Konzept
earnings ['ɜːnɪŋz] — Einkommen, Verdienst, Ertrag
economist [ɪ'kɒnəmɪst] — Wirtschaftswissenschaftler(in)
food stamp ['fuːd̮ ˌstæmp] — Essensmarke
in the long run [ɪn̮ ðə 'lɒŋ̮ ˌrʌn] — auf lange Sicht
inflow ['ɪnfləʊ] — Zustrom
native-born [ˌneɪtɪv'bɔːn] — gebürtig
poll [pəʊl] — Umfrage, Abstimmung, Wahl
short-term ['ʃɔːttɜːm] — kurzfristig
society [sə'saɪətɪ] — Gesellschaft
structure ['strʌktʃə] — Struktur
theory ['θɪərɪ] — Theorie
unemployment benefit [ˌʌnɪm'plɔɪmənt ˌbenəfɪt] — Arbeitslosenunterstützung
version ['vɜːʃn] — Version, Fassung
welfare ['welfeə] — Wohl, Wohlfahrt, Sozialhilfe
word-by-word [ˌwɜːd̮ baɪ̮ 'wɜːd] — Wort für Wort
worried ['wʌrɪd] — besorgt

D1

climate ['klaɪmət] — Klima
way of life [ˌweɪ̮ əv̮ 'laɪf] — Lebensweise

D2

editor ['edɪtə] — Herausgeber(in), Redakteur(in)
to face (a problem) [feɪs / ə 'prɒbləm] — (einem Problem) gegenüberstehen
to publish ['pʌblɪʃ] — veröffentlichen

Unit 11

A

acceptance [ək'septəns]	Akzeptanz, Annahme, Zustimmung
adolescent [ˌædə'lesnt]	Heranwachsende(r)
to adopt [ə'dɒpt]	annehmen
to analyse ['ænəlaɪz]	analysieren
briefcase ['briːfkeɪs]	Aktentasche
cardboard ['kɑːdbɔːd]	Karton
casual ['kæʒʊəl]	lässig
court case ['kɔːtkeɪs]	Rechtsfall, Streitsache vor Gericht
criminal ['krɪmɪnl]	Verbrecher(in), Kriminelle(r); verbrecherisch, kriminell
to define [dɪ'faɪn]	definieren
delinquency [dɪ'lɪŋkwənsɪ]	Kriminalität, Straffälligkeit
delinquent [dɪ'lɪŋkwənt]	Straftäter
to differentiate [ˌdɪfə'renʃɪeɪt]	unterscheiden, differenzieren
to drive someone mad [draɪv 'sʌmwʌn mæd]	jmdn. verrückt machen
farm worker ['fɑːm'wɜːkə]	landwirtschaftlicher Arbeiter
formal ['fɔːml]	formell, förmlich, formal
funny ['fʌnɪ]	lustig
to guard; guard [gɑːd]	bewachen; Wachposten, Wache
to hang around [hæŋ_ə'raʊnd]	herumhängen
to investigate [ɪn'vestɪgeɪt]	untersuchen
joke [dʒəʊk]	Witz
manner ['mænə]	Art und Weise
objective [əb'dʒektɪv]	Ziel; objektiv, sachlich
once upon a time [wʌns_əpɒn_ə 'taɪm]	es war einmal
to overlook; overlook [ˌəʊvə'lʊk]	übersehen; Aussicht
packing material ['pækɪŋ mə'tɪərɪəl]	Verpackungsmaterial
participant observation [ˌpɑː'tɪsɪpənt ˌɒbzə'veɪʃn]	teilnehmende Beobachtung
questionnaire [ˌkwestʃə'neə]	Fragebogen
researcher [rɪ'sɜːtʃə]	Forscher(in)
to search; search [sɜːtʃ]	(durch-)suchen; Suche
security [sɪ'kjʊərətɪ]	Sicherheit
sociologist [ˌsəʊsɪ'ɒlədʒɪst]	Soziologe, Soziologin
sociology [ˌsəʊsɪ'ɒlədʒɪ]	Soziologie
stranger ['streɪndʒə]	Fremde(r)
unwilling [ˌʌn'wɪlɪŋ]	nicht bereit
youngster ['jʌŋstə]	Jugendlicher

B

better off [ˌbetər_'ɒf]	(finanziell) besser gestellt
bracket ['brækɪt]	Klammer
Brazil [brə'zɪl]	Brasilien
carefree ['keəfriː]	sorgenfrei
else [els]	sonst (noch)
image ['ɪmɪdʒ]	Bild, Image
Italian [ɪ'tæljən]	Italiener(in); italienisch
on average [ɒn_'ævərɪdʒ]	im Durchschnitt
optimistic [ˌɒptɪ'mɪstɪk]	optimistisch
parent ['peərənt]	Elternteil
realistic [ˌrɪə'lɪstɪk]	realistisch
Spaniard ['spænjəd]	Spanier(in)
Spanish ['spænɪʃ]	spanisch
Sweden ['swiːdn]	Schweden
Swedish ['swiːdɪʃ]	schwedisch
up till now [ʌp_tɪl 'naʊ]	bis jetzt
violence ['vaɪələns]	Gewalt

C

at random [ət 'rændəm]	wahllos, willkürlich, zufällig
circumstances ['sɜːkəmstænsɪz]	Umstände
covert ['kʌvət]	verdeckt, heimlich
cross-section ['krɒs'sekʃn]	(repräsentativer) Querschnitt
to get on well with [get_ɒn 'wel wɪð]	gut auskommen mit
juvenile ['dʒuːvənaɪl]	jugendlich
longitudinal [ˌlɒŋgɪ'tjuːdɪnl]	längs verlaufend, Langzeit-
police force [pə'liːs fɔːs]	Polizei
to pretend [prɪ'tend]	vorgeben, tun, als ob
punishment ['pʌnɪʃmənt]	Bestrafung, Strafe
to represent [ˌreprɪ'zent]	darstellen, repräsentieren
representative [ˌreprɪ'zentətɪv]	Repräsentant(in); repräsentativ
sample ['sæmpl]	Auswahl, Probe
sexual exploits ['sekʃʊəl_'eksplɔɪts]	Sexualverhalten, sexuelle Abenteuer
social worker ['səʊʃl,wɜːkə]	Sozialarbeiter(in)
theft [θeft]	Diebstahl
to uncover [ʌn'kʌvə]	aufdecken

Unit 12

A

to abolish [ə'bɒlɪʃ]	abschaffen
acceptable [ək'septəbl]	akzeptabel, annehmbar
alcohol ['ælkəhɒl]	Alkohol
amnesia [æm'niːzjə]	Amnesie, Gedächtnisverlust
complaint [kəm'pleɪnt]	Beschwerde
confused [kən'fjuːzd]	verwirrt

crime [kraɪm] — Verbrechen
crime level ['kraɪm'levl] — Verbrechensrate
deprived [dɪ'praɪvd] — unterprivilegiert
drug [drʌg] — Droge
forgetfulness [fə'getfʊlnəs] — Vergesslichkeit
historical [hɪ'stɒrɪkl] — historisch
hooligan ['huːlɪgən] — Hooligan, Randalierer
immoral [ɪ'mɒrəl] — unmoralisch
income support ['ɪŋkʌm sə'pɔːt] — Sozialunterstützung
indicator ['ɪndɪkeɪtə] — Anzeiger, Indikator
judge [dʒʌdʒ] — Richter(in)
likely ['laɪklɪ] — wahrscheinlich
moral ['mɒrəl] — Moral; moralisch
to panic; panic ['pænɪk] — in Panik geraten, in Panik versetzen; Panik
to play truant [pleɪ 'truːənt] — (die Schule) schwänzen
to rebel; rebel [rɪ'bel] ['rebl] — rebellieren; Rebell
respectable [rɪ'spektəbl] — angesehen, anständig
rose-tinted glasses ['rəʊz'tɪntɪd 'glɑːsɪz] — rosarote Brille
to shock; shock [ʃɒk] — schockieren; Schock
shoplifting ['ʃɒp'lɪftɪŋ] — Ladendiebstahl
suicide ['sʊɪsaɪd] — Selbstmord
teenage ['tiːneɪdʒ] — im Teenageralter
unfulfilled ['ʌnfʊl'fɪld] — unerfüllt
variety [və'raɪətɪ] — Auswahl
victim ['vɪktɪm] — Opfer
violent ['vaɪələnt] — gewalttätig
youth training place [juːθ 'treɪnɪŋ pleɪs] — Ausbildungsplatz für Jugendliche

B

to ban [bæn] — verbieten
drive-by shooting [ˌdraɪvbaɪ 'ʃuːtɪŋ] — Schießen im Vorbeifahren
for fun [fə 'fʌn] — zum Spaß
gun [gʌn] — Gewehr, Schusswaffe
to kick; kick [kɪk] — treten; Tritt
to kick out of school [kɪk aʊt əv 'skuːl] — aus der Schule werfen
neighbourhood ['neɪbəhʊd] — Nachbarschaft
to pass by [pɑːs baɪ] — vorbeigehen, vorbeifahren
pick-up ['pɪkʌp] — Kleinlastwagen
prison ['prɪzn] — Gefängnis
to respect; respect [rɪ'spekt] — respektieren; Respekt
self-help [ˌself'help] — Selbsthilfe
to shoot, (shot, shot) [ʃuːt ʃɒt ʃɒt] — schießen
statement ['steɪtmənt] — Aussage, Angabe
truck [trʌk] — Lastwagen
weapon ['wepən] — Waffe

C

case study ['keɪsˌstʌdɪ] — Fallstudie
to get caught [get kɔːt] — ertappt werden
joyride ['dʒɔɪraɪd] — (wilde) Vergnügungsfahrt
to label; label ['leɪbl] — etikettieren, klassifizieren; Etikett
mate [meɪt] — Kumpel
movie ['muːvɪ] — Film
scrap yard ['skræpjɑːd] — Schrottplatz

Unit 13

A

to abuse; abuse [ə'bjuːz] [ə'bjuːs] — missbrauchen; Missbrauch
alcoholic [ˌælkə'hɒlɪk] — alkoholisch
birth control ['bɜːθkən'trəʊl] — Geburtenkontrolle
charity ['tʃærətɪ] — karitative Organisation, Wohlfahrt
church-run [ˌtʃɜːtʃ'rʌn] — kirchlich
to come to hand [kʌm tʊ 'hænd] — zur Verfügung stehen
to declare [dɪ'kleə] — verkünden
dependent [dɪ'pendənt] — abhängig, hier: minderjährig
deprivation [ˌdeprɪ'veɪʃn] — Entbehrung, Entzug
expectation [ˌekspek'teɪʃn] — Erwartung
expenses [ɪk'spensɪz] — Ausgaben
gambler ['gæmblə] — Spieler(in)
genius ['dʒiːnjəs] — Genie
illusion [ɪ'luːʒn] — Illusion, Einbildung
to insist (on) [ɪn'sɪst ɒn] — beharren, bestehen (auf)
junk [dʒʌŋk] — Gerümpel, Ramsch
kid [kɪd] — Kind, Jugendlicher
kindness ['kaɪndnəs] — Güte, Freundlichkeit
to live on welfare [lɪv ən 'welfeə] — von Sozialhilfe leben
loaf of bread [ləʊf əv 'bred] — Laib Brot
to make do [meɪk 'duː] — auskommen
middle-class [ˌmɪdl'klɑːs] — Mittelklasse
to mind one's own business [maɪnd wʌnz əʊn 'bɪznɪs] — sich um seine eigenen Angelegenheiten kümmern
to misuse; misuse [ˌmɪs'juːz] [ˌmɪs'juːs] — missbrauchen; Missbrauch
open air [ˌəʊpn'eə] — Freiluft-, draußen
recipient [rɪs'ɪpɪənt] — Empfänger
second hand [ˌsekənd'hænd] — aus zweiter Hand, gebraucht
sex [seks] — Geschlechtsverkehr, Geschlecht
to sign up for [saɪn 'ʌp fɔː] — sich einschreiben, anmelden
stereotype ['sterɪəʊtaɪp] — Stereotyp, Klischee

survival [sə'vaɪvl] — Überleben
uneducated [ˌʌn'edjʊkeɪtɪd] — ungebildet
vast [vɑːst] — riesig, weit
whatever [wɒt'evə] — was auch immer

B

absent ['æbsənt] — abwesend
agency ['eɪdʒənsɪ] — Agentur, Geschäftsstelle
granddaughter ['græn,dɔːtə] — Enkelin
low-paid [ˌləʊ'peɪd] — schlecht bezahlt
monthly ['mʌnθlɪ] — monatlich
Northern Ireland [ˌnɔːðən_'aɪələnd] — Nordirland
president ['prezɪdənt] — Präsident(in), Vorsitzende(r)
retirement [rɪ'taɪəmənt] — Ruhestand
retirement benefit [rɪ'taɪəmənt 'benɪfɪt] — Rente, Pension
social security [ˌsəʊʃl sɪ'kjʊərətɪ] — staatliche Sozialleistungen, Sozialversicherung
workday ['wɜːkdeɪ] — Arbeitstag

C

clothing ['kləʊðɪŋ] — Kleidung
cultural ['kʌltʃərəl] — kulturell
damp [dæmp] — feucht
encouragement [ɪn'kʌrɪdʒmənt] — Ermutigung
gang [gæŋ] — Bande
inadequate [ɪn'ædɪkwət] — nicht ausreichend, unangemessen
material [mə'tɪərɪəl] — materiell
peer group ['pɪəgruːp] — Gruppe von Gleichgesinnten
poorly paid ['pɔːlɪ peɪd] — schlecht bezahlt
unstable [ˌʌn'steɪbl] — unstabil
voluntary organization ['vɒləntrɪ_ˌɔːgənaɪ'zeɪʃn] — freiwillige Organisation

Unit 14

A

authority [ɔː'θɒrətɪ] — Autorität
authorities [ɔː'θɒrətɪz] — Behörde(n)
counterpart ['kaʊntəpɑːt] — Gegenspieler(in)
to criticize ['krɪtɪsaɪz] — kritisieren
to do badly in school [duː 'bædlɪ_ɪn 'skuːl] — in der Schule schlecht abschneiden
to do well in school [duː 'wel_ɪn 'skuːl] — in der Schule gut abschneiden
to encourage [ɪn'kʌrɪdʒ] — ermutigen
to fall behind [fɔːl bɪ'haɪnd] — zurückfallen, zurückbleiben

first school [fɜːst skuːl] — Grundschule
for free [fə 'friː] — gratis, umsonst
inability [ˌɪnə'bɪlətɪ] — Unfähigkeit
insurance cover [ɪn'ʃɔːrəns 'kʌvə] — Versicherungsschutz
local government ['ləʊkl 'gʌvnmənt] — Stadtrat
open-minded [ˌəʊpn'maɪndɪd] — aufgeschlossen, vorurteilslos
ordinary ['ɔːdɪnrɪ] — normal, gewöhnlich
potential [pə'tenʃl] — Potential, Möglichkeiten; potentiell, möglich
performance [pə'fɔːməns] — Leistung
preconceived idea ['priːkənsiːvd aɪ'dɪə] — vorgefasste Meinung
race [reɪs] — Rasse
racial discrimination ['reɪʃl dɪ'skrɪmɪ'neɪʃn] — Rassendiskriminierung
racism ['reɪsɪzm] — Rassismus
ratio ['reɪʃɪəʊ] — Verhältnis
secondary school ['sekəndrɪ skuːl] — weiterführende Schule
skin [skɪn] — Haut
teaching ['tiːtʃɪŋ] — Unterricht
to threaten ['θretn] — bedrohen
tuition [tjuː'ɪʃn] — Unterricht
under-achiever [ˌʌndərə'tʃiːvə] — leistungsschwache(r) Schüler(in)
volunteer ['vɒlən'tɪə] — Freiwillige(r)
West Indies [west_'ɪndɪz] — Westindien (Karibik)

B

association [əˌsəʊsɪ'eɪʃn] — Vereinigung
Californian [ˌkælɪ'fɔːnjən] — kalifornisch
conditional [kən'dɪʃənl] — Konditional
green card [griːn kɑːd] — Aufenthaltserlaubnis
high school ['haɪskuːl] — Oberschule
Third World [θɜːd wɜːld] — Dritte Welt

C

bored [bɔːd] — gelangweilt
ethnic ['eθnɪk] — ethnisch
hero ['hɪərəʊ] — Held
proper ['prɒpə] — richtig, ordentlich

Unit 15

A

amazing [ə'meɪzɪŋ] — erstaunlich
annual ['ænjʊəl] — jährlich
art [ɑːt] — Kunst
beauty ['bjuːtɪ] — Schönheit
beyond [bɪ'jɒnd] — jenseits, darüber hinaus
Chunnel = Channel Tunnel ['tʃʌnl] ['tʃænl 'tʌnl] — Tunnel unter dem Ärmelkanal

day trip ['deɪtrɪp] — Tagesausflug
educated ['edʒʊkeɪtɪd] — gebildet
English Channel — Ärmelkanal
  ['ɪŋglɪʃ 'tʃænl]
evident ['evɪdənt] — offensichtlich, deutlich
to explore [ɪks'plɔː] — erforschen
familiar [fə'mɪljə] — vertraut
fellow countryman — Landsmann
  ['feləʊ 'kʌntrɪmən]
ferry ['ferɪ] — Fähre
for its own sake — um seiner selbst willen
  [fər_ɪts_'əʊn 'seɪk]
institution [ˌɪnstɪ'tjuːʃn] — Institution, Einführung, Anstalt
to modernize ['mɒdənaɪz] — modernisieren
negligible ['neglɪdʒəbl] — unerheblich
package holiday — Pauschalurlaub
  ['pækɪdʒ ˌhɒlɪdeɪ]
to populate ['pɒpjʊleɪt] — bevölkern
prepared [prɪ'peəd] — bereit
rare [reə] — selten
sea-going ['siː'gəʊɪŋ] — seefahrend
to seek, (sought, sought) — suchen
  [siːk sɔːt sɔːt]
to set eyes on [set — sehen
  'aɪz_ɒn]
to sink, (sank, sunk) — sinken
  [sɪŋk sæŋk sʌŋk]
to sink in [sɪŋk_ɪn] — ins Bewusstsein dringen
stained glass window — bleiverglastes Fenster
  ['steɪnglɑːs 'wɪndəʊ]
stretch of water — Wasserstraße
  [stretʃ_əv 'wɔːtə]
to tackle ['tækl] — angehen, in Angriff nehmen
tourism ['tʊərɪzm] — Tourismus
traveller ['trævlə] — Reisende(r)
weekday ['wiːkdeɪ] — Wochentag
wild [waɪld] — wild

B

action ['ækʃn] — Maßnahme, Aktion
to attract [ə'trækt] — anziehen
commission [kə'mɪʃn] — Kommission
crisis ['kraɪsɪs] — Krise
negative ['negətɪv] — negativ
presidency ['prezɪdənsɪ] — Präsidentschaft
qualified ['kwɒlɪfaɪd] — qualifiziert
regional ['riːdʒənl] — regional
sector ['sektə] — Sektor, Bereich

C

pursuit [pə'sjuːt] — Beschäftigung, Betätigung, Jagd

Unit 16

(well-)acquainted — (gut) bekannt
  [ˌwel_ə'kweɪntɪd]
accusation [ˌækjʊ'zeɪʃn] — Anschuldigung
crack addict ['kræk_ˌædɪkt] — Crack-Abhängige(r)
flight [flaɪt] — Flucht
foster care ['fɒstə_ˌkeə] — bei Pflegeeltern
homeless ['həʊmləs] — obdachlos
in care [ˌɪn_'keə] — in Pflege
to go missing [ˌgəʊ 'mɪsɪŋ] — verschwinden
to keep up with — Schritt halten mit
  [ˌkiːp_'ʌp wɪð]
needle in a haystack — Nadel im Heuhaufen
  [ˌniːdl_ɪn_ə 'heɪstæk]
painful ['peɪnfʊl] — schmerzhaft
to permit [pə'mɪt] — erlauben
runaway ['rʌnəweɪ] — Ausreißer
self-esteem [ˌselfə'stiːm] — Selbstachtung
sighting ['saɪtɪŋ] — Sichten
to be unfamiliar with sth. — etw. nicht kennen, mit
  [bɪˌʌnfə'mljə wɪð ˌsʌmðɪŋ]   etw. nicht vertraut sein

Unit 17

to affect [ə'fekt] — beeinflussen
brain [breɪn] — Gehirn
carer ['keərə] — Pfleger(in)
cerebral palsy (CP) — zerebrale Lähmung
  [ˌserəbrl 'pɔːlzɪ]
determined [dɪ'tɜːmɪnd] — fest entschlossen
disabled [dɪ'seɪbld] — behindert
failure ['feɪljə] — Versagen
to fulfill [fʊl'fɪl] — erfüllen
health and social services — Amt für Gesundheit und
  ['helθ_ənd ˌsəʊʃl 'sɜːvɪsɪz]   Soziales
muscle ['mʌsl] — Muskel
noticeable ['nəʊtɪsəbl] — bemerkbar
red tape [ˌred'teɪp] — Bürokratie
request [rɪ'kwest] — Bitte
severe [sə'vɪə] — schwerwiegend
speech aids ['spiːtʃ_ˌeɪdz] — Sprachhilfen
to triple ['trɪpl] — verdreifachen
walking frame — Gehhilfe
  ['wɔːkɪŋ_ˌfreɪm]
wheelchair ['wiːltʃeə] — Rollstuhl

Unit 18

beat [biːt] — hier: Takt
dehydration — Austrocknung, Dehydration
  [ˌdiːhaɪ'dreɪʃn]
drug counsellor — Drogenberater
  ['drʌg_ˌkaʊnsələ]
Ecstasy ['ekstəsɪ] — Ecstasy (Name einer Droge)

to fail [feɪl]	versagen
glamorous ['glæmərəs]	schick, glamourös
hopelessness ['həʊpləsnəs]	Hoffnungslosigkeit
ingredients [ɪn'gri:dɪənts]	Bestandteile
organs ['ɔːgənz]	Organe
pleasurable ['pleʒərəbl]	angenehm
rave [reɪv]	Rave (größere Tanzveranstaltung zu Technomusik)
to start off [ˌstɑːt 'ɒf]	anfangen, hier: seinen/ihren Ausgangspunkt haben
Yuppie ['jʌpɪ]	Yuppie (junger karrierebewusster großstädtischer Mensch)

Unit 19

awareness [ə'weənəs]	Bewusstsein
to block out [ˌblɒk 'aʊt]	ausblenden
bloodshed ['blʌdʃed]	Blutvergießen
to commit a crime [kəˌmɪt ə 'kraɪm]	ein Verbrechen begehen
to flash [flæʃ]	hier: zeigen
massacre ['mæsəkə]	Massaker, Blutbad
murder [mɜːdə]	Mord
psychiatrist [saɪ'kaɪətrɪst]	Psychiater(in)
psychologist [saɪ'kɒlədʒɪst]	Psychologe, Psychologin
viewing habits ['vjuːɪŋ ˌhæbɪts]	Fernsehgewohnheiten
'watershed hours' ['wɔːtəʃedˌaʊəz]	Zeitpunkt, vor dem für Kinder ungeeignetes Material nicht im Fernsehen gezeigt werden darf

Unit 20

airy ['eərɪ]	luftig
clay [kleɪ]	Ton
confident ['kɒnfɪdənt]	selbstbewusst
cosy ['kəʊzɪ]	gemütlich
craft and messy area [ˌkrɑːft ənd 'mesɪ ˌeərɪə]	Bastelecke
day nursery school [ˌdeɪ 'nɜːsərɪ ˌskuːl]	Kindertagesstätte, Hort
educational [ˌedjʊ'keɪʃənl]	pädagogisch; Lehr-
floor and tabletop toys [ˌflɔːr ənd 'teɪbltɒp ˌtɔɪz]	Boden- und Tisch-Spielzeuge
imaginative [ɪ'mædʒɪnətɪv]	phantasievoll
to incorporate [ɪn'kɔːpəreɪt]	enthalten, beinhalten
nursery school ['nɜːsərɪ ˌskuːl]	Kindergarten
nursery school assistant/child carer [ˌnɜːsərɪskuːlə'sɪstənt/ˈtʃaɪldˌkeərə]	Kinderpfleger(in)
nursery school teacher [ˌnɜːsərɪskuːl 'tiːtʃə]	Erzieher(in), Kindergärtner(in)
nutritionally balanced menu [njuːˈtrɪʃnəlɪ ˌbælənst 'menjuː]	ausgewogene Ernährung
pace [peɪs]	Geschwindigkeit
peace of mind ['piːs əv 'maɪnd]	Seelenfrieden
pre-reading and -writing [ˌpriːˈriːdɪŋ ənd 'raɪtɪŋ]	erste Versuche im Lesen und Schreiben
reception class [rɪ'sepʃn ˌklɑːs]	Vorschulklasse
role play ['rəʊlpleɪ]	Rollenspiel
session ['seʃn]	Sitzung, Zeitabschnitt
toddler ['tɒdlə]	Kleinkind
to treat [triːt]	behandeln

AE = American English
BE = British English

A

a bit	ein bisschen
a couple of*	ein paar
a little	etwas, ein bisschen
a lot of	viel
a number of	einige
ability	Fähigkeit
to be able	können
to abolish	abschaffen
to be about	sich um etwas handeln
above	oben
abroad	im/ins Ausland
absent	abwesend
to abuse; abuse	missbrauchen; Missbrauch
to accept	annehmen, akzeptieren
acceptable	akzeptabel, annehmbar
acceptance	Akzeptanz, Annahme, Zustimmung
access	Zugang, Zutritt
accident	Unfall
accommo-dation	Unterkunft, Zimmer
according to (him)/(her)	(seiner)/(ihrer) Meinung nach, laut
to account for	ausmachen, erklären
accountancy	Rechnungswesen
accurate	genau
accusation	Anschuldigung
to accuse	beschuldigen, anklagen
to ache; ache	schmerzen; Schmerz
to achieve	erreichen, erzielen
acid rain	saurer Regen
(well-)acquainted	(gut) bekannt
to acquire	sich aneignen
to act	handeln
action	Maßnahme, Aktion
active	aktiv
activity	Aktivität
actual	tatsächlich
to adapt	bearbeiten
to add	hinzufügen, addieren
addictive	süchtig machend
additional	zusätzlich
address	Adresse
adjective	Adjektiv
adolescent	Heranwachsende(r)
to adopt	annehmen

*(*Der als bekannt vorausgesetzte Grundwortschatz ist kursiv gedruckt.)*

adult	Erwachsene(r)
advanced	fortgeschritten
advantage	Vorteil
adventure	Abenteuer
advert	Kurzform von „advertisement" = Werbeanzeige
to advertise	werben, inserieren
advertisement	(Werbe-)Anzeige
advertiser	Inserent(in), Auf-traggeber(in) von Werbesendungen
advertising	Werbung
advertising campaign	Werbekampagne
advertising manager	Werbeleiter(in)
advice	Rat(schlag)
to advise	(be)raten
to affect	beeinflussen
affinity	Verbundenheit, Verwandtschaft
to afford	sich leisten
to be afraid (of)	Angst haben (vor)
after all	schließlich
afternoon	Nachmittag
afterwards	danach
again	wieder
again and again	immer wieder
against	gegen
age	(Zeit-)Alter
aged ...	... Jahre alt
agency	Agentur, Geschäftsstelle
aggressive	aggressiv
to agree	einverstanden sein, zustimmen
agreement	Übereinstimmung, Übereinkunft
agricultural	landwirtschaftlich
aid	Hilfe, Hilfsmittel
to aim (at); aim	zielen (auf); Ziel
air	Luft
airport	Flughafen
airtime	Sendezeit
airy	luftig
alcohol	Alkohol
alcoholic	alkoholisch
alive	lebend, lebendig, aktiv
all	alle(s), ganz
all but	fast
all kind(s) of	alle Arten von, alle möglichen
all over the world	in der ganzen Welt
all-inclusive	alles beinhaltend
to allow	erlauben
almost	fast, beinahe
alone	allein

along	entlang
already	schon
also	auch
alternative	Alternative, Wahl; alternativ
although	obwohl
altogether	insgesamt, völlig
always	immer
amazing	erstaunlich
ambition	Ehrgeiz, Ambition
Amerasian	amerikanisch-asiatisch
amnesia	Amnesie, Gedächtnisverlust
among	zwischen, unter
amount	Betrag, Summe
to analyse	analysieren
anger	Zorn, Wut
angry	wütend
animal	Tier
to announce	bekannt geben, ansagen
announcement	Bekanntgabe, Durchsage
annual	jährlich
annual output	Jahresproduktion
another	noch eine(r), ein(e) andere(r)
to answer; answer	(be)antworten; Antwort
antonym	Antonym, Wort mit gegensätzlicher Bedeutung
any	irgendeine(r,s)
anybody	irgendjemand
anyone	irgendjemand
anything	irgendetwas
anytime	jederzeit
to apologize	sich entschuldigen
apparatus	Gerät
to appear	(er)scheinen
apple	Apfel
appliance	Gerät
applicant	Bewerber(in)
application	Anwendung
to apply (for)	sich bewerben (um)
to appoint	ernennen, bestimmen
appointment	Verabredung, Termin, Ernennung
approach	Ansatz, Annäherung
approval	Zustimmung
archbishop	Erzbischof
area	Gebiet
to argue	argumentieren, behaupten
arms	Waffen
around	herum, um, ungefähr
to arrange	aufstellen, planen, veranlassen
arrangement	Vereinbarung, Arrangement

to arrest; arrest	verhaften; Verhaftung	back	Rücken; zurück	billion	Billion, (AE: Milliarde)
arrival	Ankunft	back-up	Unterstützung	biomass	Biomasse
to arrive	ankommen	background	Hintergrund, Herkunft, Verhältnisse	bird	Vogel
art	Kunst			birth	Geburt
article	Artikel	bad	schlecht, schlimm, böse	birth control	Geburtenkontrolle
as	wie, da, als			birthday	Geburtstag
as a result	folglich	bag	Tüte, Tasche	biscuit	Keks
as well	auch, ebensogut	baggage	Gepäck	bit	Stückchen
as well as	sowie	bagless	hier: ohne Staubsaugerbeutel	to bite, (bit, bitten)	beißen
ash	Asche				
Asian	Asiat(in); asiatisch	to bake	backen	black	schwarz
to ask (for)	fragen, bitten (um)	baker	Bäcker(in)	blackboard	(Wand-)Tafel
to assemble	zusammenbauen	balcony	Balkon	to blame (for)	verantwortlich machen (für)
assertiveness	Selbstbewusstsein	Baltic	baltisch; Ostsee		
asset	Vermögen(-swert), Besitz	to ban	verbieten	to blink	blinken
		bank	Bank (Geldinstitut)	block of flats	Wohnblock
assistance	Hilfe	bank holiday	öffentl. Feiertag	to block out	ausblenden
assistant	Assistent(in)	bar graph	Säulendiagramm	blood	Blut
to associate	assoziieren, in Verbindung bringen	base	Basis, Stützpunkt, Ausgangspunkt	bloodshed	Blutvergießen
				blue	blau
association	Vereinigung	basic	Grund-; grundlegend	board	Brett
at all costs	um jeden Preis	basket	Korb	boat	Boot
at first	anfangs	bathroom	Badezimmer	body	Körper
at home	zu Hause	to be unfamiliar with sth.	etw. nicht kennen, mit etw. nicht vertraut sein	bog	Moor
at last	schließlich, endlich			to boil	kochen
at least	wenigstens			bold type	Fettdruck
at once	sofort	beach	Strand	bone	Knochen
at present	im Augenblick, jetzt	beard	Bart	to book; book	buchen; Buch
at random	wahllos, willkürlich, zufällig	beat	hier: Takt	booking	Buchung
		beautiful	schön	bookshop	Buchhandlung
at the moment	jetzt, im Moment	beauty	Schönheit	boot	Stiefel
at work	bei der Arbeit	because	weil	border	Grenze
to attack	in Angriff nehmen, angreifen	because of	wegen	bored	gelangweilt
		to become, (became, become)	werden	boring	langweilig
to attend	(Schule) besuchen			to borrow	sich ausleihen
attendance	Besuch			both	beide
attention	Aufmerksamkeit	bed	Bett	bottle	Flasche
attitude	Haltung, Einstellung	bedroom	Schlafzimmer	bottom	Boden
to attract	anziehen	bedsitter	Einzimmerwohnung	(to be) bound (to do sth.)	(etwas) bestimmt (tun), verpflichtet, unterwegs
attraction	Anziehungskraft	beer	Bier		
attractive	reizvoll, anziehend, attraktiv	before	vorher, ehe		
		to begin, (began, begun)	beginnen	boundary	Grenze
audio	Audio, Hör-			box	Schachtel, Karton, Kiste
aunt	Tante				
Austria	Österreich	beginner	Anfänger(in)	boy	Junge
author	Autor(in), Verfasser(in)	beginning	Anfang	to boycott; boycott	boykottieren; Boykott
		behaviour	Benehmen		
authorities	Behörde(n)	behind	hinter	boyfriend	Freund
authority	Autorität	Belgian	Belgier(in); belgisch	bracket	Klammer
to automate	automatisieren	Belgium	Belgien	brain	Gehirn
automatic	automatisch	to believe	glauben	brand name	Markenname
autumn	Herbst	to belong to	gehören zu	Brazil	Brasilien
availability	Vorhandensein, Verfügbarkeit	benefit	Zuwendung, soziale Leistung	bread	Brot
				to break, (broke, broken); break	(zer)brechen; Pause
available	verfügbar, vorhanden	best	am besten		
average	Durchschnitt	best known	bekannteste(r,s)	to break down	zusammenbrechen
to avoid	vermeiden	best wishes	alles Gute	breakfast	Frühstück
awareness	Bewusstsein	better	besser	bridge	Brücke
away	weg	better off	(finanziell) besser gestellt	briefcase	Aktentasche
awful	furchtbar, schrecklich			bright	hell, strahlend
		between	zwischen	to bring, (brought, brought)	bringen
		beyond	jenseits, darüber hinaus		
B				broadband	Breitband
		bicycle	Fahrrad	to broadcast, (broadcast, broadcast)	übertragen, senden
Bachelor of Arts (B.A.)	niedrigster akad. Grad	big	groß		
		bike	Fahrrad (Kurzform)		
		bill	Rechnung		

to broaden the mind	den Horizont erweitern	capital	Großbuchstabe, Hauptstadt	China	China
brochure	Broschüre, Prospekt	car	Auto	Chinese	Chinese, Chinesin; chinesisch
brother	Bruder	car body	Karosserie	chips	Pommes Frites, Kartoffelchips
brown	braun	car park	Parkplatz		
to brush; brush	bürsten; Bürste	card	Karte	chocolate	Schokolade, Praline
BTEC National Diploma	etwa: Fachhochschul-reifeprüfung	cardboard	Karton	choice	Wahl
BTU British Thermal Unit	BTU = Brit. Wärmeeinheit	cardiologist	Herzspezialist(in)	to choose, (chose, chosen)	(aus)wählen
		to care; care	sorgen; Sorge		
bubble	Blase	career	Beruf, Laufbahn, Karriere	Christmas	Weihnachten
to build, (built, built)	bauen			Chunnel = Channel Tunnel	Tunnel unter dem Ärmelkanal
building	Gebäude	carefree	sorgenfrei		
bulb	(Glüh)birne	careful	sorgfältig	church	Kirche
bumper	Stoßstange	careless	sorglos	church-run	kirchlich
bureaucracy	Bürokratie	carer	Pfleger(in)	cigarette	Zigarette
to burn, (burnt, burnt)	brennen	cargo	Fracht, Ladung	CIM (Computer Integrated Manu-facturing)	Computerintegrierte Fertigung
		to carry	tragen		
bus pass	Busausweis	to carry out	ausführen		
business	Geschäft	cartridge	Kassette, Patrone	cinema	Kino
business studies	etwa: Fachbereich Wirtschaft	case	Fall, Koffer, Kiste	circle	Kreis, Kreislauf
		case study	Fallstudie	circumstances	Umstände
busy	beschäftigt	cash	Bargeld	citizen	Bürger(in)
but	aber	cassette	Kassette	city	Stadt
butcher	Metzger(in)	casual	lässig	civil engineering	Bauwesen, Hoch- und Tiefbau
to buy, (bought, bought)	kaufen	cat	Katze		
		to catch, (caught, caught)	fangen	civilized	zivilisiert
buyer	Käufer(in)			to claim; claim	behaupten, bean-spruchen; Anspruch
by	durch, bei, neben, bis	to cause; cause	verursachen; Ursache		
by far	bei weitem	ceiling	(Zimmer-)Decke	class	Klasse
by rail	mit der Bahn	cell	Zelle	classmate	Klassenkamerad(in)
by the way	übrigens	Central Electricity Generating Board (CEGB)	etwa: zentrale Energieversorgung (England/Wales)	classroom	Klassenzimmer
by-product	Nebenprodukt			clay	Ton
				to clean; clean	reinigen; sauber
C		centre	Zentrum, Mittelpunkt	to clear; clear	säubern, räumen; klar
		century	Jahrhundert	clever	klug
cabinet	Kabinett, Schrank	cerebral palsy (CP)	zerebrale Lähmung	climate	Klima
cable	Kabel			to climb	klettern
cable TV	Kabelfernsehen	certain	sicher	clock	Uhr
CAD (Computer Aided Design)	Computerunterstützte Zeichnung (Entwurf)	certificate	Zeugnis	to close; close	schließen; dicht, nahe
		CFC (chloro-fluorocarbon)	FCKW (Fluorchlor-kohlenwasserstoff)	to close down	schließen, zumachen (Betrieb, Firma)
cake	Kuchen				
to calculate	(be)rechnen	chain	Kette	clothes	Kleidung
Californian	kalifornisch	chair	Stuhl	clothing	Kleidung
to call; call	(an)rufen, nennen; Anruf	chalk	Kreide	cloud	Wolke
		to change; change	wechseln, (sich) (ver)ändern; Wechsel(-geld), Änderung	coach	Trainer(in)
to call up	anrufen			coaching days	Postkutschenzeit
call centre	Callcenter, telefon. Auskunftsdienst			coal	Kohle
				coast	Küste
CAM (Computer Aided Manu-facturing)	Computerunter-stützte Fertigung	channel	Kanal	coastal	Küsten-
		charity	karitative Organi-sation, Wohlfahrt	coat	Mantel
				to code; code	kodieren; Kode
camera	Kamera	chart	Schaubild, Tabelle, Karte	coffee	Kaffee
to camp; camp	zelten, lagern; Lager			coin	Münze
campaign	Kampagne, Werbefeldzug	cheap	billig	cold	kalt
		to check; check	kontrollieren; Kontrolle	colleague	Kollege, Kollegin
campus	Campus, Universitäts-gelände			to collect	sammeln, abholen
		cheers	Tschüs!, Prost!	collection	Sammlung
can	Büchse, Dose; können	cheese	Käse	college	College, Fach(hoch)schule
can't stand	nicht ausstehen können	chemist	Chemiker(in)		
		child	Kind	Colombia	Kolumbien
candidate	Bewerber(in)	child carer	Kinderpfleger(in)	colour	Farbe
canteen	Kantine	childcare assistant	Kinderpfleger(in)	column	Spalte
capacity	Kapazität, Leistungsfähigkeit			to comb; comb	kämmen; Kamm
		childhood	Kindheit	to combine	verbinden, vereinigen

to come, (came, come) — kommen
to come into operation — in Kraft treten
to come to hand — zur Verfügung stehen
to come true — wahr werden
comfortable — bequem
command — Befehl
to comment; comment — kommentieren; Bemerkung, Kommentar
commercial — Werbespot; kaufmännisch
commission — Kommission
to commit a crime — ein Verbrechen begehen
to communicate — kommunizieren, übermitteln
communication — Kommunikation, Übermittlung
communist era — kommunistisches Zeitalter
community — Bevölkerungsgruppe, Gemeinde
commuter — Pendler(in)
company — Gesellschaft, Firma
to compare — vergleichen
competition — Wettbewerb, Konkurrenz
competitive — wettbewerbsfähig
competitor — Konkurrent(in), Teilnehmer(in)
complaint — Beschwerde
to complete; complete — vervollständigen; vollständig
complex — komplex, kompliziert
complicated — kompliziert
complication — Komplikation
composting — Kompostierung
comprehension — Verständnis
comprehensive school — Gesamtschule
to concentrate (on) — sich konzentrieren (auf)
concentration — Konzentration
concerned — betroffen, interessiert
condition — Bedingung
conditional — Konditional
conference — Konferenz, Tagung
confident — selbstbewusst
to confirm — bestätigen
confused — verwirrt
congested — überfüllt, verstopft
congestion — Stau
to connect — verbinden
connection — Verbindung, Zusammenhang
connector — Verbinder, Stecker
conscious — bewusst
conservative — konservativ
to consider — betrachten, denken (an), berücksichtigen
to consist of — bestehen aus
constant — ständig, gleichbleibend

constituency — Wahlkreis
constructive — konstruktiv
to consult — (sich) beraten, zu Rate ziehen
consumer — Verbraucher(in)
consumption — Verbrauch
to contact; contact — sich in Verbindung setzen mit; Verbindung, Kontakt
to contain — enthalten
container — Behälter
continent — Kontinent, Erdteil
continental — kontinental
to continue — fortsetzen, weitermachen, weitergehen
contract — Vertrag
to contrast; contrast — gegenüberstellen, vergleichen; Gegensatz
to contribute — beitragen
contribution — Beitrag
to control; control — kontollieren, steuern; Kontrolle, hier: Regeltechnik
convenient — günstig, praktisch
conversation — Unterhaltung, Gespräch
conveyor — Förderband
conveyor belt — Förderband, Fließband
convinced — überzeugt
to cook; cook — kochen; Koch, Köchin
cooker — Herd
cookie — Keks, Plätzchen
to cooperate — zusammenarbeiten
cooperation — Zusammenarbeit
to cope with — mit etwas zurechtkommen
to copy; copy — abschreiben, kopieren; Kopie, Exemplar
corn — Getreide, Mais, Korn
corner — Ecke
corporation — Gesellschaft, Körperschaft
to correct; correct — korrigieren, verbessern; richtig
correction — Verbesserung, Korrektur
to correspond — entsprechen, übereinstimmen, korrespondieren
cosmopolitan — kosmopolitisch
to cost, (cost, cost); cost — kosten; Kosten
cost-efficient — kostengünstig
cosy — gemütlich
cotton — Baumwolle
council — (Stadt-, Grafschafts-) Rat
to count — zählen, ins Gewicht fallen
counter — Ladentisch, Schalter
to counteract — entgegenwirken
counterpart — Gegenspieler(in)
country — Land
countryside — Landschaft

county — Grafschaft, Bezirk
couple — (Ehe-)Paar
courage — Mut
course — Kurs, Lauf, Gang, Strecke
court case — Rechtsfall, Streitsache vor Gericht
to cover; cover — (be)decken; Abdeckung, Umschlag
coverage — hier: Ausstattung
covert — verdeckt, heimlich
cow — Kuh
crack addict — Crack-Abhängige(r)
craft and messy area — Bastelecke
crane — Kran
to crash — zusammenbrechen
crazy — verrückt
to create — schaffen, verursachen
creative — kreativ
crime — Verbrechen
crime level — Verbrechensrate
criminal — Verbrecher(in), Kriminelle(r); verbrecherisch, kriminell
crisis — Krise
critical — kritisch
to criticize — kritisieren
to cross — überqueren
crossing — Kreuzung
crossroads — Kreuzung
cross-section — (repräsentativer) Querschnitt
crowd — (Menschen-)Menge
crowded — dicht gedrängt, voll
to cry; cry — schreien, weinen; Schrei
cultural — kulturell
cultural shock — Kulturschock
culture — Kultur
cup — Tasse, Pokal
curious — neugierig, seltsam
currency — Währung
current — aktuell, gegenwärtig
curtain — Vorhang
customer — Kunde, Kundin
customer-orientated — kundenorientiert
customs — Zoll, Zoll-
to cut, (cut, cut); cut — schneiden; Schnitt
CV = curriculum vitae — Lebenslauf
to cycle — Fahrrad fahren

D

daily — täglich
to damage; damage — beschädigen; Schaden
damp — feucht
to dance; dance — tanzen; Tanz
dancer — Tänzer(in)
danger — Gefahr

dangerous	gefährlich	Denmark	Dänemark	disabled	behindert
dark	dunkel	department	Abteilung	disadvantage	Nachteil
darkness	Dunkelheit	department	Kaufhaus	to disagree	anderer Meinung
dashboard	Armaturenbrett	store		(with)	sein, nicht über-
data	Daten	to depend (on)	abhängen (von)		einstimmen (mit)
data	Datenverarbeitung	dependent	abhängig, hier:	disagreement	abweichende Mei-
processing			minderjährig		nung, Meinungs-
date	Datum, Zeitpunkt,	deposit	Lagerstätte,		verschiedenheit
	Verabredung		Guthaben	disappearance	Verschwinden
date of birth	Geburtsdatum	deprivation	Entbehrung, Entzug	disaster	Katastrophe
daughter	Tochter	deprived	unterprivilegiert	discount	Rabatt
day	Tag	to describe	beschreiben	to discover	entdecken
day by day	Tag für Tag	description	Beschreibung	to discuss	besprechen,
day nursery	Kindertagesstätte,	to design;	entwerfen,		diskutieren
school	Hort	design	konstruieren;	discussion	Gespräch, Unter-
day trip	Tagesausflug		Entwurf, Muster		redung, Diskussion
dead	tot	designer	Zeichner(in),	to dislike	nicht mögen
to deal, (dealt,	handeln (mit, von);		Designer(in)	to dismantle	zerlegen,
dealt) (in,	Geschäft	desk	Schreibtisch		demontieren
with); deal		desperate	verzweifelt	disorder	Durcheinander,
dealer	Händler(in)	destination	Reiseziel, Zielort		Funktionsstörung
dear	lieb	to destroy	zerstören	to display;	zeigen; Anzeige
Dear Madam	Sehr geehrte Dame	destruction	Zerstörung	display	
Dear Sir	Sehr geehrter Herr	detail	Einzelheit, Detail	disposal	Beseitigung,
death	Tod	determination	Entschlossenheit,		Entsorgung
to debate;	debattieren,		Bestimmung	distance	Entfernung, Strecke,
debate	diskutieren;	determined	fest entschlossen		Abstand
	Debatte	to develop	entwickeln	district	Gegend
decade	Jahrzehnt, Dekade,	developer	Entwickler(in), Bau-	diversion	Umleitung
	zehn Jahre		unternehmer(in)	diversity	Vielfalt,
to decide	(sich) entscheiden	developing	Entwicklungsland		Verschiedenheit
decision	Entscheidung	country		to divide	teilen
decision-	Entscheidungs-	development	Entwicklung	to do badly in	in der Schule schlecht
making	prozess	device	Gerät	school	abschneiden
process		diagram	Diagramm	to do well in	in der Schule gut
to declare	verkünden	to dial	(Telefon) wählen	school	abschneiden
to decline;	sich verschlechtern,	dialogue	Dialog	doctor	Arzt, Ärztin
decline	sinken; Niedergang,	diamond	Diamant	document	Dokument, Unterlage
	Verschlechterung	diary	Tagebuch,	dog	Hund
to decrease;	abnehmen,		Terminkalender	domestic	häuslich
decrease	vermindern;	to dictate	diktieren	domestic trip	Inlandsausflug
	Abnahme	dictation	Diktat	to dominate	beherrschen,
deep	tief	dictionary	Wörterbuch		dominieren
to defend	verteidigen	to die	sterben	door	Tür
defender	Verteidiger(in)	to differ (from)	sich unterscheiden	to double	(sich) verdoppeln
to define	definieren		(von)	down	hinunter, unten
definite	eindeutig, bestimmt	difference	Unterschied	down payment	Anzahlung
degree	akad. Grad, Diplom,	different	unterschiedlich	downstairs	die Treppe hinunter,
	Grad (Temperatur)	to differentiate	unterscheiden,		unten, im
dehydration	Austrocknung,		differenzieren		Erdgeschoss
	Dehydration	difficult	schwierig	to draft; draft	entwerfen; Entwurf,
to delay; delay	verzögern;	difficulty	Schwierigkeit		Konzept
	Verzögerung,	to dig, (dug,	(aus)graben	draughtsman	Zeichner(in)
	Verspätung	dug) (up)		to draw	zeichnen, ziehen
delinquency	Kriminalität,	digital	digital	drawing	Zeichnung
	Straffälligkeit	dining-room	Esszimmer	to dream;	träumen; Traum
delinquent	Straftäter	dinner	(Mittag-, Abend-)	dream	
to deliver	liefern, (Rede) halten		Essen	to dress; dress	(sich) anziehen;
delivery	Lieferung	to dip	(in Farbe) eintauchen		Kleid, Kleidung
delivery hall	An-/Auslieferungs-	direct speech	direkte Rede	to drink, (drank,	trinken; Getränk
	halle	to direct (to);	richten, lenken (auf);	drunk); drink	
to demand;	verlangen; Nachfrage	direct	direkt	to drive, (drove,	fahren, (an)treiben;
demand		direction	Richtung	driven); drive	Fahrt, Laufwerk
democracy	Demokratie	director	Leiter(in), Direktor(in),	to drive some-	jmdn. verrückt
democrat	Demokrat(in)		Regisseur(in)	one mad	machen
democratic	demokratisch	dirty	schmutzig		

drive-by shooting	Schießen im Vorbeifahren	to eject	auswerfen	enthusiastic	begeistert
driver	*Fahrer(in)*	*to elect*	*wählen*	*entrance*	*Eintritt, Eingang*
to drop	fallen, fallen lassen	*election*	*Wahl*	entrance exam	Aufnahmeprüfung
drug	Droge	*electric*	*elektrisch*	entrepreneur-	Unternehmertum,
drug counsellor	Drogenberater	electrical	Elektrotechnik	ship	unternehmerische
to dry; dry	*trocknen; trocken*	engineering			Vorhaben
dual	doppelt, Doppel-	electrically-	elektrisch	entry	Einreise, Eingang,
due to	aufgrund von	driven	angetrieben		Eintritt
to dump; dump	(Müll) abladen;	electrician	Elektriker(in)	envelope	Umschlag
	Müllkippe	*electricity*	*Elektrizität*	*environment*	*Umwelt*
dumping	Müllablageplatz	electronic	elektronisch	environmental	Umwelt-
ground		*electronics*	*Elektronik*	environ-	Umweltschützer(in)
during	*während*	to eliminate	beseitigen	mentalist	
dustbin	*Mülltonne*	*else*	*sonst*	*equal*	*gleich*
Dutch	niederländisch;	elsewhere	woanders	to equip	ausrüsten
	Niederländer(in)	embassy	Botschaft	*equipment*	*Ausrüstung,*
duty	*Pflicht, Zoll*	*emergency*	*Notfall*		*Ausstattung*
DVD recorder	DVD-Rekorder	to emigrate	auswandern	*especial*	*besondere(r,s)*
		emigration	Auswanderung	essential	wesentlich
E		emission	Emission, Ausstoß	to estimate	schätzen
		emphasis	Betonung	estimated	geschätzter Wert
e.g.	z.B. (zum Beispiel)	to emphasize	betonen	value	
each	*jede(r,s)*	*to employ*	*beschäftigen,*	Estonia	Estland
each other	*einander, sich*		*einstellen*	etc. (et cetera)	und so weiter
ear	*Ohr*	employed	beschäftigt	ethnic	ethnisch
early	*früh*	employee	Angestellte(r),	European	Europäische
to earn	*verdienen*		Arbeitnehmer(in)	Commission	Kommission
earnings	Einkommen,	employer	Arbeitgeber(in)	European	Europäische Union
	Verdienst, Ertrag	employment	Beschäftigung,	Union	
earth	*Erde*		Anstellung, Arbeit	*even*	*sogar, selbst, eben,*
east	*Osten, östlich, Ost-,*	*empty*	*leer*		*gleich*
	ostwärts	to enable (s.o.	es (jmdm.) möglich	*evening*	*Abend*
eastern	Ost-, östlich	to do sth.)	machen (etwas zu	*event*	*Ereignis*
easy	*leicht*		tun)	eventual(ly)	am Ende, schließlich
easy-to-use	einfach zu bedienen	to enclose	beilegen	*ever*	*je*
to eat, (ate,	*essen*	to encourage	ermutigen	*every*	*jede(r,s)*
eaten)		encouragement	Ermutigung	everybody	jeder
ecological	ökologisch, umwelt-	*to end; end*	*(be)enden; Ende*	everyone	jeder
	freundlich	*energy*	*Energie, Kraft*	everything	alles
ecology	Ökologie	energy	Energierück-	everywhere	überall
economic	Wirtschafts-, wirt-	recovery	gewinnung	evident	offensichtlich,
	schaftlich	*engine*	*Motor, Triebwerk,*		deutlich
economical	sparsam, wirtschaft-		*Lokomotive*	*exact*	*genau*
	lich	*engineer*	*Ingenieur(in),*	exam(ination)	Prüfung
economics	Wirtschaft(swissen-		*Techniker(in)*	to examine	untersuchen,
	schaft)	*engineering*	*Technik; technisch*		überprüfen
economist	Wirtschaftswissen-	engineering	etwa: Fachbereich	*example*	*Beispiel*
	schaftler(in)	studies	Technik	*excellent*	*ausgezeichnet,*
economy	*Wirtschaft*	English	Ärmelkanal		*hervorragend*
Ecstasy	Ecstasy (Name einer	Channel		except	außer
	Droge)	*to enjoy*	*genießen, sich freuen*	exchange	Austausch
edge	*Kante, Rand, Schneide*		*an*	exchange rate	Wechselkurs
edition	Ausgabe	*enjoyable*	*schön, angenehm,*	*exciting*	*aufregend*
editor	Herausgeber(in),		*unterhaltsam*	*to excuse;*	*(sich) entschuldigen;*
	Redakteur(in)	enormous	gewaltig, enorm	*excuse*	*Entschuldigung*
to educate	*erziehen*	*enough*	*genug*	exercise	Übung
educated	gebildet	to enquire	sich erkundigen	exhaust pipe	Auspuffrohr
education	*Erziehung*	(about)	(nach), fragen	*to exist*	*existieren, bestehen*
educational	pädagogisch; Lehr-		(nach)	existence	Existenz, Dasein
to effect; effect	*durchführen, erzielen,*	*enquiry*	*Anfrage, Erkundigung,*	*exit*	*Ausgang, Ausfahrt*
	leisten; Wirkung		*Untersuchung*	to expand	ausdehnen
efficiency	Leistungsfähigkeit	*to enter*	*eintreten*	expansion	Ausweitung
efficient	leistungsfähig	enthusiasm	Begeisterung,	*to expect*	*erwarten*
egg	*Ei*		Enthusiasmus	expectation	Erwartung
either ... or	*entweder ... oder*	enthusiast	Begeisterte(r),	expenditure	Ausgabe(n), Aufwand
			Enthusiast(in)	expenses	Ausgaben

expensive	teuer	fashionable	modisch	fog	Nebel
experience	Erfahrung	fast	schnell	to follow	folgen
expert	Experte, Expertin	fast running	schnell fließend	food	Nahrung, Essen
to explain	erklären	fat	Fett; dick	food stamp	Essensmarke
explanation	Erklärung	father	Vater	foot	Fuß
to explore	erforschen	fault	Fehler, Schuld,	football	Fußball
to export;	ausführen, exportie-		Mangel	footballer	Fußballspieler(in)
export	ren; Ausfuhr, Export	favourite	Lieblings-; Liebling	for example	zum Beispiel
export	etwa: Außenhandels-	fear	Furcht	for free	gratis, umsonst
assistant	kaufmann/-frau	feature	Merkmal, Bestandteil	for fun	zum Spaß
exposed	ungeschützt,	to feed,	füttern	for instance	beispielsweise
	ausgesetzt	(fed, fed)		for its own sake	um seiner selbst
to express;	ausdrücken, äußern;	feedback	Rückwirkung,		willen
express	Schnellzug; als		Feedback	force	Kraft, Stärke, Gewalt,
	Eilsache	to feel, (felt,	fühlen		Macht
expression	Ausdruck	felt)		foreign	ausländisch, fremd
extension	Streckung,	feeling	Gefühl	forever	für immer
	Verlängerung,	fellow	Landsmann	to forget, (for-	vergessen
	Erweiterung,	countryman		got, forgotten)	
	Durchwahl (Telefon)	female	weiblich	forgetfulness	Vergesslichkeit
to a great	in großem Umfang	ferry	Fähre	fork	Gabel
extent		fertilizer	Dünger	to form; form	gestalten; Form,
extinction	Aussterben	few	wenige		Formular, Klasse
extra	besonders	field	Feld	formal	formell, förmlich,
to extract;	gewinnen,	to fight, (fought,	kämpfen; Kampf		formal
extract	entnehmen;	fought); fight		former	ehemalig
	Auszug, Extrakt	figure	Zahl, Figur	formula	Formel
eye	Auge	to fill	füllen	fortunate	glücklich
		final	Finale, Endrunde;	fortune	Glück, Reichtum
F			letzte(r,s), endgültig	forward(s)	vorwärts
		finance	Finanzwesen	fossil fuels	fossile Brennstoffe
to face; face	sich gegenübersehen,	financial	finanziell	foster care	bei Pflegeeltern
	gegenübertreten;	financial	Finanzdienst-	to found	gründen
	Gesicht	services	leistungen	frame	Rahmen
facility	Einrichtung,	to find, (found,	finden	France	Frankreich
	Möglichkeit	found)		to free; free	befreien; frei
fact	Tatsache	fine	Strafe; fein, gut, schön	freedom	Freiheit
factor	Faktor	to finish; finish	beenden; Ziel,	freeway	Autobahn (AE)
factory	Fabrik		Vollendung	French	französisch; Franzose,
to fade (away)	verblassen,	to fire; fire	feuern; Feuer		Französin
	nachlassen,	firm	Firma; fest,	frequent	häufig
	verwelken		verbindlich	fresh	frisch
to fail	scheitern, versagen	first	erste(r,s), zuerst	fridge	Kühlschrank
failure	Versagen	first of all	zuerst, vor allem		(Kurzform)
fair	Messe, Markt;	first school	Grundschule	friend	Freund(in)
	gerecht, fair	to fish; fish	fischen; Fisch	friendly	freundlich
fairytale	Märchen	to fit; fit	(zusammen)passen,	Friends of the	Name einer Umwelt-
to fall, (fell,	fallen; Fallen, Sturz,		einbauen; gesund, in	Earth	schutzorganisation
fallen); fall	Herbst (AE)		Form; geeignet	to frighten	erschrecken, Angst
to fall behind	zurückfallen,	to fix	befestigen, reparieren,		machen
	zurückbleiben		besorgen	front	Vorderseite
false	falsch	fixed-route	schienengebunden	fruit	Frucht, Früchte, Obst
familiar	vertraut	flag	Fahne	fuel	Kraftstoff, Brennstoff
family	Familie	to flash	hier: zeigen	fuel cell	Brennstoffzelle
famous	berühmt	flat	Wohnung; flach	to fulfil	erfüllen, entsprechen
fanatic	fanatisch;	to flee (fled,	fliehen, flüchten	full	voll
	Fanatiker(in)	fled)		full-time	Vollzeit
far	weit	flexibility	Flexibilität	fumes	Rauch, Dämpfe,
fare	Fahrpreis	flexible	flexibel		Abgase
farm	Bauernhof, Farm	flight	Flug, Flucht	fun	Spaß
farm worker	landwirtschaftlicher	flight attendant	Flugbegleiter(in)	function	Funktion, Aufgabe
	Arbeiter	floor	Boden	funny	lustig
farmer	Landwirt(in), Bauer,	floor and	Boden- und Tisch-	furnace	Ofen
	Bäuerin	tabletop toys	Spielzeuge	furniture	Möbel
farming	Landwirtschaft	flower	Blume	further	weiter
fascination	Faszination	to fly, (flew,	fliegen; Fliege	furthermore	außerdem
		flown); fly		future	Zukunft; zukünftig

G

gadget	Gerät, Apparat
to gain; gain	gewinnen; Gewinn
galactic	galaktisch, Weltraum-
gambler	Spieler(in)
game	*Spiel*
gang	Bande
garage	*Autowerkstatt, Garage*
garden	*Garten*
gate	*Tor*
GCSE = General Certificate of Secondary Education	etwa: Fachober-schulreife
gearbox	Getriebe
general	allgemein
general science	allgemeine Natur-wissenschaften
to generate	erzeugen
generator	Generator, Lichtmaschine
genetic	genetisch, Erb-
genius	Genie
gentleman	*Herr*
geographical	geographisch
Germany	Deutschland
to get, (got, got)	*bekommen, werden*
to get caught	ertappt werden
to get married	*heiraten*
to get on like a house on fire	sich sehr gut verstehen
to get on (well) with	(gut) auskommen mit
to get rid of	loswerden, abschaffen
to get to know	kennen lernen
to get up	*aufstehen*
to get used to	sich gewöhnen an
girl	*Mädchen*
girlfriend	*Freundin*
to give, (gave, given)	*geben*
to give up	*aufgeben*
glad	*froh*
glamorous	schick, glamourös
glance	*Blick*
glass	*Glas*
glasses	*Brille*
glass-walled	mit Wänden aus Glas
global	global, weltweit
global warming	weltweiter Temperaturanstieg
glory	*Ruhm*
glove	*Handschuh*
to go, (went, gone)	*gehen*
to go down	*untergehen, sinken, fallen*
to go missing	verschwinden
to go on	*weitergehen, weitermachen*
to go on strike	in den Streik treten
to go shopping	*einkaufen*

to go up	*hinaufgehen, wachsen, steigen*
good	*gut*
goodbye	auf Wiedersehen
goods	*Güter, Waren*
to govern	*regieren*
government	Regierung
GPS (Global Positioning System)	GPS-Navigations-system
gradual	allmählich, sanft (an-steigen, abfallen)
to graduate	das Studium beenden, einen akad. Grad erwerben
granddaughter	Enkelin
grandfather	*Großvater*
grandmother	*Großmutter*
grandparents	*Großeltern*
grant	Zuschuss, Bafög
graph	Schaubild, mathematische Kurve
grateful	*dankbar*
great	*großartig, groß*
Great Britain	Großbritannien
Greece	Griechenland
Greek	griechisch; Grieche, Griechin
green	*grün*
green card	Aufenthaltserlaubnis
greenhouse	Treibhaus, Gewächshaus
to greet	*grüßen*
grey	*grau*
grid	Versorgungsnetz
to grip; grip	Griff, Halt; (er)greifen, fesseln
grocer	*Lebensmittel-händler(in)*
ground	*Boden*
group	*Gruppe*
to grow, (grew, grown)	*wachsen*
to grow up	aufwachsen
grown-up	*Erwachsene(r); erwachsen*
growth	*Wachstum*
to guard; guard	bewachen; Wachposten, Wache
to guess	*erraten*
guest	*Gast*
to guide	leiten, führen
guilty	schuldig
gun	Gewehr, Schusswaffe

H

habit	Gewohnheit
hair	*Haar*
hairdresser	Friseur(in)
half	*Hälfte; halb*
hall	*Flur, Saal*
ham	*Schinken*
handbag	*Handtasche*

handbook	Handbuch
handful	Handvoll
handkerchief	*Taschentuch*
to hang, (hung, hung)	*(auf)hängen*
to hang around	herumhängen
to happen	*geschehen*
happiness	Glück, Heiterkeit, Zufriedenheit
happy	*glücklich, heiter*
harbour	*Hafen*
hard	*hart, schwierig, anstrengend*
hard-working	fleißig
hardly	*kaum*
to harm	schädigen
hat	*Hut*
to hate	*hassen*
to have, (had, had)	*haben, lassen*
to have in common	gemeinsam haben
to have to	*müssen*
hazard	Gefahr
to head; head	*anführen, fahren nach; Kopf, Leiter*
head of department	hier: Fachbereichsleiter
to head off	(hin) fahren (nach), losfahren
headache	*Kopfschmerz*
heading	Überschrift
headlight	Scheinwerfer
headline	*Überschrift*
health	*Gesundheit*
health and social services	Amt für Gesundheit und Soziales
health care	Gesundheitsfürsorge
healthy	*gesund*
to hear, (heard, heard)	*hören*
heart	Herz
heart attack	Herzanfall
to heat; heat	*heizen; Hitze*
heating	Heizung
heavy	*schwer*
heavy metal	Heavy Metal (harte Rockmusik)
height	*Höhe*
hello	Hallo
to help; help	*helfen; Hilfe*
helpful	hilfreich
here	*hier*
here you are	*bitte(schön)!*
hereditary peer	Peer mit vererbtem Adelstitel
hero	Held
to hesitate	*zögern*
Hi Tech (High Technology)	*Hochtechnologie*
to hide, (hid, hidden)	*(sich) verstecken*
high	*hoch*
high class	hochwertig, erstklassig
high school	Oberschule

high-speed	Hochgeschwindig-keits-
highway	Landstraße
hill	*Hügel*
historical	historisch
history	*Geschichte*
to hit, (hit, hit); hit	schlagen; Schlag, Treffer, Erfolg
to hold, (held, held)	halten
hole	*Loch*
holiday	*freier Tag, Feiertag, Urlaub*
holidaymaker	Urlauber(in)
home	*Wohnung, Heimat; zu/nach Hause*
homeless	obdachlos
homework	*Hausaufgabe*
honest	*ehrlich*
hooligan	Hooligan, Randalierer
to hope; hope	*hoffen; Hoffnung*
hopeful	zuversichtlich, vielversprechend
hopelessness	*Hoffnungslosigkeit*
horse	*Pferd*
hospital	*Krankenhaus*
host	Gastgeber(in)
hot	*heiß*
hour	*Stunde*
hourly	stündlich
house	*Haus*
House of Commons	Unterhaus
House of Lords	Oberhaus
household	Haushalt
housewife	*Hausfrau*
housework	*Hausarbeit*
housing	Unterkunft, Wohnungen
housing estate	Siedlung
how	*wie*
how are you?	*wie geht es Dir/Ihnen?*
however	*jedoch*
huge	riesig
human	menschlich
hundred	*Hundert*
Hungary	Ungarn
hungry	*hungrig*
to hurry; hurry	*sich beeilen; Eile*
to hurt	verletzen
husband	Ehemann
hydro	Wasser-
hydrogen-based	auf Wasserstoffbasis arbeitend
hypnotic	hypnotisch

I

ice	Eis
ice cream	*Eis*
icon	Idol, Ikone
idea	*Idee*
to identify	identifizieren
identity	Identität, Über-einstimmung
if	*wenn, falls*

ill	*krank*
illegal	illegal, gesetzlich unzulässig
illness	*Krankheit*
illusion	Illusion, Einbildung
image	Bild, Image
imaginative	phantasievoll
to imagine	*sich vorstellen*
immediate	*unmittelbar, unverzüglich*
immigrant	*Einwanderer, Einwanderin*
to immigrate	*einwandern*
immigration	Einwanderung
immoral	unmoralisch
to import; import	*importieren, einführen; Einfuhr, Import*
importance	*Wichtigkeit*
important	*wichtig*
impossible	*unmöglich*
to impress	beeindrucken
impression	Eindruck
to improve	*(sich) verbessern*
improvement	Verbesserung
in addition	zusätzlich
in care	in Pflege
in conclusion	abschließend
in contrast	im Gegensatz
in fact	*tatsächlich*
in favour of	zugunsten von
in front of	*vor*
in general	im Allgemeinen
in italics	*kursiv*
in my opinion	*meiner Meinung nach*
in my view	meiner Ansicht nach
in order to	um zu
(in) preference (to)	(unter) Bevorzugung (von)
in the end	schließlich
in the long run	auf lange Sicht
(in the) meantime	*inzwischen*
in the mid	in der Mitte von, in der Mitte der …
in time	*rechtzeitig*
inability	Unfähigkeit
inadequate	nicht ausreichend, unangemessen
inch	*(Maßeinheit) Zoll*
to be inclined to do sth.	dazu neigen, etwas zu tun
to include	*einschließen*
income	*Einkommen*
income support	Sozialunterstützung
to incorporate	enthalten, beinhalten
to increase	*zunehmen, steigen, erhöhen*
indeed	*tatsächlich*
independent	unabhängig
India	Indien
indicator	Anzeiger, Indikator
individual	individuell
to induce	verursachen, herbeiführen
industrial	industriell
industrialized	industrialisiert

industry	*Industrie*
infinitive	Infinitiv, Grundform
inflexible	unflexibel
inflow	Zustrom
to influence	beeinflussen
to inform	*informieren*
informal	informell
information sheet	Informationsblatt
ingredients	Bestandteile
injury	Verletzung
ink	Tinte
ink jet printer	Tintenstrahldrucker
inner	Innen-, inner-
innocence	Unschuld
innovation	Neuerung
innovative	innovativ
to insert	einlegen (Diskette, Kassette)
inside	*in, innerhalb*
to insist (on)	beharren, bestehen (auf)
to install	einbauen
installation	Installation, Anschluss
instead (of)	*anstatt*
institute	Institut
institution	Institution, Ein-führung, Anstalt
to instruct	*unterrichten, anweisen*
instruction	*Unterricht, Anweisung, (Gebrauchs-) Anleitung*
instrumen-tation	Messtechnik
to insulate	isolieren
insulation	Isolierung
insurance	*Versicherung*
insurance cover	Versicherungsschutz
to insure	versichern
to integrate	integrieren
inter-continental	interkontinental
interest	*Interesse, (Plural) Zinsen*
to be interested (in)	interessiert sein (an)
interesting	interessant
interface	Schnittstelle
interval	Abstand
to be into sth.	Fan von etwas sein
to introduce	*einführen, vorstellen*
introduction	Einführung, Vorstellung
introductory	einleitend
to invent	erfinden
invention	*Erfindung*
inventor	Erfinder(in)
to invest	*investieren*
to investigate	untersuchen
investment	Investition, (Kapital-) Anlage
invitation	*Einladung*
to invite	*einladen*

to involve	beteiligen, verwickeln	labour	Arbeit
Ireland	Irland	labour market	Arbeitsmarkt
island	*Insel*	*ladder*	*Leiter*
to isolate	isolieren	*lady*	*Dame*
issue	Frage, Angelegenheit, Problem	*lake*	*See*
Italian	Italiener(in); italienisch	*lamp*	*Lampe*
		land	*Land*
Italy	Italien	*landlady*	*Vermieterin, Wirtin*

J

jacket	*Jacke*
jam	*Marmelade*
Japanese	japanisch; Japaner(in)
jersey	*Trikot*
job	*Arbeit, Stelle, Aufgabe*
jobless	arbeitslos
to join	*(sich) anschließen, beitreten*
joint	gemeinsam
joke	Witz
journey	*Reise*
joyride	(wilde) Vergnügungsfahrt
judge	Richter(in)
juice	*Saft*
to jump; jump	*springen; Sprung*
junk	Gerümpel, Ramsch
just	*genau, soeben, nur*
juvenile	jugendlich

K

to keep, (kept, kept)	*(be)halten*
to keep up with	Schritt halten mit
key	*Schlüssel*
key point	springender Punkt
to kick; kick	treten; Tritt
to kick out of school	aus der Schule werfen
kid	Kind, Jugendlicher
to kill	*töten*
kilogram(me)	*Kilogramm*
kind	*Art, Sorte; freundlich*
kindness	Güte, Freundlichkeit
king	*König*
to kiss; kiss	*küssen; Kuss*
kit	Ausrüstung, Bausatz, Set
kitchen	*Küche*
knee	Knie
knee-cap	Kniescheibe
knife	*Messer*
to knock; knock	*klopfen; Klopfen*
to know, (knew, known)	*wissen*
knowledge	*Wissen*
kph	km/h (Kilometer pro Stunde)

L

to label; label	etikettieren, klassifizieren; Etikett

landlord	*Vermieter, Wirt*
language	*Sprache*
large	*groß*
to last; last	*dauern; letzte(r,s)*
late	*spät*
later on	*später*
latest	*neueste(r,s)*
Latin America	Lateinamerika
to laugh	*lachen*
laughter	*Gelächter*
law	*Gesetz*
to lay, (laid, laid)	*legen*
lazy	*faul*
to lead, (led, led)	*führen, leiten*
leadership	Führung, Leitung
leaflet	*(Hand-)Zettel, Flugblatt*
league	Liga
lean management	„schlankes" Management
to learn, (learnt, learnt)	*lernen*
learner	*Lernende(r), Anfänger(in)*
least	*wenigste(r,s), geringste(r,s)*
to leave, (left, left)	*verlassen*
lecture	Vorlesung
left	*links*
(to feel) left out	(sich) ausgeschlossen (fühlen)
leg	*Bein*
legal	legal, gesetzlich zulässig
legal services	Rechtsberatungen, -dienstleistungen
legislation	Gesetzgebung
leisure	*Freizeit*
lemon	*Zitrone*
to lend, (lent, lent)	*verleihen*
length	*Länge*
less	*weniger*
lesson	*Unterrichtsstunde*
letter	*Brief*
level	Stufe, Niveau
library	Bibliothek
to lie, (lay, lain)	*liegen*
to lie, (lied, lied)	*lügen*
life	*Leben*
life peer	Peer auf Lebenszeit
lifestyle	Lebensstil
to lift; lift	*anheben, aufheben; Aufzug, Mitfahrgelegenheit*

light	*Licht, Lampe; hell, leicht*
to light, (lit, lit)	anzünden, (be)leuchten
light industry	Leichtindustrie
lighting	Beleuchtung
to like; like	*mögen; wie*
likely	wahrscheinlich
limit	*Grenze, Beschränkung*
line	*Linie, Zeile*
lined with	gesäumt von
to link; link	*verbinden; Verbindung*
to link together	miteinander verbinden
lip	*Lippe*
to list; list	*aufführen, auflisten; Liste*
to listen	*zuhören*
listener	Zuhörer(in)
literature	Literatur, Informationsmaterial
litre	Liter
litter	Streu, Stroh
little	*klein, wenig*
to live; live	*leben, wohnen; lebend, direkt, live*
to live on welfare	von Sozialhilfe leben
living room	*Wohnzimmer*
to load; load	*laden; Ladung*
loaded with	beladen mit
loaf of bread	Laib Brot
local	*lokal, ortsansässig, örtlich*
Local Education Authority (L.E.A.)	örtliche Schulbehörde
local government	Stadtrat
locals	Einwohner
location	Lage, Standort
logical	logisch
logo	Logo, (Firmen)Emblem
long	*lang*
long-term	langfristig
long time no see	lange nicht gesehen
longitudinal	längs verlaufend, Langzeit-
to look	*schauen, (aus)sehen*
to look after	*sich kümmern um*
to look for	*suchen*
to look forward to	*sich freuen auf*
to look into	untersuchen, prüfen
to look like	aussehen wie
to look out	*aufpassen, hinaussehen*
to look up	*nachschlagen, heraussuchen, aufblicken*
to loot	plündern
lorry	*Lastwagen*
to lose, (lost, lost)	*verlieren*

loss	Verlust
(a) lot	viel; Los
lots of	viel
loud	laut
to love; love	lieben; Liebe
lovely	hübsch
low	niedrig
low-cost	preiswert
low-paid	schlecht bezahlt
to lower	senken, herabsetzen
luck	Glück, Schicksal
lucky	glücklich (im Sinne von: Glück haben)
luggage	Gepäck
lunch	Mittagessen
Luxembourg	Luxemburg

M

machine	Maschine
machinery	Maschinen
mad	verrückt
madam	Gnädige Frau
magazine	Zeitschrift
mail	Post
main	Haupt-
mainly	hauptsächlich
to maintain	behaupten
maintenance	Wartung, Instandhaltung
major	bedeutend, Haupt-
major road	Hauptstraße
majority	Mehrheit
to make, (made, made)	machen, herstellen
to make do	auskommen
to make matters worse	zu allem Unglück
to make sense	einen Sinn ergeben
to make sure	sich überzeugen
to make up one's mind	sich entschließen
maker	Hersteller(in)
Malaysia	Malaysia
male	männlich
man	Mann
to manage	zu Stande bringen, schaffen, leiten, verwalten
management	(Geschäfts-)Leitung, Verwaltung, Durch-führung
managing director	Geschäftsführer(in)
mankind	Menschheit
manner	Art und Weise
manpower	Arbeitskräfte
to manufacture	herstellen
manufacturer	Hersteller(in)
manure	Dung
many	viele
map	(Land-)Karte
marital status	Familienstand
mark	Zensur, Note
market	Markt

market development	Marktentwicklung
marmalade	(Orangen-) Marmelade
marriage	Ehe, Hochzeit
married	verheiratet
to marry	heiraten
mass	Masse
massacre	Massaker, Blutbad
to match; match	zusammenbringen, passen; Wettkampf, Streichholz
mate	Kumpel
material	materiell
mathematics	Mathematik
to matter; matter	etwas ausmachen; Angelegenheit
may	dürfen
maybe	vielleicht
mayor	Bürgermeister(in)
meal	Mahlzeit
to mean, (meant, meant)	bedeuten, meinen
meaning	Bedeutung
means	Mittel, Möglichkeiten
meanwhile	inzwischen
measure	Maßnahme
meat	Fleisch
mechanic	Mechaniker(in)
mechanical engineering	Maschinenbau
media	Medien
medicine	Medizin, Medikament
medium-sized	mittelgroß
to meet, (met, met)	(sich) treffen, kennen lernen
to meet the growing demand	der wachsenden Nachfrage gerecht werden
meeting	Treffen
megawatt	Megawatt
to melt	schmelzen
member	Mitglied
membership	Mitgliedschaft
memory	Gedächtnis
to mend	reparieren
to mention	erwähnen
menu	Speisekarte
message	Mitteilung, Nachricht
metal	Metall
method	Methode
metre	Meter
Mexican	Mexikaner(in); mexikanisch
Mexico	Mexiko
microphone	Mikrofon
microwave	Mikrowelle
middle	Mitte
middle-class	Mittelklasse
midnight	Mitternacht
might	Gewalt, Macht; könnte(n)
mile	Meile
mileage	Meilen, Meilenstand

milk	Milch
millennium	Jahrtausend
Millennium Wheel	Millennium-Riesen-rad (in London)
to mind; mind	etwas ausmachen; Meinung, Gedanken, Verstand
to mind one's own business	sich um seine eigenen Angelegen-heiten kümmern
mine	Bergwerk
mining	Bergbau
minor	kleiner, weniger bedeutend, leicht
minority	Minderheit
minus	minus, ohne, abzüglich
minute	Minute
mirror	Spiegel
Miss	Fräulein
to miss	vermissen, verfehlen, verpassen
mistake	Fehler
to misuse; misuse	missbrauchen; Missbrauch
to mix; mix	mischen; Mischung
to mix up	vertauschen
mobile phone	Handy
modal	Hilfsverb
model	Modell
to modernize	modernisieren
molecular	molekular
moment	Augenblick
money	Geld
to monitor	überwachen
monotonous	eintönig, monoton
month	Monat
monthly	monatlich
moon	Mond
moor	Moor
moral	Moral; moralisch
more	mehr
moreover	überdies, außerdem
morning	Morgen
most	die meisten
mother	Mutter
motorist	Autofahrer(in)
motorway	Autobahn
mountain	Berg
mouth	Mund
to move; move	bewegen, umziehen; Umzug
movement	Bewegung
movie	Film
MP (Member of Parliament)	Mitglied des Parlaments
mph (miles per hour)	Meilen pro Stunde
Mr	Herr
Mrs	Frau (verheiratet)
Ms	Frau (verheiratet oder unverheiratet)
much	viel
multi-	Mehr-, Viel-
murder	Mord
muscle	Muskel

music	Musik	noun	Substantiv	opinion	Meinung
must	müssen	novel	Roman	opportunity	Gelegenheit, Möglichkeit
must not	nicht dürfen	now	jetzt		
		nowadays	heutzutage	opposite	Gegensatz; gegensätzlich
N		nowhere	nirgendwo		
		number	Zahl, Nummer, Anzahl	optimistic	optimistisch
to name; name	benennen; Name	nurse	Krankenschwester	or	oder
namely	nämlich	nursery school	Kindergarten	to order; order	bestellen, befehlen; Bestellung, Befehl
narrow	eng	nursery school assistant	Kinderpfleger(in)		
nationality	Nationalität			ordinary	normal, gewöhnlich
nationwide	landesweit	nursery school teacher	Erzieher(in), Kindergärtner(in)	ore	Erz
native-born	gebürtig			organization	Organisation
natural	natürlich	nutritionally balanced menu	ausgewogene Ernährung	to organize	organisieren
nature	Natur			organizer	Veranstalter(in)
navigation system	Navigationssystem			organs	Organe
		O		original	ursprünglich, originell
near	nahe			other	andere(r,s)
nearby	nahe gelegen	o'clock	Uhr (Zeitangabe)	otherwise	sonst, anderenfalls
nearly	fast, beinahe	object	Gegenstand	ought to	sollte(n)
neat	ordentlich, gelungen, schlau	objective	Ziel; objektiv, sachlich	out of town	außerhalb der Stadt
		to obtain	bekommen, erhalten	out of work	arbeitslos
necessary	notwendig	obvious	offensichtlich	outbound	ins Ausland
to need; need	benötigen; Notwendigkeit	to occupy	einnehmen, besetzen	to outdo	übertreffen, überbieten
		to occur	auftreten		
needle in a haystack	Nadel im Heuhaufen	ocean	Meer, Ozean	outdoor	draußen, im Freien
		of course	natürlich	output	(Produktions-) Leistung
negative	negativ	off	von ... weg		
to neglect	vernachlässigen	off-the-grid	nicht an das Versorgungsnetz angeschlossen	outside	Außenseite; draußen, außerhalb
negligible	unerheblich				
neighbour	Nachbar(in)			outsider	Außenseiter(in)
neighbourhood	Nachbarschaft	to offer; offer	anbieten; Angebot	outstanding	hervorragend, außergewöhnlich
neither ... nor	weder ... noch	office	Büro, Amt		
Netherlands	Niederlande	office skills	Bürofertigkeiten	over and over again	immer wieder
network	Netz	office worker	Büroangestellte(r)		
never	nie	officer	Beamte(r), Offizier(in)	over-training	zu häufiges Training
nevertheless	dennoch	official	offiziell; Beamte(r), Funktionär(in)	over-use	zu häufiger Gebrauch
new	neu			overcrowded	überfüllt
news	Nachrichten, Neuigkeit			to overestimate	überschätzen
newspaper	Zeitung	often	oft	to overlook; overlook	übersehen; Aussicht
next	nächste(r,s)	oil	Öl		
nice	nett	old	alt	overseas	in Übersee
night	Nacht	on average	im Durchschnitt	to own; own	besitzen; eigene(r,s)
no	kein; nein	(on the) left-hand (side)	auf der linken (Seite)	owner	Eigentümer(in)
no longer	nicht mehr			ozone hole	Ozonloch
no one	niemand	on the one hand	auf der einen Seite		
nobody	niemand			**P**	
noise	Lärm	on the other hand	auf der anderen Seite		
noisy	geräuschvoll			pace	Geschwindigkeit
non-	Nicht-	on the right	rechts	to pack; pack	packen; Packung
non-returnable	Einweg-	on the road	auf dem Weg, unterwegs	package holiday	Pauschalurlaub
noon	Mittag				
north	Norden; nördlich, Nord-, nordwärts	on time	pünktlich	package tour	Pauschalreise
		on top of	zusätzlich zu	packaging	Verpackung
Northern Ireland	Nordirland	on your own	allein	packet	Paket
		once	einmal	packing	Verpackung
nose	Nase	once again	noch einmal	packing material	Verpackungsmaterial
not	nicht	once upon a time	es war einmal		
not any more	nicht länger			page	Seite
not either	auch nicht	only	nur	pain	Schmerz
not even	nicht einmal	to open; open	öffnen; offen	painful	schmerzhaft
not yet	noch nicht	open air	Freiluft-, draußen	to paint; paint	malen; Farbe
to note; note	notieren; Notiz	open-minded	aufgeschlossen, vorurteilslos	pair	Paar
nothing	nichts			panel	Schalttafel
noticeable	bemerkbar	to operate	bedienen, verkehren	to panic; panic	in Panik geraten, in Panik versetzen; Panik
to notice; notice	bemerken; Aushang, Kenntnis, Beachtung	operator	Bediener(in), Telefonvermittler(in)		

paper — Papier
paradise — Paradies
paragraph — Absatz
to paraphrase; paraphrase — umschreiben; Umschreibung
parent — Elternteil
parents — Eltern
to park; park — parken; Park
parliament — Parlament
parliamentary — parlamentarisch
part — Teil
part-time — Teilzeit
participant observation — teilnehmende Beobachtung
to participate — teilnehmen
particular — besondere(r,s)
to pass — vorbeigehen, (Prüfung) bestehen
to pass by — vorbeigehen, vorbeifahren
passenger — Passagier, Fahrgast
passive (voice) — Passiv
passport — Pass
past — Vergangenheit
past tense — Vergangenheitsform
patience — Geduld
to pay, (paid, paid); pay — (be)zahlen; Bezahlung
payment — Zahlung
peace — Friede
peace of mind — Seelenfrieden
peaceful — friedlich
to peak; peak — seine Spitzenform erreichen; Spitze, Gipfel, Höhepunkt
peak time — Stoßzeit
peat — Torf
peat bog — Torfmoor
peer group — Gruppe von Gleichgesinnten
pen — Füllhalter
pence — Plural von Penny
pencil — Bleistift
penny — Penny (engl. Münze)
people — Leute; Volk
per — pro
per cent — Prozent
per head/capita — pro Kopf
percentage — prozentualer Anteil
perfect — vollkommen, perfekt
to perform — ausführen, vollbringen
performance — Leistung
perhaps — vielleicht
period — Periode, Zeitraum, Schulstunde
permanent — (be)ständig, bleibend
permission — Erlaubnis
to permit — erlauben
persecution — Verfolgung
personal — persönlich
personality — Persönlichkeit
personnel — Personal
petrol — Benzin
petrol station — Tankstelle
to phone; phone — telefonieren; Telefon

phone call — Anruf
photograph — Foto
photographer — Fotograf(in)
photovoltaic (pv) — photoelektrisch
phrase — Ausdruck
to pick — pflücken, wählen
to pick up — nehmen, aufheben
pick-up — Kleinlastwagen
picture — Bild
piece — Stück
to pinpoint — genau anzeigen, genau bestimmen
pipe — Pfeife, Röhre
pit — Grube
pitch — Spielfeld
to place; place — stellen, legen; Platz
to plan; plan — planen; Plan
plane — Flugzeug
planner — Planer(in)
to plant; plant — pflanzen; Pflanze, Werk
plastic — Kunststoff, Plastik
plate — Teller
platform — Bahnsteig
to play; play — spielen; (Schau-) Spiel
to play truant — (die Schule) schwänzen
player — Spieler(in)
playground — Spielplatz
pleasant — angenehm
please — bitte
pleased — zufrieden, erfreut
pleasurable — angenehm
pleasure — Vergnügen
plentiful — reichlich, häufig
plenty — viel, eine Menge
to plug — stecken
pocket — Tasche
pocket money — Taschengeld
to point; point — zeigen; Punkt
point of view — Standpunkt
to point out — hinweisen auf
Poland — Polen
Pole — Pole, Polin
police — Polizei
police force — Polizei
policeman — Polizist
policewoman — Polizistin
Polish — polnisch
polite — höflich
political — politisch
politician — Politiker(in)
politics — Politik
poll — Umfrage, Abstimmung, Wahl
to pollute — verschmutzen
polluted — verschmutzt
pollution — Umweltverschmutzung
poor — arm
poorly paid — schlecht bezahlt
popular — beliebt, populär
to populate — bevölkern
population — Bevölkerung
port — Hafen

portable — tragbar
possession — Besitz
possibility — Möglichkeit
possible — möglich
post office — Post
postcard — Postkarte
postman — Briefträger
pot — Topf
potato — Kartoffel
potential — Potential, Möglichkeiten; potentiell, möglich
poultry — Geflügel
pound — Pfund
pound note — Pfundnote
poverty — Armut
power — Kraft
power line — (Stark-) Stromleitung
power plant — Kraftwerk
power station — Kraftwerk
powered — angetrieben, betrieben
powerful — stark, mächtig
practical — praktisch
practice — Übung
to practise — üben
Prague — Prag
precise — genau
preconceived idea — vorgefasste Meinung
to predict — vorhersagen
predictable — vorhersagbar, vorhersehbar
to prefer — vorziehen
prefix — Vorsilbe
to prepare — vorbereiten
prepared — bereit
pre-reading and -writing — erste Versuche im Lesen und Schreiben
to present; present — schenken, vorstellen; Geschenk, Gegenwart; anwesend, gegenwärtig
presidency — Präsidentschaft
president — Präsident(in), Vorsitzende(r)
to press; press — drücken, pressen; Presse
pressure — Druck
to pretend — vorgeben, tun, als ob
pretty — hübsch
previous — vorhergehend, früher
price — Preis
pride — Stolz
primary school — Grundschule
prime minister — Premierminister(in)
principle — Grundsatz, Prinzip
to print — drucken
printer — Drucker(in)
printing — Druckwesen
prison — Gefängnis
private — privat
prize — Preis, Gewinn
probable — wahrscheinlich
process — Vorgang, Prozess

to produce	produzieren, herstellen	to put on	aufsetzen	to receive	erhalten, bekommen
producer	Hersteller(in), Produzent(in)	to put (s.o./sth.) to the test	jmdn./etwas auf die Probe stellen	recent	jüngst, kürzlich
product	Produkt	to put up	(Hand) heben, bauen,	recently	kürzlich
production	Herstellung, Produktion		aufstellen	reception	Empfang
production line	Fertigungsstraße, Fließband	puzzle	Rätsel	reception class	Vorschulklasse
productivity	Produktivität, Leistungsfähigkeit	**Q**		receptionist	Empfangschef, Empfangsdame
professional	beruflich	qualification	Qualifikation, Befähigung	recession	Flaute
to profit; profit	profitieren; Gewinn			recipient	Empfänger
profitable	rentabel, einträglich, lohnend	qualified	qualifiziert	to recognize	erkennen, wiedererkennen
program(me)	Programm	quality	Qualität	recommen-dation	Empfehlung
progress	Fortschritt	quantity	Menge		
project	Projekt	quarter	Viertel	to record; record	aufnehmen; Rekord, Aufnahme
projection	Prognose, Projektion	queen	Königin	recording	(Ton-)Aufnahme
proliferation	Ausbreitung, Umsichgreifen	question	Frage	recording instruction	Aufnahmeanleitung
to promise; promise	versprechen; Versprechen	questionnaire	Fragebogen	to recover	sich erholen
promotion	Werbung, Beförderung	quick	schnell	recovery	Erholung
		quiet	ruhig	rectangular	rechteckig
to pronounce	aussprechen	to quit	verlassen, aufhören, aufgeben	recyclable	wiederverwertbar
pronounced	ausgeprägt, deutlich	quite	ganz, ziemlich	to recycle	wiederverwerten, wiederverwenden
pronunciation	Aussprache	quotation	Zitat, Kosten-voranschlag		
proper	richtig, ordentlich			red	rot
proportion	Verhältnis, Teil, Anteil	**R**		red tape	Bürokratie
proportional represen-tation	Verhältniswahl	race	Rasse	to reduce	verringern, senken
		racial discrimination	Rassen-diskriminierung	reduction	Verminderung
to prosper	gedeihen	racing bicycle	Rennrad	to refer to	(sich) beziehen auf
prosperous	erfolgreich, florierend	racism	Rassismus	reference	Referenz, Bezug
to protect	schützen	rack	Ständer, Regal	with reference to	mit Bezug auf
protection	Schutz	rail	Schiene		
proud	stolz	railway	Eisenbahn	to reflect	widerspiegeln
to provide	sorgen für, liefern, bereitstellen	to rain; rain	regnen; Regen	to refuse	ablehnen, verweigern
		to raise	(hoch)heben, erheben,	region	Gebiet, Bezirk
psychiatrist	Psychiater(in)	range	Sortiment, Umfang, Reichweite, Reihe	regional	regional
psychologist	Psychologe, Psychologin			to register	registrieren, anmelden
		rare	selten		
psychology	Psychologie	rate	Rate, (Prozent-)Satz	regular	regelmäßig
pub	Kneipe	rather	ziemlich	to regulate	regulieren
public	Öffentlichkeit; öffentlich	ratio	Verhältnis	related	verwandt
		rave	Rave (größere Tanzveranstaltung zu Technomusik)	relation	Beziehung
public library	Stadtbücherei			relative	Verwandte(r); relativ
public service	öffentlicher Dienst			to relax	(sich) entspannen
to publish	veröffentlichen	raw	Roh-, roh	to relocate	(Geschäftssitz) verlegen, umziehen
publishing	Verlagswesen	re-route	Umleitung		
to pull	ziehen	to re-use	wiederverwenden	to rely on	abhängig sein von, sich verlassen auf
to punch; punch	schlagen; Schlag	to reach; reach	erreichen; Reichweite		
		to react	reagieren	to remain	bleiben
punctual	pünktlich	reaction	Reaktion	to remark; remark	bemerken; Bemerkung
to punish	(be)strafen	to read, (read, read)	lesen		
punishing	mörderisch, hart			to remember	sich erinnern an
punishment	Bestrafung, Strafe	reader	Leser(in)	to remind (of)	erinnern (an)
pupil	Schüler(in)	ready	fertig, bereit	reminder	Erinnerung, Mahnung
purpose	Zweck, Absicht	real	wirklich		
pursuit	Beschäftigung, Betätigung, Jagd	realistic	realistisch	remote control	Fernbedienung
		reality	Wirklichkeit	to remove	entfernen
to push; push	schieben, stoßen; Stoß	to realize	erkennen, bemerken	renewable	erneuerbar
to put, (put, put)	setzen, stellen, legen	reason	Grund	to rent; rent	mieten, vermieten; Miete
to put into practice	in die Praxis um-setzen, realisieren	reasonable	vernünftig, günstig	to repair; repair	reparieren; Reparatur
		to rebel; rebel	rebellieren; Rebell	to repeat; repeat	wiederholen; Wiederholung
		to recalculate	neu berechnen	repetitive	(sich) wiederholend, eintönig
				to replace	ersetzen

to reply; reply	antworten; Antwort
to report; report	berichten; Bericht
reported speech	indirekte Rede
to represent	darstellen, stehen für
representative	Repräsentant(in); repräsentativ
request	Bitte
to require	benötigen, erfordern
requirement	Bedarf, Erfordernis
to rescue; rescue	retten; Rettung
research	Forschung
research department	Forschungs-abteilung
researcher	Forscher(in)
to reserve	reservieren
to reset	zurückstellen
to resign	zurücktreten
resolution	Auflösung
resort	Urlaubsort
resources	Boden-, Naturschätze, Mittel
to respect; respect	respektieren; Respekt
respectable	angesehen, anständig
responsibility	Verantwortung
responsible	verantwortlich
to rest; rest	ruhen; Rest, Ruhe
to result; result	resultieren; Ergebnis
retailer	Einzelhändler(in)
retirement	Ruhestand
retirement benefit	Rente, Pension
to return; return	zurückkommen; Rückkehr, Rückgabe
returnable	Mehrweg-
revival	Wiederaufleben, (-aufblühen)
to rewind	zurückspulen
to rewrite	neu schreiben, umschreiben
rich	reich
to ride, (rode, ridden); ride	reiten, fahren; Ritt, Fahrt
right	rechts
to ring, (rang, rung); ring	klingeln, anrufen; Ring, Anruf
riot	Aufruhr, Krawall
to rise, (rose, risen); rise	(auf)steigen, zunehmen; Aufstieg, Zunahme
to risk; risk	riskieren; Risiko
river	Fluss
road	Straße
road works	Straßenbauarbeiten
to roar away	„wegdonnern"
robot	Roboter, vollauto-matische Vorrichtung
role	Rolle
role play	Rollenspiel
romantic	romantisch
roof	Dach
room	Zimmer
rose-tinted glasses	rosarote Brille

rotation	Drehung
round	Runde; rund, herum
rubber	(Radier-)Gummi
rubbish	Abfall, Müll
to rule; rule	herrschen; Regel, Herrschaft
to run, (ran, run)	laufen
to run on	laufen mit
run-down	heruntergekommen
runaway	Ausreißer
to rush (s.o. to)	eilen, jmdn./etwas schnell an einen Ort bringen
rush-hour	Hauptverkehrszeit
Russia	Russland

S

sad	traurig
safe	sicher
safety	Sicherheit
salary	Gehalt
sale	(Schluss-)Verkauf
sales	Absätze
sales department	Verkaufsabteilung
sales figures	Verkaufszahlen
salesman/ woman	Verkäufer(in)
salt	Salz
same	gleiche(r,s), der-, die-, dasselbe
sample	Auswahl, Probe
satisfaction	Zufriedenheit
satisfied	zufrieden
sausage	Wurst
to save	retten
to say, (said, said)	sagen
sceptical	skeptisch
schedule	(Zeit-, Fahr-) Plan, Programm
scheme	Projekt, Plan, Programm
school	Schule
scientist	Wissenschaftler(in)
to score; score	(Treffer) erzielen; Spielstand
scramble	Gerangel, Gedrängel
scrap	Schrott, Fetzen
scrap yard	Schrottplatz
screen	Bildschirm, Leinwand
to screw; screw	schrauben; Schraube
sea	Meer
sea-going	seefahrend
to search; search	(durch-)suchen; Suche
seaside resort	Seebad
seat	Sitz
second	Sekunde; zweite(r,s)
second hand	aus zweiter Hand, gebraucht
secondary school	weiterführende Schule
secret	Geheimnis; geheim
secretary	Sekretär(in)

sector	Sektor, Bereich
secure	sicher
security	Sicherheit
to see, (saw, seen)	sehen
to seek, (sought, sought)	suchen
to seem	scheinen
to select	auswählen
self-employed	selbstständig
self-esteem	Selbstachtung
self-help	Selbsthilfe
to sell, (sold, sold)	verkaufen
seller	Verkäufer(in)
seminar	Seminar
to send, (sent, sent)	schicken, senden
sensor	Sensor, Fühler
to sentence; sentence	verurteilen; Satz, Urteil
to separate; separate	trennen; getrennt
series	Reihe, Folge
serious	ernst
to serve	(be)dienen, servieren
serve	Aufschlag (Tennis)
to service; service	(Auto) warten; Dienst, Betrieb
service industry	Dienstleistungsbranche
session	Sitzung, Zeitabschnitt
to set, (set, set)	setzen, stellen, legen
to set eyes on	sehen
to sever	durchtrennen, abbrechen
several	mehrere
severe	ernst, schwerwiegend
sex	Geschlechtsverkehr, Geschlecht
sexual exploits	Sexualverhalten, sexuelle Abenteuer
to shake (off), (shook, shaken)	(ab)schütteln
shall	sollen
to share; share	teilen; Anteil
sharp	scharf, deutlich, steil
sheet	Blatt, Bogen
shelf	Regal
to shift	verlagern
to shine, (shone, shone)	scheinen, leuchten
to ship; ship	verschicken; Schiff
shipbuilding	Schiffbau
shipyard	Werft
shirt	Hemd
to shock; shock	schockieren; Schock
shoe	Schuh
to shoot, (shot, shot)	schießen
shop	Geschäft, Laden
shop assistant	Verkäufer(in)
shop floor	Produktionsstätte, -halle

shoplifting	Ladendiebstahl	slow moving	zäh fließender	speech	Rede
shopper	Käufer(in)	traffic	Verkehr	speech aids	Sprachhilfen
shopping	Einkauf(en)	small	klein	to speed; speed	schnell fahren;
short	kurz	to smell; smell	riechen; Geruch		Geschwindigkeit
short cut	Abkürzung	to smile; smile	lächeln; Lächeln	to speed up	beschleunigen
short-term	kurzfristig	to smoke;	rauchen; Rauch	speedy	schnell
should	sollte(n)	smoke		to spell; spell	buchstabieren;
shoulder	Schulter	smoker	Raucher(in)		Zauber(spruch)
to shout; shout	rufen; Ruf	to snap	einrasten	to spend,	ausgeben, verbringen
to show,	zeigen; Ausstellung,	to snow; snow	schneien; Schnee	(spent, spent)	
(showed,	Vorstellung	so far	bisher, bis jetzt	spending	Kaufkraft
shown); show		so-called	so genannt	power	
shower	Dusche	soap	Seife	to spin	(sich) drehen
to shut, (shut,	schließen	to soar	(stark) ansteigen	spokesman	Sprecher
shut)		soccer	Fußball	spoon	Löffel
sick	krank	social	gesellschaftlich,	sports	Sport
sick leave	krankheitsbedingte		sozial	sportsman	Sportler
	Abwesenheit	social security	staatliche	sportswoman	Sportlerin
side	Seite		Sozialleistungen,	to spray; spray	sprühen, spritzen,
sight	Sicht, Anblick,		Sozialversicherung		lackieren; Spray
	Sehenswürdigkeit	social studies	Sozialwissen-	spring	Frühling
sighting	Sichten		schaften	square	Quadrat
to sign; sign	unterschreiben;	social worker	Sozialarbeiter(in)	to squeeze	sich drängen,
	Zeichen	society	Gesellschaft		quetschen
to sign up for	sich einschreiben,	sociologist	Soziologe, Soziologin	stable	stabil, dauerhaft
	anmelden	sociology	Soziologie	staff	Belegschaft,
significant	bedeutend,	sock	Socke		Kollegium
	bedeutsam	soft	weich	staffroom	Lehrerzimmer
similar	ähnlich	solar power	Sonnenenergie	stained glass	bleiverglastes
simple	einfach	soldier	Soldat(in)	window	Fenster
simple majority	Mehrheitswahl-	solitary	einsam	stamp	Briefmarke
voting system	system	solution	Lösung	to stand, (stood,	stehen, aushalten;
to simulate	simulieren	to solve	lösen	stood); stand	Stand
since	seit	some	einige	standard	Niveau, Standard,
since then	seitdem	somebody	jemand		Maßstab
to sing, (sang,	singen	someone	jemand	standard of	Lebensstandard
sung)		something	etwas	living	
singer	Sänger(in)	sometimes	manchmal	standstill	Stillstand
single	einzig, hier:	somewhere	irgendwo, ungefähr	to stare	starren
	einheitlich	son	Sohn	to start; start	anfangen; Anfang
to sink, (sank,	sinken	song	Lied	to start off	anfangen, hier:
sunk)		soon	bald		seinen/ihren
to sink in	ins Bewusstsein	sorry	betrübt, tut mir Leid!,		Ausgangspunkt
	dringen		Entschuldigung!		haben
Sir	Herr (Anrede)	sort	Art, Sorte	to start up	(Geschäft) anfangen
sister	Schwester	to sound; sound	klingen; Geräusch,	(business)	
to sit, (sat, sat)	sitzen		Klang	to state; state	erklären, darlegen;
to sit down	sich hinsetzen	sound wave	Schallwelle		Staat, Zustand
site	Grundstück, Sitz,	source	Quelle	statement	Aussage, Angabe
	Standort	south	Süden, südlich, Süd-,	station	Bahnhof
size	Größe		südwärts	statistics	Statistik
skill	Fertigkeit, Fähigkeit,	southern	Süd-, südlich	to stay	bleiben
	Können	sovereign	Souverän, Herrscher	steady	stabil, gleichbleibend
skilled	qualifiziert,	space	Raum, Platz,	to steal	stehlen
	ausgebildet		Weltraum	steam	Dampf
skin	Haut	Spain	Spanien	steel	Stahl
skirt	Rock	Spaniard	Spanier(in)	steering wheel	Lenkrad
sky	Himmel	Spanish	spanisch	step	Schritt, Stufe
to sleep, (slept,	schlafen; Schlaf	spare time	Freizeit	stereotype	Stereotyp, Klischee
slept); sleep		to speak,	sprechen	still	dennoch, noch
slight	leicht, schwach,	(spoke,		stone	Stein
	gering	spoken)		to stop; stop	(an)halten; Halt
slim	schlank	speaker	Sprecher(in)	storage	Lagerung, Aufbewah-
slogan	Slogan, Werbespruch	special	besondere(r,s),		rung, Speicherung
slow	langsam		spezielle(r,s)	to store; store	lagern, speichern;
to slow down	verlangsamen	specialist	Spezialist(in)		Laden (AE),
					Kaufhaus, Lager

storm	Sturm
story	Geschichte
straight in	(gerade) direkt hinein
to strain; strain	(sich) anstrengen; Belastung, Anstrengung
strange	merkwürdig
stranger	Fremde(r)
strap	Riemen, Träger
strategy	Strategie
street	Straße
strength	Stärke
stretch of water	Wasserstraße
to strike; strike	streiken, schlagen; Streik
striker	Streikende(r)
strong	stark
structure	Struktur
to struggle with	kämpfen mit
studies	Kurs, Studium
to study; study	studieren; Studium
style	Stil, Art
subject	Fach, Thema
subject matter	Stoff, Inhalt
substantial	beträchtlich, erheblich
to substitute; substitute	ersetzen; Ersatz
suburb	Vorort
to succeed (in)	Erfolg haben (in, bei)
success	Erfolg
successful	erfolgreich
such	solche(r,s)
such as	wie (zum Beispiel)
sudden	plötzliche(r,s)
to suffer from	leiden unter
sugar	Zucker
to suggest	vorschlagen
suggestion	Vorschlag
suicide	Selbstmord
to suit; suit	passen; Anzug
suitable	passend, geeignet
suitcase	Koffer
sum	Summe
to sum up	zusammenfassen
summary	Zusammenfassung
summer	Sommer
sun	Sonne
sunchair	Liegestuhl
sunshine	Sonnenschein
superb	erstklassig
superfast	außerordentlich schnell
supermarket	Supermarkt
supper	Abendessen
supplier	Lieferant(in)
to supply; supply	versorgen, liefern; Versorgung
to suppose	annehmen, vermuten
sure	sicher
surface	Oberfläche
to surprise; surprise	überraschen; Überraschung
surprised	überrascht

survey	Überblick, Umfrage
survival	Überleben
to survive	überleben
suspicious of	misstrauisch gegenüber
Sweden	Schweden
Swedish	schwedisch
sweet	süß
to swim, (swam, swum)	schwimmen
to switch; switch	schalten, wechseln; Schalter
syndrome	Syndrom

T

table	Tisch, Tabelle
to tackle	angehen, in Angriff nehmen
to take, (took, taken)	nehmen
to take a test	einen Test machen
to take action	etwas unternehmen
to take away	wegnehmen
to take care	aufpassen
to take notes	Notizen machen
to take off	abnehmen, starten (Flugzeug)
to take over	übernehmen
to take part in	teilnehmen an
to take place	stattfinden
to take the view	der Ansicht sein
to take to pieces	zerlegen
to talk; talk	sprechen, reden; Gespräch
tall	hoch(gewachsen), groß
tape	Band, Klebstreifen
target group	Zielgruppe
task	Aufgabe
to taste; taste	probieren, schmecken; Geschmack
tasty	lecker
tax	Steuer
tea	Tee
to teach, (taught, taught)	lehren, unterrichten
teacher	Lehrer(in)
teaching	Unterricht
team	Mannschaft
team work	Teamarbeit
technical	technisch
technological	technologisch, technisch
technologist	Technologe, Technologin, Techniker(in)
technology	Technik, Technologie
teenage	im Teenageralter
telephone	Telefon
television (TV)	Fernsehen
to tell, (told, told)	erzählen

temperature	Temperatur
to tend	tendieren, neigen
tense	Zeitform
tension	Spannung
tent	Zelt
term	Ausdruck, Wort
terrible	schrecklich
to test; test	testen, überprüfen untersuchen; Klassenarbeit, Versuch
textile	Stoff
than	als
to thank; thank	danken; Dank
thanks to	wegen, dank
that	dass, jene(r,s), welche(r,s)
theft	Diebstahl
then	dann, damals
theory	Theorie
there	dort
there is/are	es gibt
therefore	deshalb
these	diese
these days	heutzutage
thick	dick
to thicken	dicker werden, dicker machen
thin	dünn
thing	Ding
to think, (thought, thought)	denken
Third World	Dritte Welt
thirsty	durstig
this	diese(r,s)
those	jene
though	obwohl, trotzdem
thought	Gedanke
thousand	Tausend
to threaten	bedrohen
through	durch
throughout	die ganze Zeit, stets
to throw, (threw, thrown)	werfen
thus	so
ticket	Fahrkarte
tidy	ordentlich, aufgeräumt
to tighten	(fest) anziehen, verschärfen
till	bis
time	Zeit
times	Mal(e)
to tip	kippen
tired	müde
title	Titel
tobacco	Tabak
today	heute
toddler	Kleinkind
toe	Zeh
together	zusammen
toilet	Toilette
tomato	Tomate
tomorrow	morgen
ton(ne)	Tonne

tongue	Zunge
tonight	heute Abend
too	auch
tool	Werkzeug
tooth, teeth	Zahn, Zähne
top	Spitze
topic	Thema
total	gesamt
to touch; touch	berühren; Berührung
tour	(Rund-)Reise, Tour
tourism	Tourismus
tourist board	Fremdenverkehrsamt
tourist guide	Fremdenführer(in)
toward(s)	in Richtung
tower	Turm
town	Stadt
town hall	Rathaus
toy	Spielzeug
to trace; trace	nachgehen, nachspüren; Spur
to trade (in); trade	handeln (mit); Gewerbe, Handwerk, Handel
trading centre	Handelszentrum
traditional	traditionell, herkömmlich
traffic	Verkehr
traffic flow	Verkehrsfluss
traffic jam	Verkehrsstau
traffic light(s)	Ampel
to train; train	ausbilden, eine Ausbildung machen, trainieren; Zug
training	Ausbildung, Training
tram	Straßenbahn
tramway	Straßenbahngleis
to transfer	übertragen
to translate	übersetzen
translation	Übersetzung
transmission	Übertragung
to transmit	übermitteln
to transport; transport	transportieren; Transport
to travel	reisen, fahren
traveller	Reisende(r)
to treat	behandeln
treaty	Vertrag
tree	Baum
trillion	Trillion (AE: Billion)
trip	(Kurz-)Reise
to triple	verdreifachen
trouble	Schwierigkeit(en)
trousers	Hose
truck	Lastwagen
true	wahr, richtig
truth	Wahrheit
to try; try	versuchen; Versuch
tuition	Unterricht
turbine	Turbine
to turn	(sich) drehen, wenden
to turn into	umwandeln in
to turn left/right	links/rechts abbiegen
to turn on/off	ein-/ausschalten
to turn over	umdrehen, überschlagen

to turn to	sich zuwenden
turnover	Umsatz
twice	zweimal
to type; type	(Maschine)schreiben, tippen; Art, Typ
typewriter	Schreibmaschine
typical	typisch
typist	Schreibkraft

U

ultimate	vollendet, perfekt
umbrella	Schirm
unable	nicht in der Lage (sein)
unavoidable	unvermeidbar
uncle	Onkel
to uncover	aufdecken
undemocratic	undemokratisch
under-achiever	leistungsschwache(r) Schüler(in)
underground	Untergrund, U-Bahn
to underline	unterstreichen
underpaid	unterbezahlt
to understand, (understood, understood)	verstehen
undesirable	unerwünscht
uneducated	ungebildet
unemployed	arbeitslos
unemployment	Arbeitslosigkeit
unemployment rate	Arbeitslosenquote
unemployment benefit	Arbeitslosenunter-stützung
unfortunate	unglücklich
unfortunately	leider
unfriendly	unfreundlich
unfulfilled	unerfüllt
unhappy	unglücklich
union	Gewerkschaft
unit	Einheit, Gruppe, Kapitel
united	vereinigt
United Kingdom	Vereinigtes Königreich
unity	Einheit
university	Universität
unknown	unbekannt
unlikely	unwahrscheinlich
unlimited company	Gesellschaft mit unbeschränkter Haftung
unpopular	unpopulär
unreliable	unzuverlässig
unstable	unstabil
unsuitable	unpassend, ungeeignet
until (till)	bis
unusual	ungewöhnlich
unwilling	nicht bereit
up till now	bis jetzt
up to	bis zu
up to now	bis jetzt
up until now	bis jetzt
upon	auf

upstairs	(nach) oben, im Obergeschoss
to urge; urge	drängen; Drang
to use; use	gebrauchen; Gebrauch
used	gebraucht, gewohnt
useful	nützlich
useless	nutzlos
user	Benutzer(in)
user-friendly	benutzerfreundlich
usual	gewöhnlich

V

vacancy	freie Stelle
vacation	Ferien (AE)
vacuum-cleaner	Staubsauger
value	Wert
van	Lieferwagen
variety	Auswahl
to vary	sich ändern, unterschiedlich sein
vast	riesig, weit
vegetable(s)	Gemüse
vehicle	Fahrzeug
version	Version, Fassung
very	sehr
via	über
victim	Opfer
video production	Videoproduktion
Vienna	Wien
Vietnamese	Vietnamese, Vietnamesin; vietnamesisch
view	Sicht, Ansicht, Aussicht
viewer	Zuschauer(in)
viewing habits	Fernseh-gewohnheiten
viewpoint	Standpunkt
village	Dorf
violence	Gewalt
violent	gewalttätig
virtual	virtuell
visa	Visum
to visit; visit	besuchen; Besuch
visitor	Besucher(in)
vital	lebenswichtig, entscheidend
vocabulary	Wortschatz, Vokabelverzeichnis
voice	Stimme
voice recognition	Spracherkennung
volume	Lautstärke
voluntary organization	freiwillige Organisation
volunteer	Freiwillige(r)
to vote; vote	abstimmen, wählen; Abstimmung, Stimme
voter	Wähler(in)
voting system	Wahlsystem

W

wage	Lohn
to wait	warten
waiter	Kellner
waitress	Kellnerin
to wake (up), (woke, woken)	wecken, aufwachen
to walk; walk	gehen; Spaziergang
walking frame	Gehhilfe
wall	Wand, Mauer
to want	wollen
war	Krieg
warehouse	Lager
to warm; warm	wärmen; warm
to warn	warnen
warning	Warnung
Warsaw	Warschau
to wash	waschen
washing machine	Waschmaschine
to waste; waste	verschwenden; Abfall, Verschwendung
waste management	Abfallwirtschaft
wasteful	verschwenderisch
to watch; watch	beobachten, sehen; Uhr
water	Wasser
'watershed hours'	Zeitpunkt, vor dem für Kinder ungeeignetes Material nicht im Fernsehen gezeigt werden darf
way	Weg, Art und Weise
way of life	Lebensweise
weak	schwach
wealth	Wohlstand, Reichtum
wealthy	wohlhabend
weapon	Waffe
to wear, (wore, worn)	(Kleidung) tragen
weather	Wetter
wedding	Hochzeit
week	Woche
weekday	Wochentag
weekend	Wochenende
weight	Gewicht
to welcome; welcome	willkommen (heißen); Willkommen, Empfang
to weld	schweißen
welfare	Wohl, Wohlfahrt, Sozialhilfe
well	gut, gesund; na ja …
well-known	bekannt
well-meaning	wohlmeinend
well-paid	gut bezahlt
west	Westen, westlich, West-, westwärts
West Indies	Westindien (Karibik)
western	West-, westlich
wet	nass, feucht
what	was
what about?	was ist mit?

what else	was noch
what for	wofür, wozu
what … like?	wie …?
whatever	was auch immer
wheel	Rad
wheelchair	Rollstuhl
when	wann
where	wo
whereas	während
whether	ob
which	welche(r,s)
while	während
white	weiß
who	wer
whole	ganz
whom	wem, wen
whose	wessen
why	warum
wide	weit
wife	Ehefrau
wild	wild
will	Wille; werden
willing	bereit
to win, (won, won)	gewinnen
window	Fenster
windscreen	Windschutzscheibe
wine	Wein
winner	Gewinner(in)
wired	verkabelt
wireless	drahtlos
to wish; wish	wünschen; Wunsch
within	innerhalb
without	ohne
woman	Frau
to wonder; wonder	sich fragen, sich wundern; Wunder
wonderful	wunderbar
wood	Holz, Wald
wool	Wolle
word	Wort
word-by-word	Wort für Wort
to work; work	arbeiten; Arbeit
to work out	herausfinden, ausarbeiten, lösen
workday	Arbeitstag
worker	Arbeiter(in)
working class	Arbeiterklasse
working hours	Arbeitszeit
working week	Arbeitswoche
workmate	Kollege
workshop	Werkstatt
world	Welt
worldwide	weltweit
worried	besorgt
to worry	sich sorgen
worse	schlechter
worst	am schlechtesten
worth	wert
would like	würde(n) gerne
to write, (wrote, written)	schreiben
writer	Verfasser(in), Schriftsteller(in)
wrong	falsch

Y

year	Jahr
yearly	jährlich
(… years) ago	vor (… Jahren)
yellow	gelb
yesterday	gestern
yet	jedoch, schon
you're welcome	gern geschehen!
young	jung
youngster	Jugendlicher
Yours	Dein(e)
Yours faithfully	Mit freundlichen Grüßen
Yours sincerely	Mit freundlichen Grüßen
youth	Jugend
youth hostel	Jugendherberge
youth training place	Ausbildungsplatz für Jugendliche
Yuppie	Yuppie (junger karrierebewusster großstädtischer Mensch)

Z

zinc	Zink

AE = American English

A	
a couple of	ein paar
a little	etwas, ein bisschen
a lot of	viel
a number of	einige
to be able	können
abroad	im/ins Ausland
to accept	annehmen, akzeptieren
accident	Unfall
accurate	genau
activity	Aktivität
to add	hinzufügen, addieren
address	Adresse
advantage	Vorteil
to advertise	werben, inserieren
advertisement	Werbeanzeige, Anzeige
advertising	Werbung
advice	Rat, Ratschlag
to advise	(be)raten
to be afraid (of)	Angst haben (vor)
afternoon	Nachmittag
afterwards	danach
again	wieder
against	gegen
age	Alter, Zeitalter
ago	vor
to agree	einverstanden sein, zustimmen
agreement	Übereinstimmung, Übereinkunft
air	Luft
airport	Flughafen
all	alle(s), ganz
to allow	erlauben
almost	fast, beinahe
alone	allein
along	entlang
already	schon
also	auch
alternative	Alternative, Wahl; alternativ
although	obwohl
always	immer
among	zwischen, unter
amount	Betrag, Summe
angry	wütend
animal	Tier
to announce	bekannt geben, ansagen
announcement	Bekanntgabe, Durchsage
another	noch eine(r,s), ein(e) andere(r,s)
to answer; answer	(be)antworten; Antwort
any	irgendeine(r,s)
any time	jederzeit
anybody	irgendjemand
anyone	irgendjemand
anything	irgendetwas
to appear	(er)scheinen
apple	Apfel
to apply (for)	sich bewerben (um)
area	Gebiet

around	herum, um, ungefähr
arrival	Ankunft
to arrive	ankommen
article	Artikel
as	wie, da, als
as well	auch, ebensogut
to ask (for)	fragen, bitten (um)
at first	anfangs
at home	zu Hause
at last	schließlich, endlich
at least	wenigstens
at once	sofort
at present	im Augenblick, jetzt
at the moment	im Moment, jetzt
at work	bei der Arbeit
to attend (school)	(Schule) besuchen
attention	Aufmerksamkeit
aunt	Tante
autumn	Herbst
away	weg
awful	furchtbar, schrecklich

B	
back	Rücken; zurück
bad	schlecht, schlimm, böse
bag	Tüte, Tasche
baggage	Gepäck
to bake	backen
baker	Bäcker(in)
balcony	Balkon
bank	Bank (Geldinstitut)
basket	Korb
bathroom	Badezimmer
beach	Strand
beard	Bart
beautiful	schön
because	weil
because of	wegen
to become, (became, become)	werden
bed	Bett
bedroom	Schlafzimmer
before	vorher, ehe
to begin, (began, begun)	beginnen
beginning	Anfang
behind	hinter
to believe	glauben
to belong to	gehören
best	am besten
best wishes	alles Gute
better	besser
between	zwischen
bicycle	Fahrrad
big	groß
bike	Fahrrad (Kurzform)
bill	Rechnung
bird	Vogel

birth	Geburt
birthday	Geburtstag
bit	Stückchen
to bite, (bit, bitten)	beißen
black	schwarz
blackboard	(Wand-)Tafel
to blame (for)	verantwortlich machen (für)
block of flats	Wohnblock
blood	Blut
blue	blau
board	Brett
boat	Boot
body	Körper
to boil	kochen
to book; book	buchen; Buch
boot	Stiefel
border	Grenze
bored	gelangweilt
boring	langweilig
to borrow	sich ausleihen
both	beide
bottle	Flasche
bottom	Boden
box	Schachtel, Karton, Kiste
boy	Junge
boyfriend	Freund
bread	Brot
to break, (broke, broken); break	(zer)brechen; Pause
to break down	zusammenbrechen
breakfast	Frühstück
bridge	Brücke
to bring, (brought, brought)	bringen
to broadcast, (broadcast, broadcast)	übertragen, senden
brochure	Broschüre, Prospekt
brother	Bruder
brown	braun
to brush; brush	bürsten; Bürste
to build, (built, built)	bauen
building	Gebäude
to burn, (burnt, burnt)	brennen
business	Geschäft
busy	beschäftigt
but	aber
butcher	Metzger(in)
to buy, (bought, bought)	kaufen
buyer	Käufer(in)
by	durch, bei, neben, bis
by the way	übrigens

C	
cake	Kuchen
to calculate	(be)rechnen
to call; call	(an)rufen, nennen; Anruf
camera	Kamera
to camp; camp	zelten, lagern; Lager
can	können; Büchse, Dose
capital	Großbuchstabe, Hauptstadt
car	Auto

card	Karte
to care; care	sorgen; Sorge
career	Beruf, Laufbahn, Karriere
careful	sorgfältig
careless	sorglos
cargo	Fracht, Ladung
to carry	tragen
case	Fall, Koffer, Kiste
cash	Bargeld
cat	Katze
to catch, (caught, caught)	fangen
to cause; cause	verursachen; Ursache
ceiling	Zimmerdecke
centre	Zentrum, Mittelpunkt
century	Jahrhundert
certain	sicher
chair	Stuhl
chalk	Kreide
to change; change	wechseln, (sich) (ver)ändern; Wechsel(geld), Änderung
channel	Kanal
chart	Schaubild, Tabelle, Karte
cheap	billig
to check; check	kontrollieren; Kontrolle
cheers	Tschüs, zum Wohl
cheese	Käse
child	Kind
chips	Pommes Frites, Kartoffelchips
chocolate	Schokolade, Praline
choice	Wahl
to choose, (chose, chosen)	(aus)wählen
Christmas	Weihnachten
church	Kirche
cigarette	Zigarette
cinema	Kino
city	Stadt
class	Klasse
classmate	Klassenkamerad(in)
classroom	Klassenzimmer
to clean; clean	reinigen; sauber
to clear; clear	säubern, räumen; klar
clever	klug
to climb	klettern
clock	Uhr
to close; close	schließen; dicht, nahe
clothes	Kleidung
cloud	Wolke
coal	Kohle
coast	Küste
coat	Mantel
coffee	Kaffee
coin	Münze
cold	kalt
to collect	sammeln, abholen
collection	Sammlung
college	College, Fach(hoch)schule
colour	Farbe
to comb; comb	kämmen; Kamm
to come, (came, come)	kommen
comfortable	bequem
to communicate	kommunizieren, übermitteln
communication	Kommunikation, Übermittlung

company	Gesellschaft, Firma
to compare	vergleichen
competition	Wettbewerb, Konkurrenz
competitor	Konkurrent(in), Wettbewerbs-teilnehmer(in)
to complete; complete	vervollständigen; vollständig
to connect	verbinden
connection	Verbindung, Zusammenhang
to contact; contact	sich in Verbindung setzen mit; Verbindung, Kontakt
to contain	enthalten
container	Behälter
to continue	fortsetzen, weitermachen, weitergehen
to cook; cook	kochen; Koch, Köchin
cooker	Herd
to cooperate	zusammenarbeiten
cooperation	Zusammenarbeit
to copy; copy	kopieren, abschreiben; Kopie, Exemplar
corner	Ecke
to correct; correct	korrigieren, verbessern; richtig
correction	Verbesserung, Korrektur
to cost, (cost, cost); cost	kosten; Kosten
cotton	Baumwolle
to count	zählen, ins Gewicht fallen
counter	Ladentisch, Schalter
country	Land
couple	Ehepaar, Paar
course	Kurs, Lauf, Gang, Strecke
to cover; cover	(be)decken; Abdeckung, Umschlag
cow	Kuh
to cross	überqueren
crossing	Kreuzung
crowd	Menschenmenge, Menge
crowded	dicht gedrängt, voll
to cry; cry	schreien, weinen; Schrei
cup	Tasse, Pokal
curious	neugierig, seltsam
curtain	Vorhang
customer	Kunde, Kundin
customs	Zoll, Zoll-
to cut, (cut, cut); cut	schneiden; Schnitt
to cycle	Fahrrad fahren

D	
daily	täglich
to damage; damage	beschädigen; Schaden
to dance; dance	tanzen; Tanz
danger	Gefahr
dangerous	gefährlich
dark	dunkel
darkness	Dunkelheit
date	Datum, Zeitpunkt, Verabredung
date of birth	Geburtsdatum
daughter	Tochter
day	Tag
dead	tot
to deal, (dealt, dealt) (in, with); deal	handeln (mit, von); Geschäft

dear	lieb
death	Tod
to decide	(sich) entscheiden
decision	Entscheidung
deep	tief
to deliver	liefern, (Rede) halten
delivery	Lieferung
department	Abteilung
department store	Kaufhaus
to depend (on)	abhängen (von)
to describe	beschreiben
description	Beschreibung
to design; design	entwerfen, konstruieren; Entwurf, Muster
desk	Schreibtisch
to destroy	zerstören
destruction	Zerstörung
detail	Einzelheit, Detail
to develop	entwickeln
development	Entwicklung
to dial	(Telefon) wählen
to dictate	diktieren
dictation	Diktat
dictionary	Wörterbuch
to die	sterben
to differ (from)	sich unterscheiden (von)
difference	Unterschied
different	unterschiedlich
difficult	schwierig
difficulty	Schwierigkeit
dining room	Esszimmer
dinner	(Mittag-, Abend-)Essen
to direct (to); direct	richten, lenken (auf); direkt
direction	Richtung
dirty	schmutzig
disadvantage	Nachteil
to disagree (with)	anderer Meinung sein, nicht übereinstimmen mit
to discuss	besprechen, diskutieren
discussion	Gespräch, Unterredung, Diskussion
to dislike	nicht mögen
distance	Entfernung, Strecke, Abstand
doctor	Arzt, Ärztin
dog	Hund
door	Tür
down	hinunter, unten
downstairs	die Treppe hinunter, unten, im Erdgeschoss
to draw	zeichnen, ziehen
drawing	Zeichnung
to dream; dream	träumen; Traum
to dress; dress	(sich) anziehen; Kleid, Kleidung
to drink, (drank, drunk); drink	trinken; Getränk
to drive, (drove, driven); drive	fahren, (an)treiben; Fahrt
driver	Fahrer(in)
to dry; dry	trocknen; trocken
during	während
dustbin	Mülltonne
duty	Pflicht, Zoll

E	
each	jede(r,s)
each other	einander, sich
ear	Ohr
early	früh
to earn	verdienen
earth	Erde
east	Osten, östlich, Ost-, ostwärts
easy	leicht
to eat, (ate, eaten)	essen
economy	Wirtschaft
edge	Kante, Rand, Schneide
to educate	erziehen
education	Erziehung
to effect; effect	durchführen, erzielen, leisten; Wirkung
egg	Ei
either … or	entweder … oder
to elect	wählen
election	Wahl
electric	elektrisch
electricity	Elektrizität
electronics	Elektronik
else	sonst
emergency	Notfall
to employ	beschäftigen, einstellen
employed	beschäftigt
employee	Angestellte(r), Arbeitnehmer(in)
employer	Arbeitgeber(in)
employment	Beschäftigung, Anstellung, Arbeit
empty	leer
to end; end	(be)enden; Ende
energy	Energie, Kraft
engine	Motor, Triebwerk, Lokomotive
engineer	Ingenieur(in), Techniker(in)
engineering	Technik, technisch
to enjoy	genießen, sich freuen an
enjoyable	schön, angenehm, unterhaltsam
enough	genug
to enquire (about)	sich erkundigen (nach), fragen (nach)
enquiry	Anfrage, Erkundigung, Untersuchung
to enter	eintreten
entrance	Eintritt, Eingang
envelope	Umschlag
environment	Umwelt
equal	gleich
equipment	Ausrüstung, Ausstattung
especial	besondere(r,s)
even	sogar, selbst; eben, gleich
evening	Abend
event	Ereignis
ever	je
every	jede(r,s)
everybody	jeder
everyone	jeder
everything	alles
everywhere	überall

exact	genau
exam(ination)	Prüfung
example	Beispiel
excellent	ausgezeichnet, hervorragend
exciting	aufregend
to excuse; excuse	(sich) entschuldigen; Entschuldigung
exercise	Übung
to exist	existieren, bestehen
exit	Ausgang, Ausfahrt
to expect	erwarten
expensive	teuer
experience	Erfahrung
to explain	erklären
explanation	Erklärung
to export; export	exportieren, ausführen; Ausfuhr, Export
to express; express	ausdrücken, äußern; Schnellzug, als Eilsache
expression	Ausdruck
extra	besonders
eye	Auge

F	
to face; face	(einer Sache) ins Auge sehen, gegenübertreten; Gesicht
fact	Tatsache
factory	Fabrik
fair	Messe, Markt; gerecht, fair
to fall, (fell, fallen); fall	fallen; Fallen, Sturz; (AE) Herbst
false	falsch
family	Familie
famous	berühmt
far	weit
fare	Fahrpreis, Fahrgeld
farm	Bauernhof, Farm
farmer	Landwirt
farming	Landwirtschaft
fast	schnell
fat	Fett; dick
father	Vater
favourite	Lieblings-; Liebling
to feed, (fed, fed)	füttern
to feel, (felt, felt)	fühlen
feeling	Gefühl
few	wenige
field	Feld
to fight, (fought, fought); fight	kämpfen; Kampf
to fill	füllen
final	Finale, Endrunde; letzte(r,s), endgültig
to find, (found, found)	finden
fine	Strafe; fein, gut, schön
to finish; finish	beenden; Ziel, Vollendung
to fire; fire	feuern; Feuer
firm	Firma; fest, verbindlich
first	erste(r,s), zuerst
first of all	zuerst, vor allem
to fish; fish	fischen; Fisch

to fit; fit	(zusammen) passen, einbauen; gesund, in Form
to fix	befestigen, reparieren, besorgen
flat	Wohnung; flach
flight	Flug
floor	Boden
flower	Blume
to fly, (flew, flown); fly	fliegen; Fliege
to follow	folgen
food	Nahrung, Essen
foot	Fuß
football	Fußball
for example	zum Beispiel
foreign	ausländisch, fremd
forever	für immer
to forget, (forgot, forgotten)	vergessen
fork	Gabel
to form; form	formen, gestalten; Form, Formular, Klasse
fortunate	glücklich
forward(s)	vorwärts
to free; free	befreien; frei
freeway	(AE) Autobahn
frequent	häufig
fresh	frisch
fridge	Kühlschrank
friend	Freund(in)
friendly	freundlich
front	Vorderseite
fruit	Frucht, Früchte, Obst
full	voll
fun	Spaß
furniture	Möbel
further	weiter
future	Zukunft; zukünftig

G	
game	Spiel
garage	Autowerkstatt, Garage
garden	Garten
gate	Tor
gentleman	Herr
to get, (got, got)	bekommen, werden
to get married	heiraten
to get up	aufstehen
girl	Mädchen
girlfriend	Freundin
to give, (gave, given)	geben
to give up	aufgeben
glad	froh
glass	Glas
glasses	Brille
glove	Handschuh
to go, (went, gone)	gehen
to go down	untergehen, sinken, fallen
to go on	weitergehen, weitermachen
to go shopping	einkaufen
to go up	hinaufgehen, wachsen, steigen
good	gut
goodbye	auf Wiedersehen

goods	Güter, Waren
to govern	regieren
government	Regierung
grandfather	Großvater
grandmother	Großmutter
grandparents	Großeltern
grateful	dankbar
great	großartig, groß
green	grün
to greet	grüßen
grey	grau
grocer	Lebensmittelhändler(in)
ground	Boden
group	Gruppe
to grow, (grew, grown)	wachsen
grown-up	Erwachsene(r); erwachsen
growth	Wachstum
to guess	erraten
guest	Gast

H	
hair	Haar
half	Hälfte; halb
hall	Flur, Saal
ham	Schinken
handbag	Handtasche
handkerchief	Taschentuch
to hang, (hung, hung)	(auf)hängen
to happen	geschehen
happy	glücklich, heiter
harbour	Hafen
hard	hart, schwierig, anstrengend
hardly	kaum
hat	Hut
to hate	hassen
to have, (had, had)	haben, lassen
to have to	müssen
to head; head	anführen, fahren nach; Kopf, Leiter
headache	Kopfschmerz
headline	Überschrift
health	Gesundheit
healthy	gesund
to hear, (heard, heard)	hören
heart	Herz
to heat; heat	heizen; Hitze
heating	Heizung
heavy	schwer
height	Höhe
hello	Hallo
to help; help	helfen; Hilfe
helpful	hilfreich
here	hier
here you are	bitte(schön)!
to hesitate	zögern
Hi Tech (High Technology)	Hochtechnologie
to hide, (hid, hidden)	(sich) verstecken
high	hoch
hill	Hügel
history	Geschichte
to hit, (hit, hit); hit	schlagen; Schlag, Treffer, Erfolg

to hold, (held, held)	halten
hole	Loch
holiday	freier Tag, Feiertag, Urlaub
home	Wohnung, Heimat; zu/nach Hause
homework	Hausaufgabe
honest	ehrlich
to hope; hope	hoffen; Hoffnung
horse	Pferd
hospital	Krankenhaus
hot	heiß
hour	Stunde
house	Haus
housewife	Hausfrau
housework	Hausarbeit
how	wie
how are you?	wie geht es Dir/Ihnen?
however	jedoch
hundred	Hundert
hungry	hungrig
to hurry; hurry	sich beeilen; Eile
to hurt	verletzen
husband	Ehemann

I

ice cream	Eis
idea	Idee
if	wenn, falls
ill	krank
illness	Krankheit
to imagine	sich vorstellen
immediate	unmittelbar, unverzüglich
immigrant	Einwanderer, Einwanderin
to immigrate	einwandern
to import; import	importieren, einführen; Einfuhr, Import
importance	Wichtigkeit
important	wichtig
impossible	unmöglich
to improve	(sich) verbessern
in fact	tatsächlich
in front of	vor
in italics	kursiv
in my opinion	meiner Meinung nach
in time	rechtzeitig
inch	(Maßeinheit) Zoll
to include	einschließen
income	Einkommen
to increase	zunehmen, steigen, erhöhen
indeed	tatsächlich
industry	Industrie
to inform	informieren
inside	in, innerhalb
instead (of)	anstatt
to instruct	unterrichten, anweisen
instruction	Unterricht, Anweisung, (Gebrauchs-)Anleitung
insurance	Versicherung
interest	Interesse, (Plural) Zinsen
interesting	interessant
to introduce	einführen, vorstellen

introduction	Einführung, Vorstellung
to invent	erfinden
invention	Erfindung
to invest	investieren
invitation	Einladung
to invite	einladen
island	Insel

J

jacket	Jacke
jam	Marmelade
job	Arbeit, Stelle, Aufgabe
to join	(sich) anschließen, beitreten
journey	Reise
juice	Saft
to jump; jump	springen; Sprung
just	genau, soeben, nur

K

to keep, (kept, kept)	(be)halten
key	Schlüssel
to kill	töten
kilogram(me)	Kilogramm
kind	Art, Sorte; freundlich
king	König
to kiss; kiss	küssen; Kuss
kitchen	Küche
knee	Knie
knife	Messer
to knock; knock	klopfen; Klopfen
to know, (knew, known)	wissen
knowledge	Wissen

L

ladder	Leiter
lady	Dame
lake	See
lamp	Lampe
land	Land
landlady	Vermieterin, Wirtin
landlord	Vermieter, Wirt
language	Sprache
large	groß
to last; last	dauern; letzte(r,s)
late	spät
later on	später
latest	neueste(r,s)
to laugh	lachen
laughter	Gelächter
law	Gesetz
to lay, (laid, laid)	legen
lazy	faul
to lead, (led, led)	führen, leiten
leaflet	(Hand-)Zettel, Flugblatt
to learn, (learnt, learnt)	lernen
learner	Lernende(r), Anfänger(in)
least	wenigste(r,s), geringste(r,s)

to leave, (left, left)	verlassen
left	links
leg	Bein
leisure	Freizeit
lemon	Zitrone
to lend, (lent, lent)	verleihen
length	Länge
less	weniger
lesson	Unterrichtsstunde
to let, (let, let)	lassen
letter	Brief
to lie, (lay, lain)	liegen
to lie, (lied, lied)	lügen
life	Leben
to lift; lift	anheben, aufheben; Aufzug, Mitfahrgelegenheit
light	Licht, Lampe; hell, leicht
to like; like	mögen; wie
limit	Grenze, Beschränkung
line	Linie, Zeile
lip	Lippe
to list; list	aufführen, auflisten; Liste
to listen	zuhören
little	klein, wenig
to live; live	leben, wohnen; lebend, direkt, live
living room	Wohnzimmer
to load; load	laden; Ladung
local	lokal, ortsansässig, örtlich
long	lang
to look	schauen, (aus-)sehen
to look after	sich kümmern um
to look for	suchen
to look forward to	sich freuen auf
to look out	aufpassen, hinaussehen
to look up	nachschlagen, heraussuchen, aufblicken
lorry	Lastwagen
to lose, (lost, lost)	verlieren
loss	Verlust
lot	Menge, Los
lots of	viel
loud	laut
to love; love	lieben; Liebe
lovely	hübsch
low	niedrig
luck	Glück, Schicksal
lucky	glücklich (im Sinne von: Glück haben)
luggage	Gepäck
lunch	Mittagessen

M	
machine	Maschine
mad	verrückt
madam	gnädige Frau
magazine	Zeitschrift
mail	Post
main	Haupt-
mainly	hauptsächlich
to make, (made, made)	machen, herstellen

man	Mann
to manage	zu Stande bringen, schaffen, leiten, verwalten
management	(Geschäfts-)Leitung, Verwaltung, Durchführung
many	viele
map	(Land-)Karte
market	Markt
marmalade	(Orangen-)Marmelade
married	verheiratet
to marry	heiraten
mass	Masse
to match; match	zusammenbringen, passen; Wettkampf, Streichholz
mathematics	Mathematik
to matter; matter	etwas ausmachen; Angelegenheit
may	dürfen
maybe	vielleicht
meal	Mahlzeit
to mean, (meant, meant)	bedeuten, meinen
meaning	Bedeutung
(in the) meantime	inzwischen
meanwhile	inzwischen
meat	Fleisch
mechanic	Mechaniker(in)
media	Medien
to meet, (met, met)	(sich) treffen, kennenlernen
meeting	Treffen
member	Mitglied
to mend	reparieren
to mention	erwähnen
message	Mitteilung, Nachricht
method	Methode
metre	Meter
microwave	Mikrowelle
middle	Mitte
midnight	Mitternacht
might	Gewalt, Macht; könnte(n)
mile	Meile
milk	Milch
to mind; mind	etwas ausmachen; Meinung, Gedanken, Verstand
mine	Bergwerk
minute	Minute
mirror	Spiegel
Miss	Fräulein
to miss	vermissen, verfehlen, verpassen
mistake	Fehler
to mix; mix	mischen; Mischung
moment	Augenblick
money	Geld
month	Monat
moon	Mond
more	mehr
morning	Morgen
most	die meisten
mother	Mutter
mountain	Berg
mouth	Mund
to move	bewegen, umziehen
movement	Bewegung

Mr	Herr
Mrs	Frau (verheiratet)
Ms	Frau (verheiratet oder unverheiratet)
much	viel
music	Musik
must	müssen
must not	nicht dürfen

N	
to name; name	benennen; Name
narrow	eng
near	nahe
nearby	nahe gelegen
nearly	fast, beinahe
necessary	notwendig
to need; need	benötigen; Notwendigkeit
neighbour	Nachbar(in)
neither ... nor	weder ... noch
never	nie
new	neu
news	Nachrichten, Neuigkeit
newspaper	Zeitung
next	nächste(r,s)
nice	nett
night	Nacht
no	kein; nein
no longer	nicht mehr
no one	niemand
nobody	niemand
noise	Lärm
noisy	geräuschvoll
noon	Mittag
north	Norden; nördlich, Nord-, nordwärts
nose	Nase
not	nicht
not either	auch nicht
not even	nicht einmal
not yet	noch nicht
to note; note	notieren; Notiz
nothing	nichts
to notice; notice	bemerken; Aushang, Kenntnis, Beachtung
now	jetzt
nowadays	heutzutage
nowhere	nirgendwo
number	Zahl, Nummer, Anzahl
nurse	Krankenschwester

O	
o'clock	Uhr (Zeitangabe)
ocean	Meer, Ozean
of course	natürlich
off	von ... weg
to offer; offer	anbieten; Angebot
office	Büro, Amt
often	oft
oil	Öl
old	alt
on time	pünktlich

once	einmal
only	nur
to open; open	öffnen; offen
opinion	Meinung
opposite	Gegensatz; gegensätzlich
or	oder
to order; order	bestellen, befehlen; Bestellung, Befehl
organization	Organisation
to organize	organisieren
other	andere(r,s)
out of work	arbeitslos
outside	draußen, außerhalb; Außenseite
to own; own	besitzen; eigene(r,s)
owner	Eigentümer(in)

P	
to pack; pack	packen; Packung
packet	Paket
page	Seite
to paint; paint	malen; Farbe
pair	Paar
paper	Papier
parents	Eltern
to park; park	parken; Park
part	Teil
to pass	vorbeigehen, (Prüfung) bestehen
passenger	Passagier, Fahrgast
passport	Pass
past	Vergangenheit
to pay, (paid, paid); pay	(be-)zahlen; Bezahlung
peace	Friede
pen	Füllfederhalter
pence	Plural von Penny
pencil	Bleistift
penny	Penny (engl. Münze)
people	Leute, Volk
per cent	Prozent
perfect	vollkommen, perfekt
perhaps	vielleicht
period	Periode, Zeitraum, Schulstunde
personal	persönlich
petrol	Benzin
to phone; phone	telefonieren; Telefon
photograph	Foto
to pick	pflücken, wählen
to pick up	nehmen, aufheben
picture	Bild
piece	Stück
pipe	Pfeife, Röhre
to place; place	stellen, legen; Platz
to plan; plan	planen; Plan
plane	Flugzeug
to plant; plant	pflanzen; Pflanze
plate	Teller
platform	Bahnsteig
to play; play	spielen; (Schau-)Spiel
player	Spieler(in)
playground	Spielplatz
please	bitte

pleasure	Vergnügen
pocket	Tasche
to point; point	zeigen; Punkt
police	Polizei
policeman	Polizist
policewoman	Polizistin
political	politisch
politician	Politiker(in)
politics	Politik
to pollute	verschmutzen
polluted	verschmutzt
pollution	Umweltverschmutzung
poor	arm
popular	beliebt, populär
population	Bevölkerung
port	Hafen
possibility	Möglichkeit
possible	möglich
post office	Post
postcard	Postkarte
postman	Briefträger
pot	Topf
potato	Kartoffel
pound	Pfund
power	Kraft
power station	Kraftwerk
practice	Übung
to practise	üben
to prefer	vorziehen
to prepare	vorbereiten
to present; present	schenken, vorstellen; Geschenk, Gegenwart; anwesend, gegenwärtig
to press; press	drücken, pressen; Presse
pretty	hübsch
price	Preis
pride	Stolz
prize	Preis, Gewinn
probable	wahrscheinlich
to produce	produzieren, herstellen
producer	Hersteller(in), Produzent(in)
product	Produkt
production	Herstellung, Produktion
to profit; profit	profitieren; Gewinn
profitable	rentabel, einträglich, lohnend
program(me)	Programm
to promise; promise	versprechen; Versprechen
to pronounce	aussprechen
pronunciation	Aussprache
to protect	schützen
protection	Schutz
proud	stolz
pub	Kneipe
public	Öffentlichkeit; öffentlich
to pull	ziehen
pupil	Schüler(in)
purpose	Zweck, Absicht
to push; push	schieben, stoßen; Stoß
to put, (put, put)	setzen, stellen, legen
to put on	aufsetzen
to put up	(Hand) heben, bauen, aufstellen

Q	
quality	Qualität
quantity	Menge
quarter	Viertel
queen	Königin
question	Frage
quick	schnell
quiet	ruhig
quite	ganz, ziemlich

R	
railway	Eisenbahn
to rain; rain	regnen; Regen
to raise	(hoch-)heben, erheben
rather	ziemlich
to reach; reach	erreichen; Reichweite
to read, (read, read)	lesen
reader	Leser(in)
ready	fertig, bereit
real	wirklich
reality	Wirklichkeit
reason	Grund
reasonable	vernünftig, günstig
to receive	erhalten, bekommen
recent	jüngst, kürzlich
reception	Empfang
receptionist	im Empfang arbeitende Person
to record; record	aufnehmen; Rekord, Aufnahme
red	rot
regular	regelmäßig
relative	Verwandte(r); relativ
to relax	(sich) entspannen
to remain	bleiben
to remember	sich erinnern an
to remind (of)	erinnern an
to rent; rent	mieten, vermieten; Miete
to repair; repair	reparieren; Reparatur
to repeat; repeat	wiederholen; Wiederholung
to replace	ersetzen
to reply; reply	antworten; Antwort
to report; report	berichten; Bericht
to rescue; rescue	retten; Rettung
to rest; rest	ruhen; Rest, Ruhe
to result; result	resultieren; Ergebnis
to return; return	zurückkommen; Rückkehr, Rückgabe
rich	reich
to ride, (rode, ridden); ride	reiten, fahren; Ritt, Fahrt
right	rechts
to ring, (rang, rung); ring	klingeln, anrufen; Ring, Anruf
to rise, (rose, risen); rise	(auf)steigen, zunehmen; Aufstieg, Zunahme
river	Fluss
road	Straße
roof	Dach
room	Zimmer
round	Runde; rund, herum
rubber	(Radier-)Gummi

rubbish	Abfall, Müll
to rule; rule	herrschen; Regel, Herrschaft
to run, (ran, run)	laufen

S	
sad	traurig
safe	sicher
safety	Sicherheit
sale	(Schluss-)Verkauf
salesman/woman	Verkäufer(in)
salt	Salz
same	gleiche(r,s), der-, die-, dasselbe
to save	retten
to say, (said, said)	sagen
school	Schule
sea	Meer
seat	Sitz
second	Sekunde; zweite(r,s)
secret	Geheimnis; geheim
secretary	Sekretär(in)
to see, (saw, seen)	sehen
to seem	scheinen
to sell, (sold, sold)	verkaufen
seller	Verkäufer(in)
to send, (sent, sent)	schicken, senden
to sentence; sentence	verurteilen; Satz, Urteil
serious	ernst
to serve	(be)dienen, servieren
to service; service	(Auto) warten; Dienst, Betrieb
to set, (set, set)	setzen, stellen, legen
several	mehrere
shall	sollen
to share; share	teilen; Anteil
sheet	Blatt, Bogen
shelf	Regal
to shine, (shone, shone)	scheinen, leuchten
to ship; ship	verschicken; Schiff
shirt	Hemd
shoe	Schuh
shop	Geschäft, Laden
shop assistant	Verkäufer(in)
short	kurz
should	sollte(n)
shoulder	Schulter
to shout; shout	rufen; Ruf
to show, (showed, shown); show	zeigen; Ausstellung, Vorstellung
to shut, (shut, shut)	schließen
sick	krank
side	Seite
sight	Sicht, Anblick, Sehenswürdigkeit
to sign; sign	unterschreiben; Zeichen
simple	einfach
since	seit
since then	seitdem
to sing, (sang, sung)	singen
sir	Herr (Anrede)
sister	Schwester
to sit, (sat, sat)	sitzen
to sit down	sich hinsetzen
size	Größe

skill	Fertigkeit, Fähigkeit, Können
skirt	Rock
sky	Himmel
to sleep, (slept, slept); sleep	schlafen; Schlaf
slim	schlank
slow	langsam
to slow down	verlangsamen
small	klein
to smell; smell	riechen; Geruch
to smile; smile	lächeln; Lächeln
to smoke; smoke	rauchen; Rauch
to snow; snow	schneien; Schnee
so far	bisher, bis jetzt
soap	Seife
soccer	Fußball
sock	Socke
soft	weich
solution	Lösung
to solve	lösen
some	einige
somebody	jemand
someone	jemand
something	etwas
sometimes	manchmal
son	Sohn
song	Lied
soon	bald
sorry	betrübt, tut mir Leid!, Entschuldigung!
to sound; sound	klingen; Geräusch, Klang
south	Süden, südlich, Süd-, südwärts
space	Raum, Platz, Weltraum
spare time	Freizeit
to speak, (spoke, spoken)	sprechen
speaker	Sprecher(in)
special	besondere(r,s), spezielle(r,s)
speech	Rede
to speed; speed	schnell fahren; Geschwindigkeit
to speed up	beschleunigen
to spell; spell	buchstabieren; Zauber(spruch)
to spend, (spent, spent)	ausgeben, verbringen
spoon	Löffel
spring	Frühling
staff	Belegschaft, Kollegium
stamp	Briefmarke
to stand, (stood, stood); stand	stehen, aushalten; Stand
to start; start	anfangen; Anfang
to state; state	erklären, darlegen; Staat, Zustand
station	Bahnhof
to stay	bleiben
still	dennoch, noch
stone	Stein
to stop; stop	(an)halten; Halt
to store; store	lagern, speichern; (AE) Laden, Kaufhaus, Lager
storm	Sturm
story	Geschichte
strange	merkwürdig
street	Straße

to strike; strike	streiken, schlagen; Streik
strong	stark
to study; study	studieren; Studium
subject	Fach, Thema
suburb	Vorort
to succeed (in)	Erfolg haben (in, bei)
success	Erfolg
successful	erfolgreich
such	solche(r,s)
sudden	plötzliche(r,s)
sugar	Zucker
to suit; suit	passen; Anzug
suitcase	Koffer
sum	Summe
summer	Sommer
sun	Sonne
sunshine	Sonnenschein
supermarket	Supermarkt
supper	Abendessen
to suppose	annehmen, vermuten
sure	sicher
to surprise; surprise	überraschen; Überraschung
surprised	überrascht
survey	Überblick, Umfrage
sweet	süß
to swim, (swam, swum)	schwimmen
to switch; switch	schalten, wechseln; Schalter

T

table	Tisch, Tabelle
to take, (took, taken)	nehmen
to take part in	teilnehmen an
to take place	stattfinden
to talk; talk	sprechen, reden; Gespräch
tall	hoch(gewachsen), groß
to taste; taste	schmecken, probieren; Geschmack
tasty	lecker
tax	Steuer
tea	Tee
to teach, (taught, taught)	lehren, unterrichten
teacher	Lehrer(in)
team	Mannschaft
technical	technisch
technology	Technik, Technologie
telephone	Telefon
television (TV)	Fernsehen
to tell, (told, told)	erzählen
terrible	schrecklich
to test; test	testen, überprüfen, untersuchen; Klassenarbeit, Versuch
than	als
to thank	danken
that	dass, jene(r,s), welche(r,s)
then	dann, damals
there	dort
there is/are	es gibt
therefore	deshalb
these	diese
these days	heutzutage
thick	dick

thin	dünn
thing	Ding
to think, (thought, thought)	denken
thirsty	durstig
this	diese(r,s)
those	jene
though	obwohl, trotzdem
thousand	Tausend
through	durch
to throw, (threw, thrown)	werfen
thus	so
ticket	Fahrkarte
tidy	ordentlich, aufgeräumt
till	bis
time	Zeit
times	Mal(e)
tired	müde
tobacco	Tabak
today	heute
toe	Zeh
together	zusammen
toilet	Toilette
tomato	Tomate
tomorrow	morgen
tongue	Zunge
tonight	heute Abend
too	auch
tool	Werkzeug
tooth, teeth	Zahn, Zähne
top	Spitze
tour	(Rund-)Reise, Tour
toward(s)	in Richtung
tower	Turm
town	Stadt
toy	Spielzeug
to trade (in); trade	handeln (mit); Gewerbe, Handwerk, Handel
traditional	traditionell, herkömmlich
traffic	Verkehr
traffic light(s)	Ampel
to train; train	ausbilden, trainieren, eine Ausbildung machen; Zug
training	Ausbildung, Training
to translate	übersetzen
translation	Übersetzung
to transport; transport	transportieren; Transport
to travel	reisen, fahren
tree	Baum
trip	(Kurz-)Reise
trouble	Schwierigkeit(en)
trousers	Hose
true	wahr, richtig
truth	Wahrheit
to try; try	versuchen; Versuch
to turn	(sich) drehen, wenden
to turn left/right	links/rechts abbiegen
to turn on/off	ein-/ausschalten
to turn over	umdrehen, überschlagen
twice	zweimal
to type; type	tippen, (Maschine) schreiben; Art, Typ

typewriter	Schreibmaschine
typical	typisch
typist	Schreibkraft

U

umbrella	Schirm
uncle	Onkel
to understand, (understood, understood)	verstehen
unemployed	arbeitslos
unemployment	Arbeitslosigkeit
unfortunate	unglücklich
unfortunately	leider
unfriendly	unfreundlich
unhappy	unglücklich
university	Universität
until (till)	bis
upon	auf
upstairs	(nach) oben, im Obergeschoss
to use; use	gebrauchen; Gebrauch
used	gebraucht, gewohnt
useful	nützlich
useless	nutzlos
usual	gewöhnlich

V

vacation	(AE) Ferien
van	Lieferwagen
vegetable(s)	Gemüse
vehicle	Fahrzeug
very	sehr
village	Dorf
to visit; visit	besuchen; Besuch
visitor	Besucher(in)
vocabulary	Wortschatz, Vokabelverzeichnis
voice	Stimme
to vote; vote	abstimmen, wählen; Abstimmung, Stimme

W

to wait	warten
waiter	Kellner
waitress	Kellnerin
to wake, (woke, woken) (up)	wecken, aufwachen
to walk; walk	gehen; Spaziergang
wall	Wand, Mauer
to want	wollen
war	Krieg
warehouse	Lager
to warm; warm	wärmen; warm
to warn	warnen
to wash	waschen
washing machine	Waschmaschine
to waste; waste	verschwenden; Abfall, Verschwendung
to watch; watch	beobachten, sehen; Uhr
water	Wasser
way	Weg, Art und Weise

weak	schwach
to wear, (wore, worn)	(Kleidung) tragen
weather	Wetter
week	Woche
weekend	Wochenende
weight	Gewicht
to welcome; welcome	willkommen heißen; Willkommen, Empfang
well	gut, gesund; na ja …
well-known	bekannt
west	Westen, westlich, West-, westwärts
wet	nass, feucht
what	was
what about …	was ist mit …
what else	was noch
what for	wofür, wozu
wheel	Rad
when	wann
where	wo
whether	ob
which	welche(r, s)
while	während
white	weiß
who	wer
whole	ganz
whom	wem, wen
whose	wessen
why	warum
wide	weit
wife	Ehefrau
will	Wille; werden
to win, (won, won)	gewinnen
window	Fenster
wine	Wein
to wish; wish	wünschen; Wunsch
within	innerhalb
without	ohne
woman	Frau
wonderful	wunderbar
wood	Holz, Wald
wool	Wolle
word	Wort
to work; work	arbeiten; Arbeit
worker	Arbeiter(in)
world	Welt
worse	schlechter
worst	am schlechtesten
worth	wert
to write, (wrote, written)	schreiben
writer	Verfasser(in), Schriftsteller(in)
wrong	falsch

Y

year	Jahr
yellow	gelb
yesterday	gestern
yet	jedoch, schon
you're welcome	gern geschehen!
young	jung
youth	Jugend

Infinitive	Past tense	Past participle	German
awake	awoke	awoken	aufwachen
be	was, were	been	sein
beat	beat	beaten	schlagen
become	became	become	werden
begin	began	begun	anfangen, beginnen
bend	bent	bent	biegen
bet	bet	bet	wetten
bid	bid	bid	bieten
bite	bit	bitten	beißen
blow	blew	blown	blasen, wehen (Wind)
break	broke	broken	brechen
bring	brought	brought	bringen
broadcast	broadcast	broadcast	senden (Rundfunk)
build	built	built	bauen
burn	burned/ burnt	burned/ burnt	(ver)brennen
burst	burst	burst	platzen
buy	bought	bought	kaufen
cast	cast	cast	werfen, gießen
catch	caught	caught	fangen
choose	chose	chosen	wählen, auswählen
come	came	come	kommen
cost	cost	cost	kosten
cut	cut	cut	schneiden
deal	dealt	dealt	handeln mit, umgehen
dig	dug	dug	graben
do	did	done	tun, machen
draw	drew	drawn	ziehen, zeichnen
dream	dreamed/ dreamt	dreamed/ dreamt	träumen
drive	drove	driven	fahren
drink	drank	drunk	trinken
eat	ate	eaten	essen
fall	fell	fallen	fallen
feed	fed	fed	füttern
feel	felt	felt	fühlen
fight	fought	fought	kämpfen
find	found	found	finden
fly	flew	flown	fliegen
forget	forgot	forgotten	vergessen
forgive	forgave	forgiven	vergeben
freeze	froze	frozen	gefrieren
get	got	got	bekommen
give	gave	given	geben
go	went	gone	gehen
grind	ground	ground	mahlen, schleifen
grow	grew	grown	wachsen
hang	hung	hung	hängen
have	had	had	haben
hear	heard	heard	hören
hide	hid	hidden	verstecken

Infinitive	Past tense	Past participle	German
hit	hit	hit	schlagen, treffen
hold	held	held	halten
hurt	hurt	hurt	verletzen
keep	kept	kept	behalten
know	knew	known	wissen, kennen
lay	laid	laid	legen
lead	led	led	führen
learn	learned/ learnt	learned/ learnt	lernen
leave	left	left	lassen, verlassen
lend	lent	lent	(ver)leihen
let	let	let	lassen
lie	lay	lain	liegen
lose	lost	lost	verlieren
make	made	made	machen
mean	meant	meant	bedeuten
meet	met	met	treffen
pay	paid	paid	bezahlen
put	put	put	setzen, stellen, legen
read	read	read	lesen
ride	rode	ridden	reiten, fahren
ring	rang	rung	klingen, anrufen
rise	rose	risen	aufgehen, steigen
run	ran	run	rennen, laufen
say	said	said	sagen
see	saw	seen	sehen
seek	sought	sought	suchen
sell	sold	sold	verkaufen
send	sent	sent	schicken, senden
shake	shook	shaken	schütteln
show	showed	showed/ shown	zeigen
shut	shut	shut	schließen
smell	smelt	smelt	riechen
sing	sang	sung	singen
sit	sat	sat	sitzen
sleep	slept	slept	schlafen
speak	spoke	spoken	sprechen
spend	spent	spent	ausgeben
stand	stood	stood	stehen
swim	swam	swum	schwimmen
take	took	taken	nehmen
teach	taught	taught	lehren, unterrichten
tear	tore	torn	zerreißen
tell	told	told	sagen, erzählen
think	thought	thought	denken
throw	threw	thrown	werfen
unterstand	understood	understood	verstehen
wake	woke	woken	wecken
wear	wore	worn	tragen (v. Kleidung)
win	won	won	gewinnen
write	wrote	written	schreiben

Unit 1

■ A2   Two students meet on the campus (see Student's Book, page 11)

■ D1   An exchange visit (Exercises a and b)

Mrs Evans: So what are you doing at College this week, John?

John: We're working on the environment project until Thursday, Mum. After that there's a visit to the electronics factory near here and to the power station in Hartlepool. I'm looking forward to it, I think it's really great that we have the chance to see places like that.

Klaus: Oh yes, I'm looking forward to it, too.

Mrs Evans: I'm glad you're enjoying this week, Klaus.

Klaus: Yes, I am. I'm learning such a lot about Britain and the way you do things here.

Mrs Evans: That's why these exchanges are such a good idea in my opinion. You young people have the chance to really get to know each other and that's important.

Klaus: Oh yes, I agree with you, Mrs Evans. I don't think that tourists learn half as much about the people or the country they visit.

John: Exactly. They don't have enough contact with the locals in my view. And when they come back they still think for example that all the Germans are serious and work hard.

Klaus: Or that the British are very traditional and drink tea all day!

Mrs Evans: But I suppose it's a bit strange for you, Klaus, living with a foreign family?

Klaus: No, not at all. I mean, you're all so friendly to me. Your house is so comfortable and I love the food. In fact, I feel quite at home already! Even the T.V. programmes are the same as the ones we have at home!

Unit 2

■ A2   A radio interview (see Student's Book, page 19)

■ D   Job advertisements (Exercise d)

(Interview 1)

Interviewer: Well Miss Long, your CV seems alright. Tell me. What I'd like to know is which subjects did you enjoy most at school?

Miss Long: Ah … I liked foreign languages the most. We did French and German.

Interviewer: And can you speak them well?

Miss Long: Mm, my French isn't so good now, but I think my German is alright. I often spend my holidays in Germany as I have some friends over there and that gives me a chance to practise.

Interviewer: Hm. And why have you applied for this job?

Miss Long:	Two main reasons really. First I'd like to travel in Europe more. And secondly, I'm only 22, and I feel it is time for a change. I'd like a more interesting job. As you know, I've worked as a secretary at Hard and Soft for 2 years now in the sales department. They produce machine parts for the car industry. I don't like the work …

(Interview 2)

Interviewer:	Mr Short. I see from your CV that you now work for a large electrical company. Why do you want to change jobs ?
Mr Short:	Well, I'm 30 and I've worked at ElectroMagnum for 5 years. It's time for me to look for something else. I've been a computer operator for 8 years now.
Interviewer:	Aren't you happy in your present job?
Mr Short:	Well, not really. What I want is a new challenge. And the pay at ElectroMagnum isn't that good.
Interviewer:	Well, we can talk about that later. Now, I see from your letter of application that you did a BTEC course in electrical engineering. What did you like most on that course?
Mr Short:	The practical work was the really interesting part of the course, although I also enjoyed learning German. The trouble was I wasn't very good at it.
Interviewer:	But you do know that this job involves travelling to Europe a lot and especially to our customers in Germany?
Mr Short:	Yes, I know, and I am going to evening classes to improve my German. It's hard work though …

UNIT 3

■ **D1   Voting systems (Exercises a and c)**

(Politician 1) Brian Taylor: "Good morning ladies and gentlemen. And welcome to Westminster. My name's Brian Taylor and before I became an MP, I ran my own farm in Scotland and farming is still one of my main interests. In a way, I suppose you could say that I was fortunate to get into Parliament in the first place. You see, I belong to the Liberal Democrats. We're one of the smallest parties in the British Parliament, not because we have the fewest voters, but because of the British voting system. In Great Britain the voters have one vote, which they can use for one particular candidate. The candidate who receives the most votes becomes the Member of Parliament for that constituency. I was lucky when I won the election in Perth. But just look at these statistics … "

(Politician 2) Inge Jensen: "Hello, I'm Inge Jensen from Copenhagen. Well, we in Denmark have a different voting system to that in Great Britain. Here, the party that wins most of the votes over the whole of Denmark has the most members in our Parliament – which is called the Folketing by the way. This is certainly more democratic because the smaller parties can get into Parliament more easily. Anyway, I expect you'd like to know more about me. Well, I joined the Danish Conservative Party while I was still at school and have been a member ever since. After I left school I got a job as a computer operator. However, politics remained one of my main interests and three years ago I became a member of the Danish Parliament. It has been hard work because I've got two children and a husband to look after as well as my work in Parliament. That's one reason why I'm especially interested in family affairs in politics. But let me go back to our voting system. Now, in my opinion, …"

Unit 4

■ D1   Radio advertising (Exercises a and b)

1.

Keep on running, keep on hiding.
One fine day I'm gonna be the one to make you understand.
With Lukes you're gonna be a man!
Hey, hey, hey everyone is wearing them now. Nearly all the time. Hey, hey, hey your local store is stocking them now. At only £10.99.
Keep on running …

Lukes – the superfast running shoes. Really comfortable and built for speed! Get yours today at Simpson's Sports Store, Penarth Road.

2.

When you order your new car from Wyndham Jones, you can be confident that you're choosing from a world class range. You can be confident that every first-class car is totally safe and engineered to perfection. You can also be sure that at Wyndham Jones you will get excellent service. So whether you want a small or a family-sized car, at Wyndham Jones you know your choice will be the right one! Prices for the 'City' model start at £14,000. Wyndham Jones, Queen Street, Cardiff. Discover the difference!

3.

Shop assistant: Good afternoon sir, can I help you?

Customer: Oh, I'm looking for a personal CD player, actually. You know, one that you can carry around.

Shop assistant: I'm sure we can help you there, sir. Here at Sizzle superstore, we have a very large stock. This superb new Williams Mini-master model is very popular.

Customer: Yes, it's not bad, but it hasn't got many functions on it, has it? I mean, it's a bit basic, isn't it? Those Japanese ones, they're very good. Lots of functions on them. My mate at work bought one last week, he thinks it's marvellous.

Shop assistant: Alright sir, but I think you'll find that this Williams model is just as good. It's light and easy to use. It's got 20 functions and it only costs £99.

Customer: 99 pounds! Williams, you say, new company is it? Can't say I've heard of them. But 20 functions for 99 pounds, I'll take it!

Unit 5

■ **D1** Travel announcements (Exercises a and b)

1.
The train now standing at platform 5 is the 10.20 to Liverpool, calling at Birmingham and Manchester. Passengers for Leeds and Newcastle please change at Birmingham.

2.
Flight BA 98 to Dublin is now ready for boarding. Would all passengers please proceed to Gate A6. We apologize for the delay which was due to fog at Dublin Airport. We hope you have a pleasant flight.

3.
Travel news! Trouble again on the M4 motorway near Bristol, where there has been a serious accident. Two lorries are now blocking the westbound section of the motorway and there is a three-mile traffic jam. The police advise motorists to leave the motorway at Exit 19 and to follow the diversion signs.

Unit 6

■ **D1** Ecology or economics? (Exercises a and b)

Technologists, working for Zinc UK, a leading British mining company, have just published their plans for North Cornwall. They maintain that they have discovered large deposits of zinc ore in this beautiful part of the country not far from the seaside resorts of St. Agnes and Perranporth. The company believes that this is an extremely interesting commercial project because the ore contains a lot of zinc – up to 24 %. And according to Zinc UK there are about 50 million tonnes of the ore only 40 metres below the surface. Furthermore, Zinc UK emphasizes that this project will create about 200 new jobs in North Cornwall. However, not all the people in Cornwall are happy with the news. Local environmentalists and hotel owners have already expressed their fears. They are convinced that the mining project will destroy the area. The environmentalists believe that the beautiful countryside and the wild animals there are in danger. For this reason they have organized a demonstration to take place next week. Some hotel owners have joined the protest action because they fear that the mining company plans to turn the small seaside resorts into big ports for container ships to transport the zinc ore. According to hotel owners this will mean the death of the tourist resorts. So far Zinc UK has refused to make any further comment on this development.

Unit 7

■ D1   From poultry litter to electricity (Exercise a)

Chet: Now, this here's where our fuel arrives. The trucks drive straight in and drop the manure into those storage pits way down at the end there.

John: I see. And what about the people who live near here. Do they ever complain about the smell?

Chet: Well, no. We found a kind of neat solution to that problem. You see, the pressure here in the delivery hall is lower, so no fumes can get out. Now do you have your mask? We're going on through to the storage hall.

John: Do many people have to work in here?

Chet: No, there ain't many people here at all. From this point, the plant is fully-automated. Those conveyor belts there for example, which are taking the manure from the storage pits to burn in the furnace, are all computer-controlled.

John: And this furnace produces steam for the turbine, I suppose.

Chet: That's right. It gets real hot in that furnace – up to 800 degrees.

John: And what's your actual output here?

Chet: The generator produces 12.5 megawatts. That's enough electricity for 12,500 homes around here.

John: "Farmphos" – that's your fertilizer, isn't it? I could use some of that for my roses back home.

Chet: Yeah, I was fixing to give you a sack before you left. We produce it from the ash in the furnace. It's a quality product and very good for the environment …

Unit 8

■ D1   Sales talk (Exercises a and b)

Salesman: Good afternoon. Can I help you?

Customer: Well, actually I'm interested in one of your printers. You had an advert in the local paper.

Salesman: Ah, you mean the new laser printer. The Macprint XL7 .

Customer: Yes, that's right. Have you still got it in stock?

Salesman: Of course. If you'd like to come over here I can show it to you.

Customer: Hm, nice design.

Salesman: It not only looks good, it's one of the fastest printers on the market at the moment. It can do 20 pages per minute. And the print quality – I'll show you. What do you say to that?

Customer: Yes, it's pretty good.

Salesman: Pretty good? That's the best resolution you can get.

Customer: But what about paper? Can I use different types of paper?

Salesman: Of course. It even does envelopes as well. See this button here. You can decide what size paper you want to print, A4, A3, what you want.

Customer: That sounds good, but what about installing it? Can that be a problem?

Salesman: No, it's really easy. The handbook is so clearly written that even a complete beginner can understand it.

Customer:	And what if something goes wrong with the printer?
Salesman:	Well, that shouldn't happen. We at Microstore have a very good reputation, as you know. But if you did have a problem, we would come out right away and help you on the same day. You know, these big superstores are a little cheaper, but you don't get the same individual service as we offer.
Customer:	Right. How much does one of these cost?
Salesman:	It's yours for just £1,499 I think you'll agree that's a fantastic offer. A real bargain. And don't forget our guaranteed good service if anything goes wrong.
Customer:	I'll have to think about it first.
Salesman:	Yes, of course. May I give you my card? The name's John Clark. Please ask for me when you come in again.
Customer:	Thank you very much.
Salesman:	Thank you. May I give you this brochure …

Unit 9

■ D2   Looking for a new location (Exercises b and c)

Telephone call 1

Hello there. At the moment I'm here inside the busy shopping centre in Wetherby. Wetherby is a small town only 20 kilometres north west of Leeds, in the north of England. You've probably never heard of it but I can assure you Wetherby is a town which is developing quickly. And I think its success is mainly due to its excellent position. To give you a general idea – it's right next to the A1. And from that main road it's only half an hour's drive down to the M62 motorway which links the big ports of Liverpool and Hull. As I already said, Wetherby is expanding and the new industrial park just outside the town shows us what opportunities it in fact has. Most of the companies which have their sites there seem to be involved with light industry of one kind or another. The people in the development council I spoke to were very helpful and from my talks with them I found out that the price of land is much lower here than it is in the south of England. Despite the high unemployment rate in the area there's a positive atmosphere about the place. I would say, moreover, that the mixture of modern houses, good roads and clean modern industry makes Wetherby a pleasant place to live and work.

Telephone call 2

Hello there. Right now I'm sitting at the railway station here in Wolverhampton. Wolverhampton is about 20 kilometres north west of Birmingham, right in the middle of England.
Wolverhampton is a typical Black Country town, with both heavy and light industries, although most of the steelworks and coal mines have now been closed down. As a result Wolverhampton still has a rather high unemployment rate. The development council seems to be doing its best, but land still seems difficult to get and is also quite expensive. Most of the people I've spoken to live outside Wolverhampton. They said they prefer living in the new housing estates west of Wolverhampton rather than in the old terraced houses in town. One big advantage for companies here is that Wolverhampton is near the M6 motorway, which is a direct link to London and the Continent. This has attracted a lot of business to the area and has helped Wolverhampton to become a modern industrial centre. The visitor here gets the impression that Wolverhampton is a town which understands how to use the know-how and skills of its manufacturing tradition and at the same time be part of the 21st century.

Unit 10

■ D1   The new majority (Exercises a and d)

1.

I was told by the Russian authorities five or six times that I had no chance to get a visa. You see, back home in Minsk I was a painter. I was married and I had two sons. The only problem was – I was a Russian Jew. In spite of all the difficulties at that time I was reasonably happy, but it was my two sons who wanted to emigrate. In the end we got our visa and arrived here in San Francisco. With all our savings we opened a small fruit and vegetable store. But what I'm really proud of is how my two sons have come to terms with life in America. They are real Americans. I still have a few problems with the language but on the whole I feel happy here. Sometimes I get a little homesick, though.

2.

We came to America years ago from Cambodia as refugees. We had no luggage and no money. In Cambodia both my husband and I had worked in a restaurant until the Khmer Rouge army took over. We decided to leave our country and made our way to the refugee camps in Thailand. From there we got our visa for America. It was very hard for us at first, but now we've both got jobs near our apartment here in Los Angeles. I work on the production line of a chemical company. The pay is quite good – although it is a 45 hour working week. It's harder for my husband. He's got two part time jobs. In the mornings he works at a training center for Cambodians and the rest of the time he drives a truck for a food-processing company. He does not get home until 11 or 12 o'clock at night. That's not good for the family. The three children only really see him at weekends.

3.

I have been married now for 5 years but I've never met my wife's parents and she has not seen mine. You see, we arrived here from across the border seven years ago as so-called illegal immigrants and we do not dare leave America – we are afraid we will not be able to get across the border again. I have been working as a farm worker here in California and my wife has now got part-time work in a factory not far from our home in San Diego. Life is not easy as an "illegal" but what alternative do we have? You see, in Mexico you cannot find work – that is why we came here in the first place. And I think our daughter has a better future here than back home. Maybe we will get our visa one day.

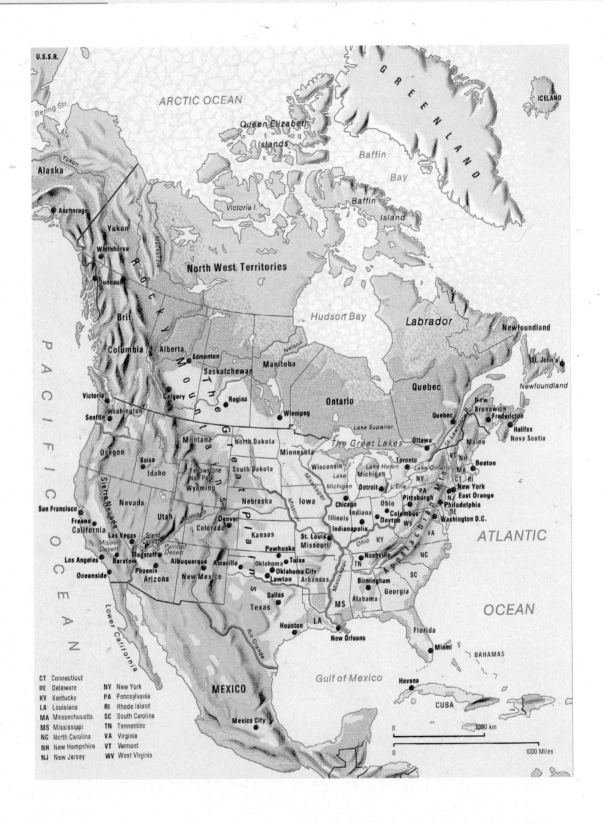